Pat Barker

MANCHESTER

Manche

D0610624

⊙ Contemporary British Novelists

Series editor Daniel Lea

already published

J. G. Ballard   Andrzej Gasiorek
Graham Swift   Daniel Lea
Irvine Welsh   Aaron Kelly

Pat Barker

John Brannigan

Manchester University Press

Manchester and New York

distributed exclusively in the USA by Palgrave

Published by Manchester University Press
Oxford Road, Manchester M13 9NR, UK
and Room 400, 175 Fifth Avenue, New York, NY 10010, USA
www.manchesteruniversitypress.co.uk

Distributed exclusively in the USA by
Palgrave, 175 Fifth Avenue, New York,
NY 10010, USA

Distributed exclusively in Canada by
UBC Press, University of British Columbia, 2029 West Mall,
Vancouver, BC, Canada V6T 1Z2

British Library Cataloguing-in-Publication Data
A catalogue record for this book is available from the British Library

Library of Congress Cataloging-in-Publication Data applied for

ISBN   0 7190 6576 3   *hardback*
EAN   9780 7190 6576 7

ISBN   0 7190 6577 1   *paperback*
EAN   9780 7190 6577 4

First published 2005

14 13 12 11 10 09 08 07 06 05   10 9 8 7 6 5 4 3 2 1

Typeset
by Northern Phototypesetting Co Ltd, Bolton
Printed in Great Britain
by Bell & Bain Ltd, Glasgow

For Moyra, Conor, and the little one, with love

Contents

Series editor's foreword

Contemporary British Novelists offers readers critical introductions to some of the most exciting and challenging writing of recent years. Through detailed analysis of their work, volumes in the series present lucid interpretations of authors who have sought to capture the sensibilities of the late twentieth and twenty-first centuries. Informed, but not dominated, by critical theory, *Contemporary British Novelists* explores the influence of diverse traditions, histories and cultures on prose fiction, and situates key figures within their relevant social, political, artistic and historical contexts.

The title of the series is deliberately provocative, recognising each of the three defining elements as contentious identifications of a cultural framework that must be continuously remade and renamed. The contemporary British novel defies easy categorisation and rather than offering bland guarantees as to the current trajectories of literary production, volumes in this series contest the very terms that are employed to unify them. How does one conceptualise, isolate and define the mutability of the contemporary? What legitimacy can be claimed for a singular Britishness given the multivocality implicit in the redefinition of national identities? Can the novel form adequately represent reading communities increasingly dependent upon digitalised communication? These polemical considerations are the theoretical backbone of the series, and attest to the difficulties of formulating a coherent analytical approach to the discontinuities and incoherencies of the present.

Contemporary British Novelists does not seek to appropriate its subjects for prescriptive formal or generic categories; rather it aims to explore the ways in which aesthetics are reproduced, refined and repositioned through recent prose writing. If the overarching architecture of the contemporary always eludes description, then the grandest ambition of this series must be to plot at least some of its dimensions.

Daniel Lea

Acknowledgements

My first debt of gratitude is to Daniel Lea and Matthew Frost for commissioning this book, and to the staff of Manchester University Press for publishing it. Thanks are especially due to Pat Barker, who has very kindly given me permission to quote from her work. She also agreed to an interview, which has helped in revisions to the book, and which will be published separately. Thanks also to Gillon Aitken Associates, Pat Barker's agents, for their help. The book has benefited greatly from Sharon Monteith's advice and suggestions in her reader's report, and she very kindly sent proof-copies of essays from *Critical Perspectives on Pat Barker*, which allowed me to revise and update sections of the book. Phil Tew generously invited me to write an essay on the *Regeneration* trilogy for a collection of essays called *Contemporary British Fiction*, ed. Richard J. Lane, Rod Mengham and Philip Tew (Cambridge, Polity, 2002). Sharon Monteith, Margaretta Jolly, Nahem Yousaf, and Ronald Paul published a shorter version of the chapter on *Union Street* in *Critical Perspectives on Pat Barker* (Columbia, University of South Carolina Press, 2005). My colleagues at University College Dublin also deserve much thanks, not least for listening to a research seminar in January 2003, but also for many helpful suggestions which have worked their way into the book. My most important debts of gratitude, of course, lie closer to home. I dedicate this book to my wife, Moyra, my son, Conor, and our little one who will be born before it is published. Moyra read and commented invaluably on many of the chapters, and Conor, when he was just six months old, typed the first few spaces of one chapter, but more significantly they have put up with my frequent absence and distraction with remarkable patience.

Chronology

1943–   Born Patricia Margaret Drake in Thornaby, near Middlesbrough, on 8th May 1943. Her mother was Moyra Drake, but she never knew her father. She was brought up mainly by her grandparents from the age of seven, first on a chicken farm, and later in a fish-and-chip shop.

1954   Attended King James Grammar School, Knaresborough. Announced to her grandparents that she had decided to be a writer.

1955   Moved to Grangefield Grammar School, Stockton-on-Tees.

1962–65   Studied International History at the London School of Economics.

1965–70   Taught A-level classes in History, Politics and English in Further Education colleges in the Teesside area.

1969   Began her relationship with David Barker, Professor of Zoology at the University of Durham, with whom she has two children, John (b. 1970) and Anna (b. 1974).

1978   Married David Barker; attended a writing course by the Arvon Foundation at Lumb Bank, Yorkshire, where Angela Carter read her work and encouraged her to publish what became *Union Street*.

1982   *Union Street* published by Virago; joint winner of the Fawcett Society Book Prize.

1983   Included among Granta's collection of the twenty *Best Young British Novelists*, chosen by the Book Marketing Council. The Granta volume included a draft from her next novel, *Blow Your House Down*.

1984   *Blow Your House Down* published by Virago.

1986   *The Century's Daughter* published by Virago (later republished by Virago in 1996 under Barker's original title, *Liza's England*); *Blow Your House Down* adapted for stage by Jane Thomas as *The Chicken Factory* (Company of Women, Hull).

1989   *The Man Who Wasn't There* published by Virago in hardback, and by Penguin in paperback the following year.

1990   The film *Stanley and Iris*, starring Jane Fonda and Robert de Niro, based very loosely on *Union Street*, is released.

1991   *Regeneration* published by Viking/Penguin.

1993   *The Eye in the Door* published by Viking/Penguin; winner of the *Guardian* Fiction Prize.

1995   *The Ghost Road*, published by Viking/Penguin, completes the *Regeneration* trilogy; winner of the Booker Prize for Fiction. *Blow Your House Down* adapted for the stage by Sarah Daniels (Live Theatre, Newcastle and Bishop Auckland).

1996   Winner of the Author of the Year Prize by the Booksellers' Association; Virago reissue her first three novels in the 'Modern Classics' series.

1997   The film, *Regeneration* (US title *Behind the Lines*), directed by Gillies MacKinnon and starring Jonathan Pryce, is released.

1998   *Another World* published by Viking/Penguin.

1999   Awarded CBE (Commander of the British Empire) in the New Year's honours list.

2001   *Border Crossing* published by Viking/Penguin.

2003   *Double Vision* published by Viking/Penguin; 'Subsidence', short story, published in the *Guardian*.

1

Critical and cultural contexts

In *Double Vision*, one of Barker's central characters, Kate Frobisher, is drawn towards the engravings of 'Green Men' or goblins that decorate the roof bosses of the local church, pagan images of faces 'angry, tormented, desperate, sly, desolate', which are believed to be symbols of renewal. 'Some of these heads were so emaciated they were hardly more than skulls. Others vomited leaves, their eyes staring, panic-stricken above the choking mouth' (29). They are not symbols of renewal, Kate decides, but 'figures of utter ruin'. Every one of Barker's novels contains some such figures – the skull visible through the skin, the tortured, screaming mouth, or the staring, petrified eyes. They are figures of abject terror, of the inhuman torment and horror of history, of the disturbing fragility of human existence. They are images of our passive subjection to the forces of history, forces which appear to be absolute and beyond our comprehension, and yet, like the Goya paintings Kate admires so much, Barker's novels never allow us 'to feel anything as simple or as trivial as despair' (153). The images of terror are contrasted with apparently simple or trivial images of human agency and warmth. A neighbour lights a fire for Kate when she returns from hospital, for example (15), a simple, skil-ful deed which recurs in many of Barker's novels, and which symbol-ises hope, community, compassion, and the capacity for creative action. Barker's characters are never simply the victims of trauma and terror. They are also creative agents who act, sometimes positively, within the constraints of specific historical conditions.

Kate's contemplation of the meanings of the 'Green Men' illus-trates much about Barker's theme, the agency of human beings living with the terror of history, but it also reveals much about Barker's approach to the problem of representation. The 'Green Men' are cultural expressions from another time, another people, the meanings of which Kate can only begin to guess. Some concrete historical event or experience lies hidden behind the faces of those engravings, which she can barely comprehend through the dense passage of time. The origin of these engravings is obscure and, in Kate's view, they refuse the ways in which human beings have attempted to appropriate them within the symbolic architecture of the Christian Church. They remain resolutely pagan, stubbornly antithetical to the Christian iconography of hope and redemption. They fail to mean what we want them to mean. Yet, as much as Kate considers these faces as figures of abjection, of absolute otherness, they also function for her as analogies. She first noticed them at the funeral of her husband, Ben, a war photographer killed in Afghanistan, and clearly they serve to project her own feelings of terror, despair, and anger. As such, they help Kate to make sense of her own loss, to find a face for her grief. Barker explores this paradoxical condition in forms of cultural expression and representation throughout her work. Her novels draw our attention simultaneously to the alterity of artistic expression, what Walter Benjamin thought of as the 'aura' of the work of art, that it exists in historical and material forms outside what we want it to mean,[1] and to the availability of art as a means for us to construct stories about ourselves. In all her work there exists this tension between the material world beyond our control, the violence and trauma which come back to haunt us, and our persistent attempts to create meaning, to find hope by looking into the depths of despair.

This is one of the reasons why Pat Barker is among the most important and popular novelists of the twentieth century and into the twenty-first century in Britain. To early reviewers and most critics, Barker seemed to be a regional, social realist writer, preoccupied largely with the de-industrialised, working-class culture of the northeast of England. The ten novels she has published to date have repeatedly returned to that region, but her canvas has always been broader than her settings implied, and the implications of her art for problems of representation have always been more ambitious than the 'social realist' label suggests. In her most recent novel, *Double Vision*, Barker seems to have consciously extended her fiction into international settings, taking in New York, Afghanistan, The Hague, and Sarajevo. But even in *Union Street*, her first novel, Barker is concerned to trace the imprimatur of global trends and events on a local, provincial, and apparently insular community. There is no easy way of divining 'phases' in Barker's work. When she has set novels in the past, in the *Regeneration* trilogy, for example, she has often been exploring the implications of the past for the present. Similarly, her most contemporary settings are equally concerned with demythologising the past. The shift from predominantly female central characters in her first three novels to male central characters since then has marked for some critics a significant transition, but her approach to those characters, male or female, has not changed. Gender identity and formation has been a concern throughout her work, and her novels have always borne out the lesson that male and female identities are only understood in relation to each other. One of the guiding precepts of this book is that Pat Barker's oeuvre is remarkably consistent, both in the social and cultural issues she explores, and in the literary styles and forms she has drawn upon.

She almost always writes from the perspective of a third-person narrator, rarely introduces metafictional commentary, and tends to favour strong narrative patterns, which corral the events of the story into a tight unity. In many of her novels she introduces the stock devices of popular genres such as Gothic or detective fiction, but complicates or abandons the expected resolution of those narratives in order to refocus the reader's attention on social or historical themes. Barker's novels seem initially to share the formal or aesthetic conservatism of much working-class social realism, such as the novels of Alan Sillitoe, John Braine, or the early D.H. Lawrence, but this impression diminishes as her oeuvre expands into historical fiction. Her themes, despite the shift of gender focus from her fourth novel onwards, are also remarkably consistent. The most obvious and persistent theme is one of dereliction – physical, economic, social, emotional and psychological. She uses the word 'derelict' frequently, to refer not just to the ubiquitous derelict settings and landscapes of her novels, but also to some of the people who inhabit her often decimated, demoralised communities. Class is an equally prevalent theme in her work besides gender, and Barker consistently returns to the unspeakable traumatic experiences of those living close to the margins of physical and economic survival, whether this is the rape of thirteen-year-old Kelly Brown in Barker's first novel, *Union Street*, the psychological trauma of front-line combat in *Regeneration*, or the child killer explored in *Border Crossing*.

Such traumatic experiences prompt crises of representation in Barker's novels, figured partly in the confrontation between victim and authority, but also in the foregrounding of memory as the scene of cultural and political conflict. Barker's novels contain scenes of recovered memory, displaced memory, relived or anamnestic memory, and in each case there is a larger political and historical conflict being played out in the memory crises of particular individuals and communities. The inability of shell-shock victims to distinguish the remembered from the real in the *Regeneration* trilogy, for example, serves to bring into critical focus the European narratives of modernity and rationality which underpin the war. This is one of Barker's most significant achievements in social realist fiction, to bring into focus the operation of memory (always part of the formal mechanics of realist narrative), as a narrative agent, and as a site of cultural and political disquiet. In particular, Barker's fiction exhibits a heightened sensitivity to the fluidity of the time of memory, and to the unsettling, spectral effects of remembered time on the time of the real, or time of the present.

How, then, might we conceive of the relationship between narrative and time, or narrative and history, in Pat Barker's work? One approach would be to follow Fredric Jameson's argument that narrative might best be conceived as 'a "form of reasoning" about experience and society', in which narrative constructs models for understanding social and historical change.[2] Barker's novels might be seen to do this in the ways they construct striking analogies that serve to connect individual experiences of trauma to their social and cultural conditions. But to say that her novels are 'forms of reasoning' about experience and society does not do sufficient justice to Barker's sense of the ineffable, or unrepresentable, experience of trauma. Here we might think of Barker's use of recurrent images of horror or trauma, such as the image of the open mouth, which recurs in every one of her novels in a variety of forms, and tends to imply rather than represent the aporetic experience of trauma. It is this aspect of her work, this sense of the ineffable, which Barker often implies through figures of spectrality, that I want to suggest constitutes a form of negative epic in her fiction.

'What the epic did in the sphere of the admirable, the story of victims does in the sphere of the horrible', writes Paul Ricoeur. The negative epic 'preserves the memory of suffering', Ricoeur argues, and places fiction 'in the service of the unforgettable'.[3] Barker's aesthetic is driven by this ethical commitment to fictionalising the story of victims, victims of war, poverty and oppression, while never allowing her characters to be defined or objectified solely as victims. Her art functions in part by revisioning the formal characteristics of post-war social realism to accommodate the unrepresentable trauma of twentieth-century mass warfare or post-industrial urban dereliction. This represents not so much a departure from social realism as a more complex realisation of the constructed and intersubjective experience of the real. This is evident, for example, in the way Barker's characters perceive their own time. Barker's characters experience time as a series of historical resonances, through notions of cyclical recurrence and repetition, so that it is impossible to see the present except through images of its otherness. Barker's characters can only achieve some understanding of their situation in time by dislocating their place in historical chronology. To situate themselves, it is necessary, in other words, to conceive of the radical heterogeneity – the hauntedness – of their own time. What I argue, in effect, in this book, is that Barker's fiction constitutes a kind of critical realism, which gives expression to what Ricoeur called the confrontation between the 'aporetics of time and the poetics of narrative'.[4] Any attempt to explain the preoccupations and concerns of Barker's complex and distinctive oeuvre must take account both of the intricacies of the formal mechanics of her novels, and the way in which she develops a critical understanding of modern history and society. The aim of this volume is to situate and explain Barker's achievements along precisely these lines of enquiry.

Barker has always rightly insisted that her work is not autobiographical in any direct way, but brief consideration of the biographical contexts of her work will help to explain some of the notable characteristics of her fiction. She was born and brought up near Middlesbrough in the industrial northeast of England, and now lives in the same region in Durham. Apart from her student years at the London School of Economics, this area has been her home, and it is home to the vast majority of her characters. Even in the *Regeneration* trilogy, which is mostly set in Scotland and London, and partly in France, the northeast is home for Billy Prior. Once renowned for its coal pits, iron- and steelworks, shipbuilding and manufacturing industries, and for the distinctive working-class communities built around those industries, the region was decimated by economic depressions several times in the twentieth century, and experienced large-scale unemployment and de-industrialisation in the 1970s and 1980s. Many of Barker's novels reflect this state of decline, from the empty steelworks at the heart of *Union Street*, to the derelict wharves along the quayside at the beginning of *Border Crossing*, a preoccupation she shares with other writers from the region, such as the poets Tony Harrison and Simon Armitage. At the end of *Border Crossing*, however, Barker notes that landscapes recently pockmarked with wastelands and derelict factories are beginning to regenerate, and a sense of optimism for the region is also conspicuous from the trips undertaken by characters in both *Border Crossing* and *Double Vision* to the Holy Island, a local tourist attraction. The region is no longer simply synonymous with post-industrial urban decay, as in Barker's first three novels, but is also associated in her later novels with hope, regeneration, and historical significance.

Barker was brought up mainly by her grandparents. She was led to believe that her father was a RAF pilot who was killed in the Second World War, but she later discovered that this was a myth invented by her mother, who in fact never knew who her real father was. Her grandparents cared solely for her from the age of seven, when her mother married and moved out. She was raised first on a chicken farm and later in a fish-and-chip shop, where Blake Morrison suggests 'she would hear the kind of gossip and spicy vernacular that she would go on to use in her early fiction'.[5] It may also be one reason for the significance of dialogue in her work. Importantly in Barker's novels, characters are constructed by their speech, by what they say and how they say it. Barker's upbringing might be described as rooted in working-class culture, but when she was eleven she told her grandmother that she was certain she would be a writer, and she was also awarded a place in the local grammar school. In the English education system in the postwar period, the grammar school was a route out of working-class life and into middle-class professions. Barker earned a scholarship which took her through an academic secondary school education, in which she excelled and earned a place at the prestigious London School of Economics, where she read for a degree in International History. Her education effectively secured her move away from working-class culture. It is a familiar phenomenon explored by an earlier generation of writers and academics, most notably by Richard Hoggart,[6] who describes the educated working-class man or woman as the revisitor, uprooted and uneasy. The 'revisitor' is a figure Barker features in a number of novels. Stephen is a revisitor in *The Century's Daughter*, for example, but perhaps the most obvious example in Barker's oeuvre is Colin and the 'ghost' of his older, revisiting self in *The Man Who Wasn't There*. It is also worth noting that increasingly Barker has moved away from working-class characters and begun to explore more fully the dynamics of middle-class professional life, especially in her three most recent novels.

This is not the first time that Barker has shifted the class background of her characters, however. She wrote several novels in the 1970s, which she describes as middle-class novels of manners, 'rather refined and sensitive', which were rejected by publishers.[7] When she attended a writing course under Angela Carter's tutelage in 1978, however, Carter encouraged her to find the voices and social terrain of the working-class culture she grew up in for her first published novel, *Union Street*. There were obvious resonances for critics with earlier traditions of working-class writing, from D.H. Lawrence, Robert Tressell and Sid Chaplin, to the postwar writers Alan Sillitoe, Stan Barstow and John Braine. But Barker did not fit comfortably with these writers, whose female characters in particular were 'quite stereotypically restricted'. Instead, she explains in a recent interview with Sharon Monteith, she turned to African-American writers like Toni Morrison, Alice Walker and James Baldwin: 'what I discovered in their work was the sense of an individual voice emerging out of a communal voice'.[8] It has remained an important dimension to her work that characters are defined not only as individuals, but inter-subjectively in relation to social markers of class, gender, sexuality, race, and nationality. It is frequently made evident that characters are not able to speak uniquely as individuals, but that the language of their 'tribe', as it were, speaks through them. It is a device which has enabled Barker to explore the construction of gendered identities, of social class, and to a lesser extent of sexual orientation, racial group, and, infrequently and obliquely, of national identity.

Barker's pursuit of an academic education in history, and later a teaching career, and her marriage to a university professor, have all played parts in the direction and focus of her fiction. The meanings of the past, and its implications for contemporary society, are central concerns in all her novels. Many of her novels, particularly from *Regeneration* onwards, feature characters engaged in academic work. Rivers has his anthropological research, which Barker discovered through her husband, David. *Another World* explores the kinds of historical questions the historian character, Helen, is interested in pursuing with the war veteran, Geordie. Tom Seymour in *Border Crossing* is writing an academic case study of child killers. Stephen Sharkey in

Double Vision is writing a cultural-historical book about how wars are represented, presumably much like the book by Susan Sontag, *Regarding the Pain of Others*, which Barker consulted in writing her novel. As I argue in the last chapter of this book, intellectual work has become increasingly important to the questions Barker explores, particularly concerning the ethics of representation.

Like many of her contemporaries in English fiction, Barker's novels have all been interested to varying degrees in the relationship between the past and the present, and particularly in the shaping of historical memory in the present. Her achievements in the *Regeneration* trilogy in re-examining the social and psychological undercurrents of the First World War earned her widespread recognition, including the Booker Prize in 1995 and the Author of the Year Award in 1996. As Ian Jack argued in a *Granta* editorial in 1996, Barker is part of a generation of British novelists engaged in fictional excavations of the past. Jack characterised the fiction of the 1980s and 1990s as a 'literature of farewell', preoccupied with 'the country and people that seemed to be there a minute ago, before we blinked and turned away'.[9] Throughout the twentieth century, Britain has declined from its position of global dominance as an imperial and industrial power in the Victorian era, and since the Second World War in particular its ability to command a place on the world stage has largely depended upon American sponsorship. Many of Barker's contemporaries, such as Kazuo Ishiguro, Salman Rushdie, Caryl Phillips and Hanif Kureishi, have explored the historical and contemporary legacies of empire and global migration patterns in Britain. Other contemporaries such as Peter Ackroyd, A.S. Byatt, Graham Swift and Iain Sinclair have been closer to Barker's own concerns, however, with the more local meanings of history and historical geography, and the spectral filtration of the past into the present. Like these contemporaries, Barker's fictional explorations of history have never engaged in nostalgia, but as Wendy Wheeler recently argued about Graham Swift, Barker's novels have constituted an attempt to imagine forms of social solidarity through the work of mourning.[10] Barker's communities are usually besieged and under threat, sometimes on the verge of extinction, and often haunted by loss. Barker traces in her novels, however, the ways in which these communities must reinvest the world around them with symbolic significance, and must acknowledge the radical rearrangement of that world as a result of their loss. Thus, in *Union Street*, Kelly Brown finds again the meaning of home at the end of the story, while in *Double Vision* Stephen and Justine learn to cope with vulnerability, and to trust in love again. Both actions constitute a proper form of mourning, of living with loss, while re-engaging in the creative work of daily life.

While Barker's novels can be situated comfortably within general trends in contemporary British fiction, her oeuvre is obviously distinctive in a number of ways. Aside from the formal characteristics of her work, and her recurrent concern with particular kinds of historical and historiographical questions, as addressed above, Barker has developed signature themes and figures throughout her fiction. These are discussed in more detail in the chapters below, but some consideration of the nature of these signatures is worth exploring here. There is, for example, widespread use of animal symbolism, from the birds of *Union Street*, to the chickens of *Blow Your House Down*, and the foxes of *Border Crossing*, and many more. Such animals recur with distinctive regularity in Barker's novels, and sometimes appear to be indicative of a brutal, primitive world parallel to human society, yet Barker always uses animals as figures of human consciousness. They are always invested with human meaning, as symbols of hidden social communality in *Union Street*, for example, or of passivity and vulnerability in *Blow Your House Down*. One image which is repeated in several novels is that of Christ on the cross, his scars resembling the appearance of a plucked chicken. The image at once serves to demystify and historicise Christ, refusing the notion of a glorious martyr, and at the same time it invests Christ with significance as a tortured, violated body, the passive and fragile victim of historical forces. The repetition of that image in several novels constitutes a kind of signature, and serves to connect the stories of one novel with others.

Images of fragility also recur across all of the novels, particularly images of the body as a shell, or chrysalis, which can be easily broken or crushed, but which are also the bearers of life, of creativity. One of the themes which runs throughout Barker's oeuvre is the vulnerability of human society, and the vulnerability of human life. Violence, either on the massive scale of the First World War in the *Regeneration* trilogy, or as a random, isolated act in a country house in *Double Vision*, tends to expose the myth of individualism, of the monadic self-sufficiency of each person, and to act as a catalyst in Barker's novels for imagining forms of social solidarity. Barker tends to fix our attention on specific kinds of trauma and horror through bodily images and symbols, as mentioned above – the staring eyes of Kath in *Blow Your House Down*, the tortured mouth of Yealland's patient in *Regeneration*, or the skulls which recur in almost every novel.

The images of the body, and of corporeal vulnerability, are never unrelated to the recurrent images of ghosts and spectres in Barker's novels. Ghosts occupy a curious place in Barker's oeuvre, because her characters are frequently keen to dismiss them, and to find rational explanations for what are presented as instances of haunting. Yet the rational explanations never manage to work fully. The ghost of the Fanshawe girl in *Another World*, for example, seems to appear several times in the novel, possibly as an evil influence, almost resulting in the death of a toddler. But the novel attempts to explain her away, as the figment of the children's imagination, as the mistaken image of Miranda sleepwalking, or the hallucination of Nick when he is over-tired. Yet these explanations never work successfully, and the possibility that ghosts exist and influence the fate of the living can never be dismissed fully. There is a Gothic theme running through many of Barker's novels, and Gothic intertexts in some of them (*Jane Eyre* and *The Turn of the Screw* in *Border Crossing*, for example).

There is also a signature to be traced in Barker's narrative techniques, particularly in the shift from one narrative consciousness to another, which she has employed in every novel. In part, the reason for this technique lies in Barker's move away from the controlling, omniscient narrator of classic realism, but it is also a move away from the entirely subjective consciousness of the modernist novel. It is indebted to both, of course, but Barker's use of shifting narrative perspectives and free indirect discourse implies an intersubjective consciousness, which occasionally even permits a kind of community, or sense of solidarity, to emerge from the relations between her characters. This is an idea I explore more fully in the early chapters of the book in particular, and explains in part the formal analyses which preoccupy parts of those chapters.

So, too, Barker's work has become renowned formally for her use of dialogue and, more generally, her use of dialogic techniques. This has led a number of critics to comment on the Bakhtinian resonances in her fiction, that she not only reveals much about her characters and themes through the subtle interweaving of dialogue, but also pits characters and situations in dialogic relation to each other. Every 'authority' figure has an answering figure, every possible explanation has a disturbing counter-explanation, every symbol has an opposite symbol, and every utterance from an individual contains the language of community. This functions sometimes at the level of paradox, too, that silence constitutes a more meaningful response than speech, that absence is more powerful than presence, that the gaps in memory are more significant than what is remembered. This forms a structuring device for many of her novels – the empty steelworks at the heart of *Union Street*, or the five-hour gap in Danny Miller's memory of what he did to Lizzie Parks in *Border Crossing*. Barker stated in a recent interview that her novels are centred on dialogue, that dialogue shapes the key features of her art: 'There are two types of dialogue that fascinate me: the apparently unselfconscious, inconsequential dialogue, and the hyperconscious dialogue between a therapist and a patient where every word is loaded'.[11] Both types of dialogue are used widely and effectively throughout Barker's oeuvre, with the significance of the psychoanalytic encounter particularly evident in the *Regeneration* trilogy and *Border Crossing*.

The characteristic features of Barker's art evidently comprise a distinctive note within contemporary British fiction. Also distinctive is Barker's eclectic range of literary and cultural influences, which are more difficult to pinpoint. Early reviewers suggested Lawrence and the social realism of the 1950s and 1960s, but this represented a male tradition, with which Barker's indebtedness to the Second Wave feminism of the late 1960s is somewhat incongruous. Barker's immediate mentor, Angela Carter, is perhaps dimly discernible in some of her preoccupations with gender formation and subjectivity, but Barker's style and the way she handles her key themes is very different from what has habitually been characterized as the postmodernism of Carter's work. In interviews she has frequently discussed writers she has read or admires, but they are often difficult to characterise as influences. She admires the poetry of Seamus Heaney, Ted Hughes, Simon Armitage and Glyn Maxwell, for example, but confesses to being useless at writing poetry.[12] She read 'the whole of Dostoyevsky' when she was growing up,[13] borrowing the novels from her local library, but other than her interest in deep psychic disturbances, it is difficult to discern a line of inheritance between the two.

It is perhaps less useful to talk about influences on Barker's work than it is to trace the particular literary and cultural sources of inspiration for her themes and ideas, and these are largely acknowledged in her novels, and sometimes in her interviews. Goya's paintings in *Double Vision*, for example, or the publications of W.H.R. Rivers in the *Regeneration* trilogy, are obvious starting points for her ideas. Works of art have become increasingly significant points of reference in her recent novels, as the artistic process and the role of artists have become equally important as themes. Sociological and psychological case studies of post-traumatic stress and borderline personality disorders play a significant part in Barker's research for recent novels too. Equally, some critical and theoretical studies have inspired her, notably Elaine Showalter's *The Female Malady* for the *Regeneration* trilogy, and Susan Sontag's *Regarding the Pain of Others* for *Double Vision*. But sometimes her intertexts or sources of inspiration are surprising: she acknowledges a debt to V.S. Naipaul's *The Enigma of Arrival*, for instance, for the idea that the landscape will absorb a stranger as it has absorbed everything else, which becomes an important part of how Stephen adjusts his sense of belonging in *Double Vision*.[14] But such examples illustrate that Barker engages in a process of research, which is intensive but not exhaustive, thoughtful but not necessarily academic, and ultimately inspirational rather than definitive. To pinpoint Barker's sources does little to account for the uses she makes of them in her fiction, and this is where Barker is most evidently a distinctive voice in contemporary British fiction. Her work seems to follow in no one's footsteps, and testifies to her having accomplished a technical mastery and a unique vision which is all of her own making. She has clearly gained much from her wide reading and careful research, and she frequently incorporates what she has learned from others into her work. But the artistic achievements of her novels, the vision of the world which unfolds in her fiction from *Union Street* to *Double Vision*, are difficult to locate within any one tradition.

Yet for all that Barker is difficult to place in a line of literary precursors and influences, she remains one of the most rooted and consistent writers of her generation. The stability of style, setting, and theme in her work shows a remarkable continuity, all the more laudable for the fact that her repertoire of characters and concerns has constantly expanded to incorporate new ideas, discover fresh insights, and reflect current social and cultural issues. *Double Vision* is as dynamic in its engagement with contemporary rural politics in England in 2003, the burning pyres of animal carcasses dotted across her Northumbrian landscape, as *Union Street* was breathtaking in its bold depiction of the blighted industrial landscape of Teesside in 1982. What early reviewers mistook for gritty realism might instead be

understood as Barker's exceptional ability to create thoughtful, analytical fiction, which probes deeply into contemporary social and political events, while enabling readers to connect those events to wider
debates and ideas. Even her historical novels are strikingly tuned in to
contemporary debates about public memory and national myths,
while bringing historical situations to fresh and illuminating fictional
life. As this study hopes to show in the ensuing chapters, it is Barker's
ability to ground her fictions in a recognisable, material reality, past
or present, while using the aesthetic form of the novel in innovative
and exciting ways, which has secured her reputation as one of the
most important writers in modern English literary history.

Notes

1 Walter Benjamin, 'The Work of Art in the Age of Mechanical Reproduction', *Illuminations*, trans. Harry Zohn (London, Fontana, 1973).
2 Fredric Jameson, 'Ideology, Narrative Analysis, and Popular Culture',
 Theory and Society, 4 (1977), 543.
3 Paul Ricoeur, *Time and Narrative*, vol. 3, trans. Kathleen Blamey and
 David Pellauer (Chicago, University of Chicago Press, 1988), 189.
4 Ibid., 189.
5 Blake Morrison, 'War Stories', *New Yorker*, 22 January 1996, 79.
6 See Richard Hoggart, *The Uses of Literacy* (Harmondsworth, Pelican,
 1957), 291–304.
7 Morrison, 'War Stories', 79.
8 Sharon Monteith, 'Pat Barker', *Contemporary British and Irish Fiction: An
 Introduction through Interviews*, eds Sharon Monteith, Jenny Newman and
 Pat Wheeler (London, Arnold, 2004), 20.
9 Ian Jack, 'Editorial: Whatever Happened to Us?', *Granta*, 56 (1996), 7–8.
10 See Wendy Wheeler, *A New Modernity? Change in Science, Literature and
 Politics* (London, Lawrence and Wishart, 1999), 62–87.
11 Monteith, 'Pat Barker', 22.
12 Robert McCrum, 'It's a disaster for a novel to be topical', *Observer*, 1 April
 2001.
13 Morrison, 'War Stories', 79.
14 Monteith, 'Pat Barker', 31.

2

Small worlds: *Union Street*

Pat Barker's first novel, *Union Street*, published in 1982, examines the problems of sustaining community and identity in working-class culture in England in a post-industrial context. What happens to a class defined by 'work' when the source of work peters out of existence? What happens to a community built (literally) around the engines of the Industrial Revolution – the steel factories, the coal pits, the linen mills – when those industries fall into ruin? What happens in particular to women in a society once dominated by the history and identity of a male struggle for labour power when men have been rendered impotent by unemployment?[1] Barker's first novel made an immediate impact, not just as an artful novel, but also because it asked such questions about English society at a time of miners' strikes, inner-city riots, rising unemployment and, after the revived nationalism of the Falklands' War, a virulent right-wing attack on the assumptions of the postwar welfare state. This chapter explores first the ways in which Barker's novel attempts to answer these questions, specifically in relation to a tradition of working-class writing and representation, and second, the extent to which Barker experiments with narrative strategies to articulate the experiences and feelings of working-class women and their communities.

The title of the novel evokes the familiar topography of working-class community. It seems to promise the intimate neighbourliness, shift-work routines and cheerful endurance common to the popular, often nostalgic, imagination of working-class life. 'Street' has obvious significance as the parochial unit of urban, working-class community, and functions in the classic British soap opera *Coronation Street* (1960–) as a convenient, symbolic container of a knowable, familiar society, the kind of places Richard Hoggart described as 'small worlds, each as homogenous and well-defined as a village'.[2] 'Union' establishes an association with working-class labour, a history of struggle against exploitation, as well as the more suggestive resonances of unity, togetherness, family and sexual union. 'Union Street' is a symbolic space, then, which functions to delineate the imaginative contours of an urban, working-class landscape and social structure. In doing so, it connects with those earlier intrepid cartographers of working-class community, with George Orwell, Richard Hoggart, Raymond Williams, and with the social realism in literature, drama, film and television of the late 1950s and early 1960s. Pat Barker writes within the same genre of social realism as an earlier generation of male writers such as Alan Sillitoe, John Braine, Stan Barstow and David Storey, whose representations of working-class culture reached a mass audience through paperback novels and film adaptations. Barker interacts with this popular genre in two ways. First, she shifts the perspective of social realism from the male, affluent worker, to the experiences and identities of working-class women, against an emergent condition of post-industrial economic blight. Second, she experiments in a localised way with a number of literary techniques and styles less familiar to social realism, such as non-linear narrative, an emphasis on collective experience, symbolism, fractured time and stream of consciousness, and what I will suggest is a form of omnipresent rather than omniscient narration – moving between characters without moving beyond what they know and how they think.

When Barker sets out in *Union Street* to represent the plight of working-class community in a de-industrialised England, she does so in the full knowledge that 'working-class community' is already heavily inscribed in twentieth-century English culture. It should not take long to establish that Barker's working-class homes differ somewhat from those familiar in the writings of her precursors. Working-class community for George Orwell, for example, is an idea best embodied in the cosy, familial environment of a working-class home:

> In a working-class home – I am not thinking at the moment of the unemployed, but of comparatively prosperous homes – you breathe a warm, decent, deeply human atmosphere which is not so easy to find elsewhere. . . .. I have often been struck by the peculiar easy completeness, the perfect symmetry as it were, of a working-class interior at its best. Especially on winter evenings after tea, when the fire glows in the open range and dances mirrored in the steel fender, when Father, in

shirt-sleeves, sits in the rocking chair at one side of the fire reading the racing finals, and Mother sits on the other with her sewing, and the children are happy with a pennorth of mint humbugs, and the dog lolls roasting himself on the rag mat – it is a good place to be in, provided that you can be not only in it but sufficiently *of* it to be taken for granted.[3]

Barker's homes are set up from the beginning of the novel as antithetical to this sentimental depiction of 'completeness', 'symmetry' and a 'warm, decent, deeply human atmosphere'. Houses are broken, or empty. The atmosphere inside is sometimes warm, but is often fraught, showing signs of struggle, not just between their inhabitants, but against the cold, smoke and grime which these (literally) broken houses cannot help but admit. Orwell's depiction of working-class domesticity is deliberately sentimental, of course. He avoids thinking of the struggle with debt and disease, and settles instead for a comfortable image of homeliness and sufficiency. There is the hint of warning in his distinction between being *in* this home and being *of* it, which remembers that community relies upon exclusion and suspicion. But its attraction as an idea for Orwell is its rootedness, its almost mythical connection with the 'deeply human', whereas for Barker, as I hope to show, *Union Street* registers that these are communities which have been abandoned, and have become transient, rootless places.

Hoggart describes the roots and core values of this community in more detail and with less sentiment in *The Uses of Literacy*, but finds also the deep mythic structures of working-class life, the 'extraordinary changelessness' of working-class culture, in which men and women have their apparently timeless places at the hearth and the factory. Such depictions of working-class life represent as natural and fixed the rhythms and patterns of an industrialised working-class community, which runs to a daily clock of factory sirens, and the weekly cycle of pawnshops and payday. The temporal rhythm of working-class life is the subject of Alan Sillitoe's novel *Saturday Night and Sunday Morning* (1958), which figures working-class community as a solid, timeless culture, with its own mythic figures and rituals:

Fat Mrs Bull the gossiper stood with her fat arms folded over her apron at the yard-end, watching people pass by on their way to work. With pink face and beady eyes, she was a tight-fisted defender of her tribe, queen of the yard because she had lived there for twenty-two years, earning names like 'The News of the World' and the 'Loudspeaker' because she watched the factory go in every morning and afternoon to glean choice gossip for retail later on.[4]

Community for Sillitoe is figured in the familiar rhythms and routines of daily working life, revolving around the aggressive, mechanical time of factory and pub, and the seasonal, slow time of home
and nature.⁵ Arthur Seaton, Sillitoe's hero, is representative in some
respects of an emergent class of affluent workers, but the novel suggests that even the arrival of the 'affluent society', symbolised in the
novel by television sets, will do nothing to dent the temporal patterns
and deep structures of working-class society. The resilience of working-class culture to change, which is related to the persistent representation of its deep-rootedness and organicism, is a recurrent theme
in the postwar imagination of the working-class community, and one
which serves to invest symbolic significance in the working class as a
repository of 'natural', homely values. In place of this idea that working-class community is changeless and continuous, Barker's novel
shows a community in the painful process of dissolution, a community which struggles to register its existence at all.

It is against this ideological context that *Union Street* is best read, as
a novel which pays considerable attention to demythologising the
homeliness and continuity of working-class culture, and which registers the traumatic impact of the decimation of particular economic
and social structures. *Union Street* comprises the stories of seven
working-class women, ranging from Kelly Brown who is eleven years
old to Alice Bell who is in her seventies. 'Home' and 'street', the stable
anchors of existence in Hoggart's working-class community, are
derelict or dystopian sites in Barker's post-industrial imagination.
The same permeability which featured in earlier celebrations of working-class community – the open front door, the gathering of neighbours on street corners and in doorways, the popping in and out of
each other's houses – is shown in Barker's novel to have become the
mark of vulnerability. The working-class homes of *Union Street* are
falling apart, literally and metaphorically. Windows are boarded up, or
partially boarded where panes have been smashed. The floors and
stairs contain treacherous holes and gaps, which disrupt the function
of home as sanctuary. Chimney backs are broken, allowing the smoke
from neighbouring houses to pour in. For Kelly Brown, the streets are
filled with 'a smell of decay, of life ending' (13). The streets around
Union Street are in the process of complete demolition, so that Kelly
finds whole landscapes of dereliction, pockmarked with the rubble of
disused factories and crumbling houses:

She liked particularly the decaying, boarded-up houses by the river. There a whole community had been cleared away: the houses waited for the bulldozers and the demolition men to move in, but they never came. Grass grew between the cobbles, rosebay willowherb thronged the empty spaces, always threatening to encroach, but still the houses stood. Officially empty, but not in reality. You had only to walk down these streets at night to realise that life, life of a kind, still went on. (59–60)

In these abandoned streets, Kelly finds an abandoned throng of homeless, hopeless tramps and drunks, derelict people hidden in a derelict landscape. 'Derelict' is a word repeated several times in the course of the novel, and serves as a metaphor for the decrepit condition of life in the wastelands of England's post-industrial communities. It defines the economic, psychological, cultural and geographical landscape of Barker's fiction, and serves to connect the apparently isolated instances of rape, murder, domestic violence, abandonment and sickness to the social and cultural structures of this bleak, post-industrial scene.

Barker's novel depicts working-class community, then, through tropes of absence, brokenness and ruin. This might lead us to suspect that her depiction of the post-industrial plight of the working class is heavily scored by nostalgia for a lost haven of communality and rootedness. This would put the community depicted in *Union Street* in close proximity to the kind of England which Beryl Bainbridge describes in her *English Journey* (1984), as she tours abandoned mines, struggling shipyards, and deserted factories and mourns the deaths of England's industrial, maritime and cultural past.[6] The landscapes to which Bainbridge is constantly drawn, two years after the publication of *Union Street*, are ones of erasure, disappearance, decimation, the rotting, forsaken landscapes which bear the scars of once industrious communities, just as in Barker's *Union Street*. Bainbridge's narrative is structured to resemble the journey undertaken by J.B. Priestley in 1933, narrated in his *English Journey* (1934), but it is also conversing with Orwell's *The Road to Wigan Pier* (1937), upon which Bainbridge plays a sardonic joke in her subtitle, *The Road to Milton Keynes*. Much of England Bainbridge finds to be ghostly, haunted by what it has lost, paralysed into acts of perpetual remembrance and mourning. Barker's England, and specifically her northeastern corner of England, is as much a site of memory, of loss and paralysis, as the one Bainbridge depicts. But Barker in my view is not so much nostalgic as revisionist in her approach, revisionist in the sense of returning critically to the myth of homeliness and community pervasive in earlier representations of the working class.

This is particularly apparent in the first story in the novel, the story of Kelly Brown. Kelly is eleven, on the cusp of entering an adult world of work and sexuality. Barker crafts this novel as a kind of *Bildungsroman*, in which the emergence into adulthood is charted as a process of becoming conscious of class and sexual identity. Moreover, in the light of Second Wave feminist models of subjectivity, Barker shows such identity as a construction determined by social and economic structures. In the case of Kelly Brown, this is shown through Kelly's violent awakening into an understanding of the vulnerability of her home and community. The division between childhood and adulthood is conventionally figured in terms of interiority and exteriority, in which childhood is cocooned from the painful knowledge of the world outside by a series of physical, emotional and moral barriers, and in which home and family represent comfort and safety. For Kelly, however, these barriers are shown to be porous. This is the significance of the story's opening, in which Kelly is woken by the noise of a square of cardboard flapping against the broken window frame of her bedroom. It is one of a number of images of exposure, of the lack of the protective shell that 'home' should represent, which recur through the novel.

The boundary between home and outside is breached. This is exemplified further when Kelly discovers that her sister, Linda, has discarded a soiled sanitary towel in Kelly's clothes drawer. Kelly rejects the 'mucky bloody' adult world which Linda represents: 'She looked at the hair in Linda's armpits, at the breasts that shook and wobbled when she ran, and no, she didn't want to get like that. And she certainly didn't want to drip foul-smelling, brown blood out of her fanny every month' (3). Kelly's innocence is marked here by her disgust at what appears to her as the grotesque physicality of adulthood. Later, she will discover that more affluent families shroud their young girls in the cosy, pink world of glossy make-believe to preserve their innocence (52). For her, however, the boundaries between innocence and experience are as thin as the walls through which she hears her mother 'on the hump all night' with some new man dragged home from the pub (3). Her mother's latest lover is introduced to Kelly the following morning, almost comically, as *Uncle* Arthur, but the intrusion of a strange man into their home life seems expected, signalling again the permeable boundaries between the homely and the strange.

The story of 'Kelly Brown' shares in this respect the domestic situation of Shelagh Delaney's *A Taste of Honey* (1958), in which Helen's unstable sexual life leaves her daughter, Jo, in circumstances in which her childhood and the securities afforded by 'home' are compromised. Delaney's play provides a significant pretext in this case for Barker's stories about the disjunctive experiences of working-class women caught outside the familial structures of their communities. This is signalled in Delaney's play, for example, in the fact that Helen and Jo are not part of a street, but instead inhabit a transient world of defaulting tenants and serial evictions.

There are some semblances of home and community for Kelly, which are perhaps the only indications of a preserved innocence. She chooses to wear one of her mother's sweaters, for example, because 'they were warmer, somehow, and she liked the smell' (4). She shows no such signs of familial affection towards her mother, but the gesture is an indication at least of a desire for sentiment, for connection. So, too, she feels connected to the local shopkeeper and to Iris King, who embodies some degree of stability and continuity in the street (although Iris's own story in chapter five revisits and undermines this reputation as a myth). There is some trace here of the solidity and commonality of Hoggart's and Sillitoe's depictions of working-class community. It is associated in the story, however, with Kelly's childhood fictions of the world around her, and is shattered when Kelly is raped. Later in the novel, Muriel Scaife remembers such a feeling of solidarity and security as a childhood game of playing in the lamplight, 'a moment in the light' of childhood, but 'then the lamp goes out, the circle is broken, the chanting voices are silenced forever' (152).

Kelly is raped by an older man, whom she has begun to construct as a substitute father. He shapes this image of himself when they first meet in the park, when he treats her in a gentle, paternal manner, which allows her to begin 'telling herself stories again, fantasies whose warmth eased away the last ache of doubt. Her father had come back' (16). Kelly does not entertain this fantasy for long, and she knows that the man is a threat. She is drawn to him, however, because he appears to fill a void in her identity. 'Other people – her mother, Linda, the teachers at school – merely glanced at her and then with indifference or haste, passed on. But this man stared at her as if every pore in her skin mattered' (15–16). On their second encounter, after Kelly has been at the funfair, the man pretends to lead her home, but leads her instead into a deserted industrial wasteland, where he rapes her. Barker here connects the rape symbolically to a powerful matrix of absent centres. Kelly is drawn to the man because he takes the place of her absent father, and because his gaze 'creates her', where she has been ignored by her own mother, sister, teachers and everyone else. His choice of location is also symbolic, for if the community of Kelly's birth once thrived upon the monumental power of industry the deserted factory yard is now the symbolic core of a deserted, vulnerable community.

Set in such a bleak landscape of loss and dereliction, the rape has obvious allegorical significance for the community as a whole. It destroys any sense of connection, cohesion or self-validation, so that when Kelly realises that the rape defines her – 'she *was* what had just happened to her' (32) – she also recognises that she is now made in the image of her surroundings. The man has deprived her of the last tissue of protection between her and the painful, blighted landscape around her. He makes her, 'and he was . . . nothing!' (32), and so she becomes nothing too. She has been initiated into the world of dereliction, and thereafter she sees the world around her in all its terrifying mundanity:

> His face remained. And would be there always, trailing behind it, not the cardboard terrors of the fairground, those you buy for a few pennies and forget, but the real terror of the adult world, in which grown men open their mouths and howl like babies, where nothing that you feel, whether love or hate, is pure enough to withstand the contamination of pity. (57)

Kelly's newly broken vision of the world around her is suggested in the story by a series of images and metaphors of sight and specularity. She cannot escape seeing the man who has just raped her when she sits with him in a fish-and-chip shop lined with mirror-tiles (33). She cannot avoid the 'unadmitted speculation' of neighbours, the prying eyes of the street (47). She sees in her mother's beaten face a mirror of her own (58) and, when she encounters her own savage reflection in a mirror in a house she has broken into, she smashes it, 'hurling her whole body against the glass' (54).

Kelly's rage at what she has become is the rage of Caliban, born of the recognition of herself as the creation of the man's violent, sadistic desires. 'You taught me language; and my profit on't is, I know how to curse', speaks Caliban in *The Tempest* (I.ii.363–4). It is a lesson exemplified in Kelly's enraged defacement of her school, in which she daubs her shit all over the headmaster's office,[7] and chalks graffiti on her classroom blackboard:

> She careered down the corridor to her own classroom, the smell of her shit hot above the usual smells of gymshoes and custard. She almost ran at the blackboard, and wrote, sobbing, PISS, SHIT, FUCK. Then, scoring the board so hard that the chalk screamed, the worst word she knew: CUNT. (56)

These are the words signifying Kelly's entry into the physicality of adulthood. They are the emblems of rebellion against the authority of the school. She screeches in chalk the 'worst word she knew', the word which sums up her worth in a society in which she has only ever been valued by a man intent on raping her. This is Kelly's exasperated cry at the cruel knowledge of what she will become. It is the fate of her mother, of Linda, and of the characters in later stories; of Iris King, for example, whose husband invites his drunken friends to rape her. In the derelict society symbolised in Union Street, women are frequently reduced to commodities for use and exchange, their value determined in the impoverished system of social and cultural relationships of their ruined community. Blonde Dinah, the prostitute from Wharfe Street, is only the most obvious example of the determination of women as commodities.

Barker shows such oppressive constructions of women to be the products of a bankrupt social economy. In this context even the rapist is not the victor, but is reduced before Kelly's eyes to a snivelling wreck. Everywhere, in fact, in Barker's landscape are the signs of a failed social system, from Kelly's acts of outrage, to the absence of any authorities or guardians in her community, or the sicknesses paralysing the few remaining men in the street, or the dead baby which Kelly discovers buried under a heap of rubble near her home. 'Barker's main aim', Ian Haywood argues of Union Street, 'is to show that working-class femininity, as constructed by those largely absent contexts of capitalist and patriarchal power, is a process of almost unremitting gloom and entrapment'.[8] In this sense it more than superficially resembles the stories in Nell Dunn's Up the Junction (1963), in which working-class women are depicted as trapped in a relentless cycle of poverty and debt, casual underage sex, backstreet abortions, abusive relationships and early signs of illness. Barker's women, like those in Dunn's stories, or in Margaret

Lassell's *Wellington Road* (1962), are as condemned as the slum housing they live in.

It is this recognition that she is condemned to dereliction which seems to enrage Kelly into committing her acts of destruction.[9] When she wanders bewildered into an affluent Victorian house, one which had 'preserved [its] air of smug assurance into a more violent and chaotic age' (51), she marvels at how sheltered and cloistered the house is, with its enclosed garden, and delicately scented and ordered rooms. It is the opposite of her own world, in which everything is fragile, porous and disordered. Kelly discovers this to be particularly the case in the parents' bedroom, in the depiction of which Barker conjoins the symbolism of a safe, protective home with the image of venerated femininity:

> She turned her attention to the bed, rubbing her hands across the flesh-coloured satin until a roughened flap of skin from a healing blister snagged on one of the threads and tore. There was a pile of cushions at the head of the bed: big, soft, delicately scented, plump, pink, flabby cushions, like the breasts and buttocks of the woman who slept in the bed. A man slept there too, of course, but you could not imagine him. It was a woman's room, a temple to femininity. And the altar was the dressing table. (53)

As Margaretta Jolly argues, the scene plays out a kind of rape on the protected femininity of this cosy middle-class world, figured in Kelly's easy penetration of its enclosed spaces, and her prurient probing of the woman's dressing table and bed.[10] Kelly desecrates this 'temple to femininity' because it appears to be invulnerable to rape, because it is imagined as the antithesis of her own world of violence, neglect and poverty. She understands that she is excluded from this world, even if she does not comprehend the social structures which create and maintain such exclusions, and hence, in the girl's bedroom, she feels pity or hatred, but 'she would not have known how to envy her' (52). There is no more stark comparison than this middle-class domestic interior to her own broken, neglected home and childhood, no more salient reminder of the impermeability of the social and cultural barriers between classes. In contrast, the interiority of working-class culture, which Orwell celebrated as 'a good place to be', is explored in *Union Street* as an abyssal ghetto, from which there is neither respite nor escape.

The course of Kelly's life after this painful awakening is mapped out for her in the lives of the women around her. She begins to see herself, as if for the first time, in the eyes of her mother and sister. She sees herself figured as female monster when she compares herself with the angelic femininity venerated in the middle-class home, a contrast which reflects on the divergent class-bound experiences of femininity. Her mother attempts belatedly to foster an already derelict model of femininity when Kelly is given presents at Christmas which orient themselves around the preparation for adult womanhood: 'a doll that wet itself, a hairdressing set, a matching necklace and brooch' (63). But, in a phrase which is repeated frequently throughout *Union Street*, Kelly is said to be 'too far gone' (62).

The final line of the story – 'She was going home' – which seems to recover some sense of comfort in her home, suggests that Kelly finds in this vision some way of living with the confining conditions of her social situation. 'Home' is not the protective cocoon which it should be, but she resigns herself at least to what it does have to offer. *Union Street* develops this theme through a number of images of broken shells – the split shells of the conkers in 'Kelly Brown', for example (14), and the galling image of the man's face cracking open like an egg after he has raped Kelly (33); the breaking waters of Lisa Goddard as she gives birth (127) and, in the same story, symbolic images of smashed eggs and a crushed chrysalis (138); the open coffin containing the broken body of John Scaife, whose death leaves his son feeling exposed, 'with nobody now to stand between him and the great void' (167). There are many more such images, which suggest the fragility of protective shells such as body and home, and serve to identify the women symbolically with each other. 'Home' is equated through these images with figures of the womb, thus indicating the familiar configuration of home, identity, and community with security and interiority. But this configuration is fragile and troubled in Barker's novel, as each story in the novel interrogates and explodes received notions of homeliness and community. Even the provisional, fleeting notions of solidarity between the women are fractured by issues of race ('Joanne Wilson'), social class ('Iris King') and politics ('Alice Bell'), just as the possibility that some of the characters might form anything resembling Orwell's idyll of a working-class home proves illusory.

The story of Kelly Brown ends with Kelly looking at the gates of the local cake factory, which employs many of the women from *Union Street*. In the women emerging from those gates, Kelly sees a premonition of the woman she will become, just as Joanne Wilson looks around the other women in the factory and observes that 'every older woman became an image of the future' (94). The cake factory takes the place of the centres of male labour represented in earlier representations of industrial working-class communities. The relatively well-paid figure of Arthur Seaton, working on the factory assembly line in Sillitoe's *Saturday Night and Sunday Morning*, is replaced with the poorly paid figure of the female casual worker. The factory functions in *Union Street* in part to highlight the displacement of mass labour concentrations from men to women, but also on a symbolic level, to represent the commodification of labour, or what Georg Lukács calls reification.¹¹ Reification is the process whereby the social relations of labour are made to appear as commodities in a capitalist system of exchange, so that people are alienated from their productive activity. The factory scene in the story of Joanne Wilson exemplifies this process:

> The noise was horrific as usual. There was no possibility of conversation. Even the supervisor's orders had to be yelled at the top of her voice and repeated many times before anybody heard. At intervals, there were snatches of music. It was being played continuously but only the odd phrase triumphed over the roar of the machines. Some of the women moved their mouths silently, singing or talking to themselves: it was hard to tell. Others merely looked blank. After a while not only speech but thought became impossible.
>
> The first sponge cake reached Jo. She began the sequence of actions that she would perform hundreds of times that day. It took little effort once you were used to it and, provided the cakes continued to arrive in a steady stream, it could be done almost automatically.
>
> Almost. But not quite. Now that she was alone – for in this roaring cavern of sound each woman *was* alone – she wanted to think about Ken, she wanted to plan the evening, to work out exactly how she was going to tell him about the baby. (84–5)

Barker represents the reification of human labour primarily here through the metaphor of mechanical noise, which drowns out any attempts at communication, and reduces every woman to being alone. Instead of being part of a social process, every woman on the assembly line functions as a monadic unit, operating only in harmony with the mechanical process she is paid to serve. Superficially, this scene is similar to several factory scenes in Sillitoe's novel, in which the repetitive, mechanical labour of the factory worker is relieved to a certain extent by a sort of mental or imaginative escape. But Sillitoe always pits the imaginative life of Arthur Seaton against the mechanical life of the factory, so that Seaton seems to transcend the rut of working-class labour. This is not the case in Barker, who shows that the factory extends beyond its mechanical processes into the mental and emotional life of the community. Moreover, *Union Street* shows that the permeation of capitalist relations of commodification into the community in fact functions to fragment community altogether.

One danger of such an approach to the novel is that it risks nostalgia for an implied past in which the working class somehow enjoyed greater security. There is nothing new about the insecurity of working-class life, but, as Zygmunt Bauman argues, what is new about the economic insecurities of contemporary working-class life is that they embody 'a powerful *individualizing* force'.[12] The inhabitants of *Union Street*, for the most part, are left to contend with the economic and social consequences of post-industrial capitalism as individuals. There is no 'union' left in Union Street, no powerful mass movement through which to articulate resistance to the power of capital. Instead, in the new economic realities of post-union Britain, 'each woman was alone', as the stories of Barker's novel testify. Barker counters this individualising tendency in radical ways, as I will show later in this chapter, but even the most obvious attempts in the novel to solidify a sense of community – through Iris King's neighbourly deeds for the Browns or Alice Bell, for example, or through the fleeting alliances between women formed in the factory – are no more than temporary relief against the processes of fragmentation effected in advanced capitalism.

The dominance of economic structures over the social life of the inhabitants of *Union Street* is evident in the ways in which the novel uses the imagery of machinery and industry to describe a commodified subjectivity. The industrial landscape permeates into every aspect of the lives of Barker's characters. Lisa Goddard's baby is delivered by 'metal hands', after a period of labour described as 'mechanical', the pains coming with 'remorseless regularity', which felt like 'extreme heat, as though she were being forced to stand too close to a furnace' (128). The furnace dominates the imagination of this former steel town. Sex is also mechanical, like the 'impersonal, machine-like passion' Joanne Wilson finds exciting but then terrifying, with her boyfriend Ken under the railway bridge, beneath the 'deadly and monotonous' sound of a goods train (101). There is little pleasure in sex for the women of *Union Street*, as it is frequently experienced as a form of violence – the rape of Kelly Brown is, in this sense, only the most stark instance of violent sex in the novel – but it also symbolises the commodification of women's bodies as part of a mechanical process of reproduction. This is the world Kelly Brown is coming to know in the awakening depicted at the beginning of the novel.

Kelly discovers this dehumanised world of commodified subjectivity when she encounters the wasted, vagrant women with faces which show 'the outward and visible signs of an inner and spiritual collapse' (60), or in the park, where she watches a boy and girl having cold, robotic sex in the bushes. Again, she sees terror in the ordinary, when 'something mechanical in his movements, a piston-like power and regularity, began to make it seem not ridiculous, but terrible' (62–3). She identifies with the girl's alienation from this mechanical process, and later Kelly feels that she is 'turning into a machine. Her legs, pumping up and down the cold street, had the regularity and power of pistons. And her hands, dangling out of the sleeves of her anorak, were as heavy and lifeless as tools' (64). After this, the whole landscape seems to take on the character of an exhausted, mechanical world, like the former steel town in which the novel is set, with the sun imagined as a 'brutal, bloody disc', the sky a 'red furnace' and the earth exhibiting a 'steely blue radiance' (64–5). Kelly's world is hardening into a predetermining landscape of decay and entrapment, and she sees this not only in the landscape, but also in the assembly-line girls she watches emerging from the cake factory. It is her fate to work there, along with all the other women from Union Street, and to inhabit the same mechanical routines as they do.

It is her fate to live out the lives of all the women depicted in *Union Street*, which is the significance of the end of the story, when Kelly sits hand in hand with Alice Bell, the subject of the final story in the novel. The brief encounter between the two signals a barely formed possibility of communication, humanity, perhaps understanding, as Kelly 'stared at the old woman as if she held, and might communicate, the secret of life' (67). Alice Bell sits on a park bench, exposed to the freezing air, waiting to die as a salvation from what she perceives to be the spiritual death of having to go into a 'home'. Kelly finds in herself a well of compassion and empathy for the old woman, and she comforts Alice in her final moments as she slips into 'sleep, or unconsciousness, or death' (68). The story concludes with a chain of symbolic images of women as birds: from Alice, who appears to Kelly to have bird's claws for hands, and a throat 'as vulnerable as a bird's', to the association of the women emerging from the cake factory with the 'fierce, ecstatic trilling' of the starlings she has heard in the park (68). Barker relieves the painful, miserable knowledge of the stultifying existence of working-class women with this glimpsed, lyrical vision of the women of Union Street as vulnerable but trilling birds.

If there is no longer a mass movement through which working-class men and women can find community, and struggle against exploitation, Barker traces the more informal, transient hopes of community in the interrelations between the women of Union Street. This is the most significant achievement of the novel, that it picks amongst the debris of derelict streets and the aborted dreams of a broken class to pull together a narrative of women maintaining a community of sorts. *Union Street* is set in a grim, post-industrial age, and yet it ultimately finds a way of avoiding pessimism about the fate of working-class women in these derelict streets. Partly, this is achieved in the symbolic vision of a spectral community of women with which the novel ends, and to which I'll return. But it is also the product of carefully constructed narrative strategies, which enable the reader to perceive not just the monadic isolation of each character, but also the intersubjective community which begins to form from each character's apparently empathic awareness of others.

Barker experiments in *Union Street* with a consistent theoretical problem in working-class writing, a problem which Sillitoe described, perhaps unfairly, as how 'to write a book about a man who has never read a book'.[13] It is the problem of how to represent a culture which has consistently struggled to find representation. As Alan Sinfield argues, the working-class writer was always already a revisitor to working-class culture, since the impetus (and indeed the space, time and money) to write placed her in an ambivalent relationship with the class of her upbringing.[14] Working-class fiction thus runs a double risk: the risk of appropriating working-class experience for middle-class forms of representation, and the risk of marginalising working-class subject matter by attempting to invent distinctive working-class forms of expression. In terms of narrative style, this comes down to a series of choices. Is the narrative external or internal to the experiences of the characters? Does the narrator write or speak like the characters, or in a more educated diction? Does the narrator know more about the characters than they do themselves? Is the narrator reliable or unreliable, a subjective presence in the story, or an omniscient being hovering over the story? All of these questions reflect important debates about the ethics and politics of narrative authority in fictional representations of the working class, debates which owe much to Marxist thinking about the relationship between aesthetics and politics.[15]

Union Street strives to avoid the narrative stance of the omniscient observer defining and cataloguing working-class community for middle-class consumption. It avoids what Raymond Williams discusses as the fictional mode 'in which we are all signifiers, all critics and judges, and can somehow afford to be because life – given life, creating life – goes on where it is supposed to, elsewhere'.[16] For Williams, one danger with realist representation of the working class is that it risks exercising a class division in its very form, between the 'us' of narrator and reader, and the 'them' of its subject. The narrative voice of *Union Street*, however, articulates an intersubjective consciousness, which shifts from the apparently external stance of the objective narrator to the internal voices of the characters:

> There was a cold spell towards the end of January. The women of Union Street had to cope with the problem of keeping themselves and their families warm. There were continued reports that the miners were about to go on strike.
>
> Mrs Bell had a final look at the deaths, muttering the names under her breath as her magnifying glass moved down the page. The list was longer now. After making sure there were no familiar names she pushed the blankets back and added the newspaper to those already in the bed.
>
> She tried to do without a fire in the afternoon, so that she could have heat at night when the temperature dropped. Though she had a lot of faith in the newspaper, too. Tramps covered themselves with it, didn't they, and they should know.
>
> Iris had discovered some coal in one of the corner shops and was carrying it home on her back. At the corner of the street she paused to get her breath. Further along, bending down, was the large black-clad arse of Mrs Harrison. Out gathering again. George Harrison'ld drop dead if he ever found out. (239–40)

The above passage begins with objective narration, comprising general statements about the social conditions of the inhabitants of Union Street. The first paragraph consists of factual statements, none of which imply an interior or subjective experience. The second paragraph takes us inside the home of Alice Bell, observing what she is looking at, and what she is saying 'under her breath', as only an omniscient narrator can. There is, however, an implied internal perspective here, when we are told 'The list was longer now', and this is exemplified further in the imitated speech or thoughts of Alice Bell in the next paragraph, 'Tramps covered themselves with it, didn't they, and they should know'. Barker shifts subtly here from objective narration into the free, indirect discourse of speech representation, in which Alice Bell's voice is presented to the reader as if unmediated by a narrator. The same shift of perspective from objective to subjective is made in the next paragraph, from the reported actions of Iris King to the unmediated presentation of her thoughts. The objective perspective of the omniscient narrator preserves the collective vision offered in the novel, so that the novel is not confined to the solipsistic perspectives of individual characters. In this passage the narrative focus moves from all the women of Union Street, to Mrs Bell, to Iris looking at Mrs Harrison, so that there is a controlling movement from one character to another. Yet the narrative focus is never permitted to remain above and superior to the characters. Peter Hitchcock describes this method, after Bakhtin, as dialogic, and argues that the fact that 'the Bakhtinian voicing of her work cannot be read as one voice' is the 'hallmark of a significant counterhegemonic discourse'.[17] This dialogic principle of narration is one of the principal ways in which Union Street not only avoids the pitfalls of realist representations of working-class life which Williams observed, but also resists the attempt to objectify or commodify working-class community.

Similarly, the narrative idiom is never far from the ways in which the characters might describe their own experiences and feelings. Barker recalls that one difficulty in writing the novel was that she 'kept undermining characters by slipping into middle-class style language and distanced observation'.[18] Union Street is, in this sense, an experiment in closing the gap between the authoritative voice of the omniscient narrator and the recorded language of the characters. The 'community' of the novel is only possible through the distance of extradiegetic narration, but Barker's narrator is able to be omnipresent without straying beyond the knowledge and idiom of her community. There are limits to the narrator's knowledge, then, which is confined to the imagined geography of a small, knowable community of working-class streets. Every time the characters in the novel encounter the boundaries of their community, the narrative implies the hiatus between the 'us' of Union Street and the 'them' of elsewhere. 'They' include 'The Man' who rapes Kelly, and the nameless authorities –

doctors, nurses, policemen, teachers and social workers – who intervene in the lives of the street's inhabitants. The narrative sometimes peeks into the consciousness of these others – we learn that 'The Man' thinks of killing Kelly, and that the man who comes to put Alice into a 'home' takes pride in his work – but this is knowledge glimpsed through the eyes of the working-class characters, not simply told by an omniscient narrator. The narrative perspective in *Union Street*, then, moves covertly from one consciousness to another, never beyond an implied collective consciousness of the street's inhabitants.

Even as the novel depicts the decimation of working-class community, therefore, it is also in the process of constructing an imagined or symbolic community through the intersubjective consciousness of the narrative. The structure of Barker's novel resembles that of James Joyce's *Dubliners* in the sense that it is possible to argue that each of the characters are really versions of one character's progress through life. Barker indicates this in the recurrent scenes in which characters see their younger or older selves reflected in the other characters, of which the mutual recognition between Kelly Brown and Alice Bell is perhaps the most obvious example. Like *Dubliners*, too, *Union Street* develops a dark, oppressive theme in all of the stories which is both concluded and relieved in the final story. The final story in *Union Street*, 'Alice Bell', is both the most communal and the most solipsistic story, in the sense that several characters gather and converse around Alice, but she is also most alone of all the women in her battle to preserve her dignity in the face of death. This story also brings the equation between home and identity to its conclusion, as Alice struggles for a home in which to die. Home, despite the fact that it is cold, damp, broken and hazardous, is defined positively for Alice in opposition to the 'workhouse'. That she keeps herself warm with newspapers, however, like a street tramp, is indicative of the thin line distinguishing her from those sleeping on park benches.

Home symbolises the dignity of defining her own space, and determining her own death. As she begins to lose control of her own body, after a fall and a stroke, she increasingly turns to home as an instinctive shell: 'She burrowed down into her house, savouring its various textures and smells, an old fox that had reached its earth at last' (248). It is described as 'almost an extension of her own body' (234), while her desire for home is experienced as 'a physical pain' (246), which is connected symbolically to a desire to return 'in spirit to her beginnings. To her first home . . . to her mother' (249). For Alice, home is equated fully with self-identity, so that she conceives the attempt by social services to remove her from her home as equivalent both with rape and death (260). Barker's novel here suggests the ambivalence of the working-class home as a construct, for, in a culture in which 'home' is a potent and pervasive myth, it exhibits at one and the same time the marginal social status of its inhabitants and the stubborn assertion of self-identity. Union Street exists on a social scale, in which it is seldom a comforting place to be, yet still holds itself above the states of dereliction or vagrancy which exist nearby. Alice clings to what her home symbolises, therefore, long after it has ceased to afford her the comforts of a home, because even the fact of its possession is an effective social signifier of her elevation above the level of a pauper in the workhouse, her anachronistic marker of indignity.

If home is depicted as more comforting and desirable in 'Alice Bell' than in the other stories in Union Street, it is also shown to be the site of the unhomely, of the return of haunted memories, and the ghostly presence of unfamiliar voices and faces. All of the characters in Union Street experience the ghostly in some form, even if it is only in the form of seeing themselves mirrored in the lives of others. It is through such spectral visions of themselves as others that Union Street proposes an alternative conception of community, one which can only be imagined through the symbolic and psychic realm of the ghostly. In 'Alice Bell', the ghosts accumulate in the course of the story, so that the clamour of ethereal voices builds into the same crescendo of 'fierce, ecstatic trilling' which Kelly Brown hears in the park (264). For Alice, these voices are associated with an apparently communal chorus of feminine identity, which begins with indistinguishable sounds like 'speech under water' (253), becomes clearer as a 'web of voices' – 'a child shouting, a young girl laughing, a woman crooning over her child' (263) – until finally the 'electric clicks' of women talking commingles with the vision of birds trilling in a 'withered and unwithering tree' (265). As Alice Bell fades towards death, she experiences this mythical vision of women as birds in a tree, while at the same time 'her white hair and skin took on the colours of blood and fire' (264). Barker presents Alice here as the chimerical embodiment of a mythic symbol of renewal, like the 'Lady Lazarus' of Sylvia Plath's poem, at the same time as she serves to bring the disparate, troubled women of Union Street into an imaginary unity.

This is where the story of 'Alice Bell' seems most to resemble Joyce's 'The Dead', in its lyrical, generous vision of the symbolic unity achieved in the twilight moment of passing towards death. Like Gabriel Conroy in Joyce's story, her identity seems to dissolve as she passes away, so that she experiences a fusion of her memories and consciousness with those of other women. 'She had been so many women in her time' (263), Barker writes, and Alice seems ultimately to function as a mythical conduit for the spiritual or symbolic regeneration of all the women. This is symbolised in particular in the final passage of the novel:

> The world dwindled to a park bench and a litter of dead leaves in the grass.
> But there was a child there, now, a girl, who, standing with the sun behind her, seemed almost to be a gift of the light. At first she was afraid, the child had come so suddenly. Then – not afraid. They sat beside each other; they talked. The girl held out her hand. The withered hand and the strong young hand met and joined. There was silence. Then it was time for them both to go.
> So that in the end there were only the birds, soaring, swooping, gliding, moving in a never-ending spiral about the withered and un-withering tree. (265)

Barker creates in this climactic image what Isobel Armstrong calls, in her discussion of Angela Carter's *Nights at the Circus* (1984), 'a dance of possibility',[19] in which the materialist depiction of social and economic dereliction is intertwined with a sublime vision of flight and rejuvenation. Like Carter's novel, *Union Street* holds these two conflicting modes of representation in parallel, so that while the novel is thematically and formally indebted to social realist writing, it succeeds also in glimpsing the symbolic realm explored more intensively by Carter. Such a formation reproduces the dialogic tension between myth and history, the real and the symbolic, the material and the ideal, not in order to transcend the bleak depiction of dereliction presented throughout the novel, but to signal the possibility of an imaginative transformation of the structures which produce these material conditions. *Union Street* revisits the topography of the 'small worlds' of Hoggart's account, in part to offer a revisionist, feminist critique of received notions of working-class community, but (perhaps more importantly) to delineate the grounds upon which we might be compelled to conceive of the functions and forms of 'home' and community anew.

Union Street ends with a radical revision of the notion of community, holding in tension the derelict sites of an older tradition of working-class 'unionised' community with the symbolic unity of the women of a new, displaced working class. Ken Worpole predicted, in his influential study, *Dockers and Detectives*, that the working-class novel would have to be reinvented in order to represent the new realities of working-class life:

> As 'de-industrialization' and the movement of capital disrupts settled industrial communities, we shall need to make the break from the traditional working-class novel with its emphasis on the continuity of the diurnal family life. Displacement, fragmentariness, cosmopolitanism, the life on the streets rather than in the homes, cultural multiplicity are likely to be the new conditions of experience for the next generation of working-class people.[20]

Barker's novel is perhaps more of a revisitation of the dereliction wrought by de-industrialisation, rather than the substantive break with tradition which Worpole imagines here, but *Union Street* is also the beginning of a sustained attempt in Barker's work to explore the ways in which fictional narrative can represent the experiences and feelings of displaced and disrupted communities without itself displacing the voices of those communities. Barker's commitment to return to the apparent sites of working-class dissolution serves also as a renewal of faith in the possibility that these are also sites of regeneration. The ability to represent hope and survival in the darkest corners of a derelict, post-industrial society has become perhaps the most persistent attribute of Barker's work.

Notes

1 Especially when women are shown to be constantly devalued, even by women themselves, as Monica Malm argues in her short essay, '*Union Street*: Thoughts on Mothering', *Moderna Språk*, 92:2 (1998), 143–6.
2 Richard Hoggart, *The Uses of Literacy* (Harmondsworth, Penguin, 1957), 59.
3 George Orwell, *The Road to Wigan Pier* (Harmondsworth, Penguin, 1962), 104.
4 Alan Sillitoe, *Saturday Night and Sunday Morning* (London, Grafton, 1985), 31.
5 See Peter Hitchcock, *Working-Class Fiction in Theory and Practice: A Reading of Alan Sillitoe* (Ann Arbor, UMI Research Press, 1989) and *Dialogics of the Oppressed* (Minneapolis, University of Minnesota Press, 1993).
6 Beryl Bainbridge, *English Journey, or The Road to Milton Keynes* (London, Flamingo, 1984).

7 This action seems to connect with the 'dirty protests' current in Northern Ireland's prisons in the early 1980s, particularly as images of the war in Northern Ireland perforate the novel in several places.

8 Ian Haywood, *Working-Class Fiction: From Chartism to* Trainspotting (Tavistock, Northcote House, 1997), 145–6.

9 See George Wotton's argument in 'Writing from the Margins', *Peripheral Visions: Images of Nationhood in Contemporary British Fiction*, ed. Ian A. Bell (Cardiff, University of Wales Press, 1995), 194–215.

10 Margaretta Jolly, 'After Feminism: Pat Barker, Penelope Lively and the Contemporary Novel', *British Culture of the Postwar: An Introduction to Literature and Society, 1945–1999*, ed. Alistair Davies and Alan Sinfield (London, Routledge, 2000), 65).

11 See Georg Lukács, *History and Class Consciousness* (London, Merlin, 1991).

12 Zygmunt Bauman, *Liquid Modernity* (Cambridge, Polity, 2000), 148.

13 Alan Sillitoe, quoted in Stuart Laing, *Representations of Working-Class Life, 1957–1964* (Basingstoke, Macmillan, 1986), 69. Barker, on the other hand, insisted that working-class women are articulate and creative, but remained underrepresented in contemporary culture; quoted in Sharon Monteith, *Pat Barker* (Tavistock, Northcote House, 2002), 13.

14 Alan Sinfield, *Literature, Politics and Culture in Postwar Britain* (London, Athlone, 1997), 266–71. Sinfield's argument here is of course building upon Hoggart's depiction of the scholarship boy in *The Uses of Literacy*, 291–304.

15 See in particular the work of the Frankfurt school, and the debates about aesthetics and politics collected in Adorno et al, *Aesthetics and Politics* (London, Verso, 1980). See also Georg Lukács, *The Historical Novel* (London, Merlin, 1962), Fredric Jameson, *The Political Unconscious: Narrative as a Socially Symbolic Act* (London, Routledge, 1986) and, specifically in relation to feminist writing, Rita Felski, *Beyond Feminist Aesthetics* (London, Hutchinson Radius, 1989).

16 Raymond Williams, *The English Novel: From Dickens to Lawrence* (London, Hogarth, 1984), 91.

17 Hitchcock, *Dialogics of the Oppressed*, 54.

18 Quoted in Hitchcock, *Dialogics of the Oppressed*, 64.

19 Isobel Armstrong, 'Woolf by the Lake, Woolf at the Circus: Carter and Tradition', *Flesh and the Mirror: Essays on the Art of Angela Carter*, ed. Lorna Sage (London, Virago, 1994), 273.

20 Ken Worpole, *Dockers and Detectives: Popular Reading, Popular Writing* (London, Verso, 1983), 93.

3

Whoever fights monsters:
Blow Your House Down

In 1983, *Granta* magazine published a collection of new fiction by what its panel of judges decided were the best writers of their generation.[1] Pat Barker was chosen to have an extract from her next novel, *Blow Your House Down*, published alongside work by Martin Amis, Salman Rushdie, Kazuo Ishiguro, Graham Swift, Ian McEwan and Julian Barnes, among others. It is a measure of the impact Barker had already made with *Union Street* that she was chosen for inclusion among the best of her generation. It is a measure of that generation that so many of the list of twenty authors published in the *Granta* issue are now household names in contemporary fiction, proving that the 'end of the English novel' (a prediction upon which *Granta* had sponsored a symposium in 1980[2]) was very far from the case. This generation revived the flagging fortunes of the English novel, producing arguably the most successful period of fiction writing in England. Barker has a special place in this generation, too, for her commitment to social realism in an era more readily associated with postmodern and postcolonial writing marks her out from many of her contemporaries. That Barker's realism is no less experimental than the writing strategies of her contemporaries is an argument I will make throughout this volume.

Barker's contribution to the *Granta* issue in 1983 is a draft version of parts of chapters two and four of *Blow Your House Down*.[3] It signals some of the themes for which Barker had already established a reputation in *Union Street*. Brenda and Audrey arrive at a dingy pub, the Palmerston, in which women gather to shelter from the rain, and from the violence of the world outside. The women bear the hallmarks of violence – a scar on Jean's throat, bruises around Elaine's eyes – and their conversation reveals that they work as prostitutes.

Barker indicates that these women form a kind of community, bound together by their shared experiences of poverty and violence. There is a warmth to her depiction of the ways in which these women care for each other, but little sentiment, for this is community of a particularly precarious kind. Barker's piece finishes with Brenda, one of the main characters in the novel, being picked up by one of her regulars, and doing her job in serving the sexual needs of the pitiable men who visit her. *Union Street* depicted rape, unwanted teenage pregnancy, domestic violence, abortion, prostitution and an elderly pensioner committing suicide, as part of a coherent and uncompromising representation of the dereliction of community as experienced by working-class women. *Blow Your House Down* explores the same matrix of violence, sexuality, poverty and community, and the extract published in *Granta* advertises that Barker is committed to analysing the same social territory as she had brought to literary representation in *Union Street*.

This is especially noticeable if we compare the two novels. *Union Street* begins in the bedroom of two girls, Kelly and Linda Brown, as they wake up in the morning. Kelly is enraged to discover that Linda has dumped a sodden sanitary towel in one of her drawers. *Blow Your House Down* begins also in the bedroom of two girls, Brenda's daughters, as they are about to go to bed. Brenda discovers that her youngest daughter, Sharon, has wet the bed the night before, and failed to tell her. Tropes of bodily excretions pervade much of Barker's work, especially where such excretions symbolise the involuntary permeability of the body. Both novels also contain scenes in the opening chapters with suspect 'step'-fathers – the casual boyfriends of the girls' mothers – who become the objects of a kind of sexual jealousy for the elder daughter. Both novels share a common set of tropes and allusions – to bodily orifices, factory work, myths of community, dereliction, smells and senses – and both conclude with a scene in which the flight and singing of masses of birds symbolise a community of women. The similarities between the novels may indicate that Barker is exploring a narrow social world, within a conservative aesthetic form, but I argue here that Barker's second novel develops further the critique of class and gender politics of *Union Street*, and it does so in part by adopting and subverting conservative narrative forms.

The extract published in *Granta* is not just important for what it tells us about Barker's impact on the literary scene in the early stage of her career, nor just for the continuity it advertises between her first and second novel, but it also affords a significant insight into Barker's methods of writing and revising her work. If we compare a passage from the *Granta* extract with the same passage in the published novel, we can see some of the small but significant revisions which help to define the voice and tone of Barker's fiction. This is the extract from *Granta*:

> The Palmerston was crowded, as it always was by this time of night. Other pubs were livelier, with music and strip-tease shows; and more comfortable, too, for the Palmerston's dingy lino and balding plush had been there as long as anybody could remember. But to the women who drank in the back room, the Palmerston was special. It was their pub in a way that others were not, and what drew them back to it was the personality of its owner: Beattie Miller.[4]

The same passage in *Blow Your House Down* is slightly longer and contains some revisions:

> The place was crowded, as it always was by this time of night. Other pubs were livelier, with music and skin shows, and more comfortable too. The Palmerston's dingy lino and balding plush seats had been there as long as anybody could remember. But to the women who used its back room the Palmerston was special. They drank in all the pubs, moving in a nightly gavotte up and down Northgate, along Church Row, down Melbourne Terrace, under the viaduct, and back into Northgate again. But the Palmerston was different, and that was because of its owner, Beattie Miller. (9)

Both passages convey more or less the same information, but there are subtle changes of emphasis and tone. The changes in the first sentence from 'the Palmerston' to 'the place', and in the second sentence from 'strip-tease shows' to 'skin shows', refine the voice of the narrator from the language of an outsider to that of an insider. If Brenda or Audrey were describing this scene, they would not say 'The Palmerston was crowded' and talk of striptease, but would instead say 'the place was crowded' and talk of 'skin' shows. Barker brings the language of the narrative closer to the language of the characters. She also breaks up that long second sentence in the *Granta* extract, into two sentences in the novel. She changes 'balding plush' to 'balding plush seats' to clarify what is potentially an elusive image for those readers unfamiliar with the clichés of pub décor.

Two further small changes continue the process of harmonising the language of narrative with that of the characters – the change from 'the women who drank in the back room' to 'the women who used its back room' ('used' in this context being a less specific but more meaningful description of the function of this room for the women, since the room serves to bring them together for warmth and support more than simply to drink), and the change from 'the personality of its owner' to 'that was because of its owner' (again recognising that the women themselves might not have used the word 'personality' to refer to why they returned to the pub, just that it was 'because of its owner'). Beattie Miller remains an elusive but magnetic character in the novel, and this is how the women experience her in the pub, as someone to whom they feel compelled to turn and yet whom they never really know. Hence, Barker's revision helps to convey that elusive quality of Beattie's character. The most significant change to the passage is that Barker adds a more detailed topographical sense of the place inhabited by these women. In the *Granta* extract, the Palmerston pub is special in comparison to 'others' that were not. 'Others' implies that those pubs are so insignificant in comparison to the Palmerston that they are not worth naming, and also that they are not part of the same community or place. They are somewhere else, and hence the women are described as being drawn 'back' to the Palmerston. In the novel, however, Barker fills out and names the topography of streets in which these other pubs are located, but the women are completing a circle in their journey, starting from and returning to Northgate. Thus, this journey they undertake defines a contained and familiar community, creating an imagined space of streets in the minds of readers. Naming the streets and places in particular not only adds a sense of verisimilitude, but it also serves to embed these 'other' pubs in a landscape familiar to the characters, thus bringing the narrative again closer to the characters' perspectives. The only possible departure from this shift of tone from an external to an internal narrator is the use of the word 'gavotte', which alludes to an old French dance, the specific meaning of which would presumably be relatively unfamiliar to Barker's characters. But in the context of this passage 'gavotte' is emptied of this specific meaning, and is used instead simply to suggest a jaunt or journey. Indeed, it is important in this context that the word 'gavotte' is used inappropriately – or rather, that the word is appropriated into the local meaning assigned to it in this passage, since Barker is not suggesting that her characters have a good knowledge of old French cultural forms.

By comparing these two passages, then, we can see that Barker's process of revision refines the language and perspective of the narrative so that it comes closer to what the characters know, and how they would describe their own surroundings. In the previous chapter, I argued that in *Union Street* Barker sought to dissolve the barriers between the authoritative voice of omniscient narration and the voices of her characters, and this is achieved by a form of third-person narration which shifts, often in subtle ways, from extradiegetic narration to free indirect discourse. In *Blow Your House Down* Barker uses the same narrative techniques, but there are a number of ways in which she extends the repertoire of narrative perspectives to close further the gap between the narrative voice and the voices of the characters. This is most obviously the case in Jean's story, which is constructed as a first-person narrative. Moreover, it is addressed directly to a narratee, or an implied reader:

> You do a lot of walking in this job. More than you might think. In fact, when I get to the end of a busy Saturday night, it's me feet that ache. There, that surprised you, didn't it?
> I work on me own now. Nobody else fancies this place, because they've all got it worked out that he must've picked Kath up from here. I've got the whole viaduct to meself some nights. Except for Kath, who's still here in a way, stuck up there on her billboard. Hiya, Kath. (94)

The first-person narrative conveys the voice of experience and authenticity. Jean understands that the person to whom she is telling her tale is not familiar with life as a prostitute, and even that some aspects of her tale have the potential to surprise. There is, therefore, an implied gap between Jean's knowledge and the reader's knowledge, but this is in part what bonds the reader to the narrator, that the reader or narratee has something to learn from Jean's story. The first-person perspective guarantees an immediacy of access to Jean's experience, which even the most covert use of third-person narrative can never quite achieve. Those guarantees of immediacy are there not just in the pronoun 'I', but also in the 'improper' syntax and grammar of Jean's narrative. The fact that Jean's narrative also reports her speech and thoughts addressed to others – such as 'Hiya, Kath' at the end of this passage – also signals to readers the immediacy of access which the first person narrative affords.

Jean's narrative forms the third part of the novel, and functions as a subordinate level of narration to the third-person narrative in which the rest of the novel is written. There are two reasons in particular for Barker's switch into first-person narration at this point in the story. The first is that it deepens the authenticity of the experience of the women, by accessing Jean's stories and thoughts in a more direct way than is possible in third-person narrative. The second is that it brings the reader closer to the suspense of the thriller plot within the novel, so that Jean's encounter with the suspected serial killer is more immediate and real. Jean wants to find the murderer, and her story thus takes on the characteristics of an adventure or quest narrative, in which she tries 'to get inside his mind': 'It's the only way of finding him: you've got to see what he sees, you've got to know what he would do' (96). One could explain the reasons for Barker's switch into the first-person perspective in much the same way, that it enables the reader to get inside the mind of a woman troubled by the murder of her lover and intent on revenge. In hunting down the murderer, Jean becomes a murderer herself, just as the epigraph to the novel from Nietzsche warns us, 'Whoever fights monsters should see to it that in the process he does not become a monster'. We must see what she sees in order for Barker to take us to the point at which we become as muddled by the clues as Jean is, as confused by the blurring of boundaries and signs. We follow the same trail of clues – the violet-scented breath, the derelict backstreets, the tie for strangling his victims – in the order in which Jean thinks of them, so that we arrive at the same conclusions as Jean. This is the crucial difference between first-person and third-person perspectives, that we should not know more than Jean knows, and so the first-person narrative is the means by which Barker limits our perspective to what Jean knows.

In contrast, elsewhere in the novel Barker uses a combination of omniscient narrative and second-person narrative – a rare phenomenon in fictional narratives – to provide the reader with access to knowledge which is not available to any characters:

> The sleeping and the dead. Any resemblance between them is a contrivance of undertakers: they do not look alike. Kath's body seems to have shrunk inside its clothes. If you approached the mattress casually you would see nothing but a heap of old rags. You would tread on her before you realized a woman's body lay there.
>
> The window is boarded up, the room dark, except for five thin lines of moonlight that lie across the mattress like bars. One of them has just reached her eyes. They look so alive you wonder she can bear the light

shining directly into them. Any moment now, you feel, her eyes will
close. (66)

It is unusual in Barker's work for a narrator to provide generalising
comments like the first two sentences of this extract. The narrator in
these sentences is informing the reader of a general truth about the distinction between the appearance of sleep and death. In order to bring
the reader closer to the scene depicted of Kath's dead body, however, a
second-person narrative is used, at first as a hypothetical situation in
which 'you' imagine yourself at the scene. But in the final two sentences of the extract, 'you' are a character in the room with Kath, and
the narrator is describing how 'you' feel, what 'you' are thinking. Of
course, no one is in the room with Kath's body, so the sight of Kath's
eyes remaining wide open in the moonlight should not be available to
the reader. This is a key indication of omniscient narration, that the
narrator is able to access places where we know the character described
is unaccompanied, and in this case, where the character herself is dead.
The use of second-person narration here closes the gap between the
distant, 'voice-over' commentary of the omniscient narrator and the
perspective afforded to Kath or her murderer in the intimacy of this
derelict room. It hypothesises a situation in which 'you' (the implied
reader, or narratee) are asked to see yourself as an uncomfortable and
voyeuristic presence in the room with Kath's body, and so Barker
denies the reader the consoling distance of omniscient narration.[5]

When Barker writes in third-person narration, the narrator is usually as covert as possible. We should not be conscious necessarily of
the narrator as a subjective presence, and yet this scene needs to be
perceived and witnessed by someone. The third-person perspective is
capable of describing the scene to us, telling us that 'the window is
boarded up', for example, but in order for the narrative to consider
how alive Kath's eyes look, or whether her eyes will close, there needs
to be a subjective presence. Of course, Barker could have kept her
killer hanging around to perceive this, or have a wandering vagrant
stumble into this scene, but the effect would be very different. The use
of second-person narrative brings the narratee or the implied reader
into the story, and involves 'you' in witnessing the scene of Kath's
death, acknowledging the eerie vitality of Kath's eyes in the moonlight. It is an extension of Barker's techniques for dissolving the
boundaries between narrator and character, between external and
internal perspectives, between the characters and the implied reader.

Barker is working in this novel with a productive tension between narrative access and the limits of narrative knowledge. An omniscient narrator guarantees access to all characters and situations, and has unlimited knowledge of events and characters, but would also be always on the outside looking in. Such a narrator would be a voyeur, a manipulative, superior observer of the lives and perspectives of these women. The first-person narrative of Jean, and the free, indirect discourse used more widely in the novel, signals that Barker wants her readers to see these characters and events as if from the inside, but the problem with these perspectives is that they are confined to knowledge of their own subjective experiences.

There is a level of meaning, particularly symbolic meaning, however, which Barker implies her characters cannot fully see, and yet wants her readers to share. Hence, the second-person witness to Kath's dead body in the moonlight. Hence, also, the extraordinary degree of omniscient perceptibility in the following passage, in which the reader is given access even to what the wind is doing and thinking:

> Every window is shut fast, every door locked, and yet the wind gets in, finding here a gap between the floorboards and door, there a space between window and frame. It fingers the material of the curtains, tests the pile on the carpet, as if it were asking: How strong is this? Will it last? How long before it gives? (90)

Typically, the wind is personified as a character not unlike some of the women of the story, such as Brenda's mother-in-law, making fussy observations about the quality of curtains and carpets, and so is not as much beyond the limits of the characters' knowledge as might be expected of an omniscient characterisation of an atmospheric force. The fact that access is provided to the perspective of the wind, is, however, highly unusual, especially in realist fiction, and signals the extent to which Barker's novel is interested in opening up hidden levels of experience and meaning. This is particularly evident in the concluding passage of the novel, in which, like the conclusion to *Union Street*, *Blow Your House Down* ends with a lyrical vision of birds gathering together in the trees above the city streets:

> There is a moment in every evening when the streets of the city are dark although the sky is still light, almost as if the darkness is exhaled as a vapour from the pavements and cannot reach the sky. At this moment the starlings come. At first a solitary black dot against clear translucent turquoise, then later, as the sun sinks beneath the level of the bridges,

in a great black wave swelling and breaking over the city. They swarm above its streets, they descend on its buildings, covering every ledge and gutter thickly, wing to wing. But however many come down the sky remains full and the people of the city walk home through air that tingles with the starlings' cries.

The sky flames. Then, gradually, as the birds continue to descend, the red gentles through purple and gold to rose, until at last every bird is lodged, and the singing dies away.

Above the hurrying people, above the lighted windows, above the sodium orange of the street lamps, they hump, black and silent; unnoticed, unless some stranger to the city should happen to look up, and be amazed. (169–70)

As in *Union Street*, the vision of birds flocking together as a protective community functions to symbolise the underlying unity of the women depicted in the novel, a beautiful, meaningful communion of souls which can only be glimpsed above the darkness of the city streets. One problem with this vision, however, is that it appears to be available only to the omniscient narrator, and not to the women themselves. Barker's prose is at its most lyrical at this point, and seems far removed from how the women might speak and describe themselves. The poetry of their lives, the underlying sense of connectedness with a level of symbolic and spiritual meaning, appears inaccessible to the women themselves, who can barely glimpse beyond the material deprivations of their social and gendered identities.

While the novel is firmly located in the close-knit pattern of streets and houses which make up the Northgate neighbourhood, the narrator implies in this final passage that another, deeper vision of their lives is available, but notably only above those streets. Thus, it remains 'unnoticed, unless some stranger to the city should happen to look up, and be amazed' (170). And yet, that is precisely what the narrator has invited us to do, as strangers to this city; to look up and be amazed at the vision of beauty and community which appears above the city every evening. The pronoun 'you' is not used in this final sentence, but the second-person perspective is, I think, implied in the fact that the reader is led to notice what the narrator tells us is 'unnoticed'. The reader has a role to play, this suggests, in crossing the hiatus between the narrative and the characters, between the narrating subject and the narrated objects, between the dictions and visions of observer and observed. If in *Union Street* Barker made accessible to readers a community in which the lives of working-class women were shown to be interconnected, *Blow Your House Down* attempts to push this method one stage further and to imply also that the reader is both inside and outside this intersubjective network of social relations.

Barker's use of multiple narrative perspectives has led some critics, notably Peter Hitchcock and John Kirk, to describe her fiction in Bakhtinian terms as 'dialogic' and 'heteroglossic'.[6] Bakhtin argued that the novel as a form made use of 'dual-voiced discourse', offsetting the voice of the narrator with other voices and types of discourse, through the representation of speech and thought in a variety of direct and indirect ways. What this technique enables in Barker's work is the shift of perspectives between the authoritative voice of the narrator and the subaltern voices of the characters, and thus, according to John Kirk, 'the narrative encodes a heterogeneity of struggle against patriarchy, capital, and the state'.[7] The multiple narrative perspectives are just part of that articulation of heterogeneity, for Barker's fusion of realist and symbolist modes of writing, lyrical and cinematic techniques, and genres of murder mystery and social exploration, contributes to the hybrid and heteroglossic form of *Blow Your House Down*. For Bakhtin, the hybrid form of the novel, its expression of heterogenous perspectives and discourses, is not simply a formal reflection of social heterogeneity, but also functions to bring different discourses into contact with each other as a form of social critique.[8] In the case of Barker's novel, I want to argue, this is particularly apparent in the ways in which the novel articulates a critique of the commodified subjectivities of the women employed in the sex industry.

Of necessity, the women engaged in prostitution have internalised the language of commodification, and the alienated images of their own bodies as objects for consumption. They register the sliding scale of their own exchange value on the street, and even joke about comparisons with commodity goods. When Audrey describes herself as dressed to look like a 'Fry's Turkish Delight', a common confectionery product advertised as an exotic delicacy, Brenda replies, 'I hope not. They only cost 14p' (8). The language of commercial value debunks the myth of exotic or indeed erotic promise. The women attempt to maintain some degree of resistance to the commodification of their bodies – Kath tells Brenda, for example, 'always remember your mouth's your own' (46) – but this is barely effective in a system of exchange value in which, as Kath explains, 'they want more they pay more' (46). Nonetheless, this attempt to resist the process of

sexual commodification introduces a discourse of independent subjectivity, however weakly realised, to contend against the discourse of
commercial use value. Elsewhere, the language of familial love – for
children, in particular – contends against the language of prostitution, and indeed serves to motivate the women to endure the debas-
ing experiences of selling their bodies. Brenda's love for her children,
Kath's love for the children who have been taken away from her,
Jean's love for Carol, are all understood to be outside of the system of
capitalist exchange, and so serve as oppositional discourses to the
language of capitalism. But Barker shows also how these contending
discourses are also complementary, not to the women themselves,
but within the logic of the capitalist state. When Brenda is visited by
social security officials, for example, she understands that marriage to
them is not 'white weddings and the romance and all that', but is com-
parable to prostitution: 'if you're getting on your back for a fella, he
ought to pay. *That* was what they really thought. And where did that
leave you? You might as well be standing on a street corner in bloody
Northgate – at least it'd be honest' (30).

   This is what Brenda is compelled to do. Out of love for her children,
she is forced to sell her body as an object for consumption, and thus
love is not ultimately oppositional to the discourse of prostitution, but
complementary to it. This is the context in which Barker begins to
explore the possibility for resistance in a system which commodifies
every aspect of women's lives, or rather she explores the signs of
limited resistance. For in an image of passivity repeated several times
in the course of the novel, the women are shown to be troubled by the
figure of their own commodification and oppression. In the first
occurrence of this image in the novel, Brenda arrives into the chicken
factory at which many of the women in her community work, and
stumbles upon the image of the chickens waiting to be slaughtered:

> She was frightened, she needed the job so badly. In her anxiety to get the
> interview over, she blundered in at the wrong entrance and saw a line of
> live chickens fastened to a conveyor belt by their legs. They jerked past.
> At the end of the line a man hit them with something to stun them and
> another man chopped off their heads.
>   The tiles were spattered with blood. They must've been able to smell
> it, but there was no struggling, no panic after the first frantic clapping
> of wings.
>   *They didn't even squawk.* (33)

It is important that Brenda stumbles upon this scene, that it is something she is not meant to see, something which is kept secret from her. 'Oh, you don't go in there', the supervisor tells her, 'killing's for the men' (34). The factory is divided into gendered spaces and gendered tasks, and the supervisor's warning serves as a pointed reminder of the social demarcation of the licence to kill. The divisions of labour within the factory reflect the gender stereotypes which posit that men are active, rational, strong and objective, while women are passive, emotional, weak and subjective. Men go to war, while women stay at home. Such stereotypes are based upon an understanding of women as vulnerable and in need of male protection, but Barker shows that such images of passivity and vulnerability disturb the women. Brenda is shocked by the passivity of the chickens as they are brought to their deaths. The significance of this image for Brenda is made more apparent by the fact that she seems to ponder what the chickens themselves perceive ('They must've been able to smell it') as they process along the conveyor belt.

This is a disturbing image for Brenda even before it becomes symbolic of the women being slaughtered by the serial killer. It extends and develops the critique of reification offered in the stories of *Union Street*, in which the cake factory and the disused steelworks are the symbolic loci of a commodified subjectivity. Brenda seems to identify with the chickens waiting to be slaughtered, as mirrored images of the commodification of her own body as an object in the labour process. When she becomes a prostitute, Kath tells her that she must learn to 'switch off' (47), to become a passive object of consumption, like the chickens waiting to be killed. Barker ties this image of the passivity of chickens to the misogynist murders of the serial killer in a striking and explanatory image of the killer's fetishistic motives:

> At some point, unnoticed by him, Kath died.
>
> After a few minutes he was able to stop and look down. It wasn't enough that she was dead, he needed more. He gathered handfuls of feathers together and started shoving them inside her cunt. It wasn't easy: as fast as he pushed them inside her they turned red. He had to practically stuff her with them, like stuffing a chicken, before he could get the effect he wanted: a ridiculous little white frill between her legs.
> (65)

For the murderer, too, the image of the chickens being slaughtered is inextricably tied to the commodified sexuality of the prostitutes he butchers. His fetishistic stuffing of his victim with feathers, in this case, reveals a disturbing complex of emotions, both of his hatred for women (his violence towards her is expressed physically and verbally here) and also his veneration for an image of female sexuality as pubescent and delicate. The prostitute offends this notion of female sexuality, hence his evident disgust for the women he pays for sex. But the murderer is shown here to be as much the subject of commodification and alienated subjectivity as the women he murders, for he is no more able to escape from the discourse and imagery of production and exchange than they are.

The identification of the murdered women with the slaughtered chickens becomes even clearer as the novel progresses. In the final section of the novel, Maggie is on her way home from the chicken factory when she is struck on the back of the head, like one of the chickens on the conveyor belt. The assailant is interrupted before he can kill her, and when she recovers she is left to ponder the image of her own powerlessness:

> The dark shapes that had pursued her for so long suddenly closed in around her. She tried to switch her thoughts off, but across her mind's eye moved a line of faces, all women, young, old, fat, thin, smiling, serious. She knew who they were: she'd seen them in the papers, as everybody had, but then it had been just a story, something that had happened to somebody else, always to somebody else. But now it was real because it had happened to her. The image faded and was replaced by a line of chickens waiting to be killed. In each eye the same passive uncomprehending terror. (155–6)

For much of the novel, the slaughter of the chickens is a recurring trope which runs parallel to the thriller story of the women being murdered. The symbolic resonances of the chickens for the murder story are available to the reader, of course, in pointed and self-conscious ways, but Maggie is the only character for whom this parallel is clearly apparent. As Sharon Monteith argues, the focus on Maggie at the end of the novel is significant because it dislocates the contemporary media construction of the murders as a melodramatic story, and reaffirms the humanity of the women who face the realities of male misogynist violence.[9] Barker shifts our attention away from the sensationalist narrative of the evil and monstrous, and back to the social structures of gender stereotypes, divisions of labour, class divisions and commodity fetishism. There is no intrusive narrative explanation of the causal connections between male violence and such social structures, but the connections are implied. Instead of de-humanising the stories of the women with sociological justifications, Barker concludes the novel with the story of Maggie grappling with her own 'passive uncomprehending terror'.

In representing such feelings of terror, of trauma, Barker shows the inadequacy of explanation, the failure of narrative to provide con-solation or understanding. This is signalled in the fact that two of the victims of violence in the novel are shown to express the word 'why?' as they struggle to understand what has happened to them. Words fail to account for Maggie's feelings, for example: 'her worded thoughts were like dead leaves on a river, able to reveal the direction of the cur-rent, but neither its depth nor its power, and, taken together, might have amounted to no more – or less – than the single word, *Why?*' (159). As the novel comes to a close, Maggie finds no words to express her feelings to her husband, but simply holds his hand (169). There is no resolution in the novel to the search for an explanation. Even the final paragraphs of third-person omniscient narration dwell upon the enigmatic and symbolic image of birds clustering above the city, rather than tying up the 'loose ends' of the narrative. The murder mystery plot is unsolved – the killer is still at large, and so the 'clues' embedded in the thriller plot of the novel turn out to be misleading. So, too, the social realist exploration of the causal connections between misogynist violence and social structures is implied, but not accounted for and explained. That *Blow Your House Down* uses the conventions of murder mystery and social realism, however, is part of what Ross Chambers calls the 'situational self-reflexivity' of the text, part of the narrative process of seducing the reader into an engage-ment with the text.[10] It is an important part of what makes this novel dialogic that it uses the generic conventions of realism and the popu-lar thriller without being contained by those conventions. The novel invites the reader to become, like Jean, an amateur detective, follow-ing the clues which will lead to the identity of the murderer, but the comforting denouement of the conventional detective plot is neces-sarily interrupted. The reader is denied the conservative narrative of crime and punishment, and instead the novel offers a vision of the complex matrix of social relations in the dark, labyrinthine spaces of the urban ghetto.

The city space is shown in *Blow Your House Down* to be uncontain-able and ineffable. Although the novel maps out a small, familiar clus-ter of streets and buildings, the same urban topography is also an alien and inhospitable place. The police herd the prostitutes into the Northgate area as a way of containing and watching them, thus suggesting that prostitution is controlled and licensed in certain ways by the law. But this only allows other parts of the city to escape the eyes of the police. Jean stalks this other, hidden side of the city when she tries to snare the murderer:

> He'll come back, and he'll come back here, because it's impossible to police. Too many corners, factory yards, alleys leading off each other, streets with the windows boarded up, bricked up houses, and then under the arches, the timber yard, the place where the old iron foundry used to be, and the waste land beyond that. I don't suppose there's much more than a square mile if you looked at it on a map, but you'd get lost five times if you tried to walk across it. No, it's a good place from his point of view, especially if you compare it with Northgate and one or two other areas I could mention, where it's packed deep with girls – I'm not exaggerating, it's bloody ridiculous – and there's a vice-squad car in every alley. (101)

Jean draws a distinction between the visible, rational city of maps and police surveillance, and the hidden, labyrinthine city of wastelands, derelict streets and rhizomic alleys. This other city space is, according to Michel de Certeau, 'beneath the discourses that ideologise the city', and is 'impossible to administer'.¹¹ But this is not to suggest that the hidden, dark spaces of the city which the prostitutes are compelled to share with rapists and serial killers are outside of such ideological discourses, for an important part of Barker's critique is that such spaces are ideologically produced. They are the necessary opposite of the rational, civilised society, the expendable excess of sexual promiscuity and lawlessness upon which the discourses of policing and social control depend. They are, in short, the wolf at the door of the three little pigs, threatening to 'blow your house down'.

In Barker's novel this opposition between the rational society and its dark underside is expressed through modes of visibility in the city, in a way which anticipates the theme of surveillance in *The Eye in the Door*. The women are ghettoised into the boarded-up streets, railway arches and deserted factories which make up an invisible city. Throughout the novel, the social exclusion of the women is articulated partly through the metaphors of blindness and myopia, of damaged sight, which strike many of the characters. Elaine is partially blind. Beattie looks disturbing with just one eye made up. Maggie is attacked in 'Blind Lane'. Barker juxtaposes these images of disturbed sight with the fixed, staring eyes of Kath, whose stare symbolises an unwillingness to be made invisible. From the poster seeking the capture of her murderer, Kath's eyes continue to survey the ground upon which the women are herded and slaughtered. The eyes become the markers of a privileged mode of knowing the city. Barker's depiction of modes of visibility in the city makes an ironic counterpoint to the modernist representation of the male flâneur, which is understood to be made possible by the new modes of seeing and watching other people in the nineteenth-century city.[12] The flâneur is the privileged spectator of the flux of urban life in the arcades and streets. He sees through the eyes of modernity, but is himself the product of a re-organisation not only of capitalist labour relations, but also of the spatial design of the city. In contrast to the flâneur, Barker's characters see the discontents of the modern metropolis. They see the city not as a space enabling freedom and licentiousness, but rather producing surveillance, control, poverty, violence and murder. The oppression and victimisation of women in *Blow Your House Down* is thus understood, in part, to be a product of social and sexual geography.

This is especially apparent in the final section of the novel, in which Maggie seeks to understand the disparity between the aesthetic ideal of the city and the lived experience of poverty and violence within the city:

> She got up and walked to the top of the hill from where she could see the whole city spread out before her. Rain and mist together bound in the columns of yellow smoke, the clouds of steam from cooling towers. Even the tall flames of the burners could scarcely penetrate the haze. But then, as she watched, the ridge of black cloud lifted a little, and suddenly there were rays of light, or rather great shafts of golden light, falling onto the city, which looked now like an island raised up out of the sea, for there were still inlets of rain and mist in the surrounding fields.
>
> This was not the city she knew: back streets, boarded-up houses, the smell of blood in a factory yard. And yet it was the same city. She watched the columns of light move over it, until the cloud thickened and the veils of rain closed round it once again. (168)

For Maggie there is a sudden recognition in this scene that the city can be beautiful, which comes as such a shock that she must acknowledge that there are not just 'rays of light' but 'great shafts of golden light' lifting the city from its grey surroundings. But this recognition is fleeting, as such moments of aesthetic beauty or symbolic vision are only ever fleeting for Barker's characters. This is a moment of estrangement for Maggie, to realise that this vision is so different from her experience, and yet it is the same city. Significantly, Maggie can only glimpse this aesthetic ideal of the city from outside, from the surrounding countryside, which itself is difficult for Maggie to access. At first, as she recovers from the attempt to murder her, she goes in search of the countryside as a mythical haven – 'a green, moist, safe place' – which might provide 'some revelation of good to balance the evil' (162). Maggie wants to believe in an idyllic space beyond the dystopic city, but she finds that the countryside too is a regulated, controlled space, in which the fields are carefully fenced off from the tidy roads, and in which the landscape is 'grey-green and featureless', as monotonous as the 'grey, twisting streets' of the city.

Maggie's story allows Barker to pull back from the convoluted streets and congested lives of the city, to leave the detective thriller plot of Jean's narrative behind and take up instead Maggie's attempt to understand the question which Jean's victim has asked: 'why?'. The countryside provides no answers to the mysteries and horrors of the city, however. It is as much subject to ideological discourses of property and power as the city. She stumbles across a fox with 'the still-twitching body of a rabbit clamped in his jaws' (164), which proves as much an image of the murdered and violated women as the motion-less chickens on the factory assembly line. If the possibility of a haven outside the city proves illusive, so too does the promise of religious faith. Maggie wanders into a church and, when she finds it impossible to pray to the image of the resurrected Christ, she comes upon a startling and familiar image of Christ dead on the cross:

> She stared at his green mouth, and then her gaze moved down, and her attention quickened. The whole chest was deformed by the stretched-back arms and lolling head. The lower ribs flared out to a point where they seemed hardly to be human at all. There were marks all over his skin, from the flogging she supposed, and here and there a thorn had escaped from the crown and embedded itself in the flesh of hip or breast. She had seen such marks before. They were like, no, *were*, the marks left when the spine of a feather is pulled out. That was it, and that was where she had seen the flaring ribs before. . . .. The chicken Christ on his cross might claim her as his own, but the risen Christ, Christ in Majesty, pain sloughed off him like an outworn skin, had nothing to say. (160)

There is no salvation here, either; just the recognition of a common sense of pain and oppression, the familiar image of passive suffering which Maggie finds in the chickens, Christ on the cross, and the women murdered and butchered by the serial killer. Maggie recognises in Christ not the image of a way out of her suffering, not the possibility of redemption, but instead she sees in him only the 'tortured human flesh' which becomes symptomatic of the bleak state of human life subject to the larger and largely uncomprehended forces of history and power. There is, then, no answer to the question 'why', no grand design or motive which reveals itself to Maggie or the other characters in the novel. It is this bleak, secular vision of a world without answers which informs Barker's depiction of a city darkened by terror, but a city which nonetheless does yield at least fleeting glimpses of the hope, the faintest whisper, of a life beyond the grey and grinding lives of her characters.

The sense of an alternative reality felt by her characters comes in the form of the experience of spectral presence. Maggie experiences this in the chicken factory, for example:

> As she bent down the feathers that were everywhere stirred. One brushed against the back of her bare hand. It was only a draught from the door, of course, you knew that, but all the same it was a funny feeling. You felt you were not alone.
>
> She went to the window and peered out through the crack between two boards, hoping to see some of the men who worked in the yard, but there was no-one, no person, only a line of chickens, upside down, moving past on their way to be stunned and killed. As she watched, one of them, only one, started to flap its wings.
>
> She turned back to the room. Before her on the table was a half-plucked bird, its plump, naked, white thighs spread wide. Some of the surrounding feathers were still white, some blood-sodden from the severed neck. She stared at it, and as she stared the presence that she sensed all round her grew stronger and stronger until it roared in her ears. (140–1)

A recurrent feature of Barker's fiction is this experience of the uncanny presence of another force. It has no discernible association with religious faith, or even spirituality per se, but it does intimate the merest sense of a life beyond the poverty and suffering of her characters. In *Blow Your House Down*, this sense of spectral presence is partly conveyed through the aesthetic experiences of Maggie when she watches the golden light on the city, or when she catches a glimpse of Christ on the cross as a vision of her own suffering. But it is also experienced as the feeling of ghostly presence. Jean feels the

presence of Kath's eyes watching her from the police poster, or sees
fleeting images of her murdered lover, Carol. Beattie sees the ghost of
Irene, the first woman murdered by the serial killer, in the bar. The
feeling of ghostly presence is subtly interwoven with the terror of
being watched by the killer, too, so that the killer is himself at times a
spectral figure. Such spectral figures appear in the narrative in order
to signify a crisis in the distinction between the visible and the invisible, the past and the present, the living and the dead. In doing so, the
ghostly figures of Barker's novel indicate that the landscape of this
bankrupt modern city is haunted by its discontents. The prostitutes,
after all, like the murderer, or the men and women who work in the
chicken factory, are the invisible others of the rational, social order of
modernity, the ghosts whose occasional presence disturbs the image
of a progressive, clean, modern civilisation. If in *Union Street* Barker
used figures of spectrality to intimate that the last remnants of working-class community were only felt through that ghostly sense of the
presence of others, in *Blow Your House Down* the spectral takes on a
more political sense, in that it functions to register the refusal of the
other, darker side of modernity to disappear into silence and invisibility. Kath's eyes remain open, and what they see in the sliver of
moonlight, or even perhaps the concluding vision of the birds com-
mingling over the city, may be the merest signs of hope in a novel of
terror and despair.

Notes

1 'Best of Young British Novelists', *Granta*, 7 (1983).
2 The proceedings were published as 'The End of the English Novel',
   Granta, 3 (1980).
3 Pat Barker, 'Blow Your House Down', *Granta*, 7 (1983), 47–58.
4 Ibid., 49.
5 See Ann Ardis's important essay on the challenges of teaching *Blow Your
   House Down*, which makes a similar argument about the way in which the
   novel implicates the reader; Ann Ardis, 'Political Attentiveness vs Political Correctness: Teaching Pat Barker's *Blow Your House Down*', *College
   Literature*, 18:3 (1991), 44–54. An expanded version of this essay is published in Sharon Monteith, Margaretta Jolly, Nahem Yousaf and Ronald
   Paul (eds), *Critical Perspectives on Pat Barker* (Columbia, University of
   South Carolina Press, 2005).
6 Peter Hitchcock, *Dialogics of the Oppressed* (Minneapolis, University of
   Minnesota Press, 1993), 53–82, and John Kirk, 'Recovered Perspectives:

Gender, Class and Memory in Pat Barker's Writing', *Contemporary Literature*, 40:4 (1999), 603–26. Bakhtin's *The Dialogic Imagination* is particularly important, especially the essay 'Discourse in the Novel'; see M.M. Bakhtin, *The Dialogic Imagination*, trans. Caryl Emerson and Michael Holquist (Austin, University of Texas Press, 1981).

7 Kirk, 'Recovered Perspectives', 613.

8 See Bakhtin, 'Discourse in the Novel', *The Dialogic Imagination*, 259–422.

9 Sharon Monteith, *Pat Barker* (Tavistock, Northcote House, 2002), 21.

10 See Ross Chambers, *Story and Situation: Narrative Seduction and the Power of Fiction* (Manchester, Manchester University Press, 1984).

11 Michel de Certeau, *The Practice of Everyday Life*, trans. S. Rendall (Berkeley, University of California Press, 1988), 94.

12 See Walter Benjamin, *Charles Baudelaire*, trans. Harry Zohn (London, Verso, 1997), 38.

4

Telling stories: *The Century's Daughter (Liza's England)*

In *The Century's Daughter*, Barker continues to explore the post-industrial subjectivities of working-class women in northern England, but she expands her outlook from the local and contemporary focus of her first two novels to encompass a broader sense of national and historical significance.[1] The history of working-class life in the twentieth century is implied as a background in *Union Street* and *Blow Your House Down*, against which contemporary processes of dereliction, reification and long-term unemployment are to be understood. Barker's third novel develops a dialogic relationship between the historical and the contemporary, however, shifting between Liza's life-story of the century, and Stephen's experience of the contemporary dissolution of civic society in the 'sink' estates of urban, post-industrial England.

The shift between the historical and the contemporary allows Barker to elucidate the connections between the structures of working-class community in the past and the anomic, almost anarchic character of working-class existence in the present, for as much as Liza and Stephen embrace a nostalgia for lost forms of belonging and identity in the past, their stories also exemplify the inseparability of the present from the past.[2] The past occasionally erupts into the present in Barker's first two novels, usually in disturbing and haunting ways, but in *The Century's Daughter* the past is relived as if it is the present. I will argue in this chapter that Barker's third novel is especially concerned with figures of prosopopoeia, of giving breath or life to the dead.

The Century's Daughter grows out of the final chapter or story in *Union Street*, the story of Alice Bell. Like Alice, Liza is living in a cold, condemned house, and prefers to die rather than be moved to 'sheltered accommodation'. Both women serve to contrast the present, near-derelict condition of their streets, with memories of vibrant, persistent communities. Both women bear the scars of working-class labour and the struggle for survival against war, poverty and loss, and both articulate a clearer sense of working-class community than appears to be available to their younger neighbours. Both Alice and Liza are forced to confront the state authorities who presume to act in their interests, although Liza's relationship with her social welfare visitor, Stephen, develops into a warm friendship, unlike Alice who feels as if she has been raped by the impersonal bureaucrat who wants her out of her home. Both women play a therapeutic role in the lives of younger characters. Alice helps to comfort Kelly Brown, and seems to give Kelly a way of understanding the value of her home. Liza's stories of the past become addictive for Stephen, and help him to overcome a sense of loss, partly for his father, but also for the 'generation without hope' which he believes to be growing up around him.

For Barker, these two old women function as anchors for the remnants of community and, perhaps more importantly, as repositories of community memory and history. This is particularly the case in *The Century's Daughter*, since the novel is comprised largely of the story of Liza's life, and also because storytelling is more central to Liza's character than to Alice's. The role of narrative itself is a central preoccupation in *The Century's Daughter*, and especially its ability to function as an organic process of memory which connects the past and the present through the consciousness of the storyteller. As Walter Benjamin argues, 'The storyteller takes what he tells from experience – his own or that reported by others. And he in turn makes it the experience of those who are listening to his tale'.[3] Narrative is a mode of connection, of connecting not just one idea to others, but also of connecting the teller with her listeners, and with the larger community of others who have figured in the tale and the telling. If Barker's novel is exploring the dissolution of community and connection in the dereliction of working-class streets, she is also exploring the narratives of memory and belonging which may yet continue to connect people's experiences together. This is the significance of Liza's stories of the past for Stephen, the vital function of narrative, of a sense of interconnection, for the survival of civic society. Stephen is equally significant for Liza, however. For, as Benjamin suggests, an important function of storytelling is the conferral of authority from teller to listener, the passing on of experience, history and memory to the next generation.

Stories transform the teller and the listener. *The Century's Daughter* begins with a scene of transformation in which Liza's power to tell stories alters Stephen's perception of her. Liza understands that her authority to tell stories derives from her age. She is as old as the century, and this brings its own claim to having witnessed the passage of history, even when Liza's story purports to be simply her life-story. The beginning of such a story is inherently problematic, and Liza jokes about the potential of her story to exhaust the listener: 'If I started telling some poor old bugger about meself now he'd be dead by the time I'd finished' (4). Liza's joke plays off the mythical origin of the *Arabian Nights*, the 1001 nights, in which Scheherazade must keep telling stories to stay alive. Liza's story is not just about her survival, but as long as she tells it her story is her survival. It is what will keep her alive, and it is also what transforms her for her listener, Stephen:

> Telling the story of her birth had animated her: her cheeks had flushed to the same hectic colour as her shawl; and suddenly, in Stephen's eyes, she ceased to be a case, a social problem, a stubborn, possibly senile old lady, and became instead what she called herself: the century's daughter. (6)

Something magical happens in the darkened room in which Liza Jarrett begins to tell stories of her life to the young man at her bedside. A ritual of animating the dead and passing on stories from history transforms the relationship between social worker and his problem case. It is a ritual apparently enacted on the lid of the memory box which Liza keeps hidden underneath her bed:

> It was an old metal box . . . painted on the lid and sides with dancing figures, women holding their clasped hands high, dancing in a ring. Behind the women, almost in the shadow of the trees, were two other figures. One was so shrouded in a long robe that neither age nor sex was visible; the other was a young man. The draped figure held something in its hands, but the box-lid was so filmed with dirt that Stephen couldn't see what it was. (7)

The box has passed down through Liza's maternal ancestry for centuries, and is inherited by Liza's daughter at her death, but it remains a symbol for Stephen not just of Liza's repository of memories, but also of the ritual of inheritance. The draped figure, who for Stephen becomes a fusion of Liza and his father, holds something invisible to be passed on to the young man. The depiction of women dancing in

a ring repeats an image Barker used in *Union Street*, an image symbolising the joyful continuity of life. In both novels this image serves
to juxtapose mythological figures of regeneration and female creativity with the material struggles which women face every day in the
depressed communities Barker represents. There are no material
treasures in Liza's box, as the robbers who precipitate her death discover. Her only legacy is the story of her life, which Stephen repeatedly returns to hear, and it is at this scene of bedside storytelling that
the magical transformation of death into life takes place.

Stephen suspects that there is something strange about Liza's
power to tell stories from the beginning. He wrestles with the idea
that she is telepathic, when she answers questions he has thought but
not spoken (3). He is unnerved by her quirky appearance, 'her scarlet
headsquare tilted crazily over one eye, giving her the look of a senile
pirate', an impression fortified by the discovery that she keeps a parrot
called Nelson (1). His authority is also shaken by the suspicion that
Liza is imitating 'his own official voice', an act of parody which seems
to displace Stephen's investigation and to open the way for Liza to
begin her story (5). When Liza begins her story, however, it is an
impossible beginning, the story of her birth as if she has witnessed it:

> 'Me Mam'd got herself reckoned up to the end of January, and she was
> never far wrong, she was the local midwife, you know. . .. She hadn't
> even given up work. In fact she'd just got her hat on to go out to a
> woman when *whoosh!* – all over the oilcloth. Well, she got herself off to
> bed and sent for *her* midwife – mucky old bugger she was, you could've
> planted a row of taties in her neck – and settled down to wait. Then just
> before midnight, she says, "Hey up, it's coming." "Never in this world,"
> said the old wife. Didn't like me mother. Took too much of her trade.
> "*You'll* still be here this time tomorrow night." Then the clock started to
> strike midnight and, my God, did she have to stir her pins, because there
> I was, very near fighting me way out. Water everywhere, bloody great
> pool of it in the middle of the bed. And if me Mam hadn't the presence
> of mind to pick me up and wallop me I'd've drowned there and then
> because all the midwife did was gawp. But there was a piece in the paper
> about it, on the front page, and it said: "The Century's Daughter."
> Me Dad treasured that bit of paper, and then after he died it come to
> me.' (5–6)

This is the story about her coming-to-life, but she also comes to life in
telling it, as if storytelling re-enacts the event itself. It is a story similar in its sense of the mystical coincidence of the birth of a new life

and the beginning of a new historical era to Salman Rushdie's *Midnight's Children* (1981), but in Rushdie's novel Saleem Sinai's tale of his own birth is self-consciously magical. Saleem professes to have supernatural powers of consciousness, although he is also an unreliable narrator, whose story of his birth may also be read as self-fashioning fiction. In Barker's novel, there is something magical about the coincidence of Liza's birth, but the authority for Liza's perspective on her own birth must be her mother. The newspaper article which her father has passed on to her could not give the intimate details in which Liza's story revels, and the sense of competition between Liza's mother and the other midwife would appear to indicate that Liza is ventriloquising her mother's story. Thus, phrases like 'did she have to stir her pins', 'you could've planted a row of taties in her neck' and 'all the midwife did was gawp' are likely to be examples of Liza's mother's voice speaking through Liza's story. Liza's birth is obviously the beginning of her life-story, but it is obviously not just *her* story. There are other voices and other stories which are bound up with and inseparable from the story of Liza's life.

This is evident in the shift in narrative perspective as the novel progresses. The first chapter establishes a storytelling scene, in which Liza will narrate the story of her life to Stephen. In the second chapter, Liza is sitting alone and as she feels the dancing figures on the lid of her memory box, the memories of her childhood flood back to mind. The narrative in the second chapter begins to take the reader inside Liza's unspoken memories, as if from the child's perspective, referring for example to 'Mam' and 'Dad'. But it slides swiftly into third-person narrative, viewing 'Liza', 'Louise' (her mother) and 'her Dad' from an external perspective (21–2). The narrative becomes even more distant in chapter four, in which Liza is not even present in some of the scenes and events being narrated. When her brother Edward goes swimming, for example, he tells his friend 'we ought to be getting back. It's not fair leaving Liza on her own' (47). This is part of a life which Liza could not have witnessed, nor is it told as a story which she has heard from others.

The shift from the expected first-person story of Liza's life to the omniscient narration of events in her life which she could neither have witnessed nor experienced suggests that the novel is concerned with a life-story which is not limited in scope to the consciousness of one individual.[4] The unity of the self, and the coherence of a life are, as David Carr has argued, fictions necessary to the life-story but quite

impossible as an experience.[5] Birth and death are the obvious and crucial events to which the life-story teller can have no immediate experience, and yet are required as part of the comprehensive perspective
which gathers the diverse fragments of a life together into a coherent
narrative unity. This is to recognise that the life and the life-story are
structured quite differently. The life-story is organised around unity
and singularity (although Carr's focus on autobiographical writing
perhaps leads to an overemphasis on the monological characteristics
of the life-story), whereas the life itself is experienced partially, from
heterogeneous perspectives, and in constantly shifting contexts.
Barker's shifts of narrative mode recognise that Liza's life-story
cannot be told simply by Liza, for Liza's life is necessarily entangled
in other lives, larger events, and the complex interrelations of individual, community and history.

Liza's story, whether told by her or not, is populated with other lives
and other voices. More so than *Union Street* and *Blow Your House
Down*, Barker's third novel reflects upon the function of storytelling,
and the dual imperative to remember and narrate the past. Storytelling is central to the lives of many other characters in the novel
besides Liza. The young men who congregate in the community
centre in the Clagg Lane estate tell each other stories and jokes in
which, in their constant repetition, 'there was something of the magic
of fairy tales' (13). Liza's husband, Frank, tells the stories and more
importantly impersonates the voices of his dead comrades in the First
World War. As a close and comic parallel to Frank, Liza's parrot,
Nelson, impersonates the voices of the sailors from the ship on which
he was once kept. Stephen's father, Walter, spends his dying hours
telling the story of the waste and shame of the last few years of his life,
a confessional story which prepares him for death, but which leaves
Stephen with disquieting memories of his father. The compulsion to
narrate, to give voice to memory, particularly to give voice to the dead,
is a central preoccupation of the novel.

Stories function in the novel chiefly as prosopopoeia, as means of
giving life to the dead, or resurrecting the voices of the dead. This is
particularly evident in Frank's performances of the voices of his dead
comrades, which Liza witnesses in the church hall and which has all
the ambience and eeriness of a spiritualist seance:

> Then, without warning, the silence deepened, became something that
> was not merely the absence of speech, but a positive force. Positive, or
> perhaps negative, she couldn't tell. At any rate a source of power,

binding them together, drawing them in, and it was easy to believe, in that silence, that the white-faced women were no longer alone, that other figures crowded in the doorway and stood in the shadows at the back of the hall. Liza felt the hair on her neck prickle. She wanted to turn around, to stare hard into the darkness, but she didn't dare.

He began to speak again. Or rather he opened his mouth and voices poured out. One voice after another, and all different. Not as different, perhaps, as they had been in life, because there is a limit to what one damaged set of vocal cords can do, but different enough to be recognizable, and woman after woman leaned forward and strained to hear the voice of her son.

These were the voices of young men who had died; he was resurrecting an entire neighbourhood, because the attack that gave him a bullet in his throat had wiped a battalion out. He'd lain for three days in a shell-hole before he managed to crawl back to the British lines and ask for his regiment, only to be told that they were gone. Almost to a man. Gone. And as he was carried to the dressing station behind the lines perhaps he'd said, *Wait. Wait for me.*

His face shone with sweat. A snake-like vein appeared on his forehead, wriggling down from hairline to temple, the sort of vein you see only on the foreheads of old men. And still the voices poured out. Mouths, silent, mud-stopped, gaped open and spoke. Lungs, gas-blistered, blood-frothed, drew in air again. They gasped for air and for life. (60–1)

Liza reacts angrily to this performance, suspecting that Frank has passed off his impersonations of his friends as communion with the dead. At least she attempts to dismiss what she has witnessed by this explanation, but the prickles on her neck testify that she has felt something strange, felt the room crowded with the ghosts of the men who have been killed in the war. The 'white-faced women' come to this meeting not for healing or prayer, but to hear the voices of their sons from beyond the grave. What Liza witnesses in this hall is something akin to a Pentecostal meeting, at which the holy spirit is understood to pass through the faithful, causing them to speak in tongues. The voices pour out of Frank, an involuntary action, as if he has become possessed by the spirits of the dead. The visible signs of stress on his face are characteristic marks of mediumistic possession, and indicate the pose of the passive recipient of forces too strong for his body to contain. But if Frank is akin to a Pentecostal medium, there is also a significant difference, for he is not speaking in strange languages, but in the language of the all-too-familiar. He brings back to his community the uncanny voices of its dead sons, not the indecipherable babble of glossolalia.

The voices he resurrects from the dead are not perfect imitations; he strains to make them passable with his wounded throat, and the mothers must strain to hear the voices they recognise. The need he fulfils is the consolation of a neighbourhood mourning the loss of almost all of its sons, for Frank has survived the slaughter of a regiment the soldiers of which hailed from the same locality. Thus, Frank is not just impersonating one voice, or the voices of many individuals, but he is raising the voices of an 'entire neighbourhood' as one, the torn community of the living and the dead which can only be reunited in the voices he performs. This, he explains (when he himself appears to Liza from the dead), is his own special act of prosopopoeia, when he chides her form of remembering: '*I gave the dead breath, Liza. But you shut them up in a box*' (276).

This is an unfair criticism of Liza, however, even if it is her own imitation of what Frank might say, for Liza has not shut the dead up in a box. She has told stories about them, and those stories have given the dead life and breath in much the same way as Frank's voices. Her stories of her neighbours, family and friends keep them alive for the generations to come. Stephen recognises this as he looks up at boarded windows in Liza's street: 'The occupants were dead or scattered, but he could have named them all, for in the months he'd been coming to see Liza she'd talked about them often, weaving their stories in and out of her own' (169). As James Olney argues, weaving is 'a characteristic metaphor for the operation of memory', which unlike the archaeological metaphor of digging up memories, implies a generative process, in which memories are shaped into meaningful and creative patterns.[6] Liza's stories animate a sense of community long after the houses and streets of that community have become dormant, and they suggest the significance of narrative as a form not just of remembering but also of regenerating the past. Such stories presume not just to honour the dead, but to speak for the dead in the present, to keep the dead alive. What Liza reacts against in Frank's performance of voices, and what is at stake also in her own stories of the community and history in which she has lived, is that such acts of prosopopoeia enact claims to the authority of speaking for the dead.

This is an argument which J. Hillis Miller makes about storytelling in general as a form of prosopopoeia:

Storytelling, oral or written, depends on the power to create persons out
of modulated sounds in air or black marks on the page. . .. All
prosopopoeias are visits to the underworld. They depend, in a shadowy
way, on the assumption that the absent, the inanimate, and the dead are
waiting somewhere to be brought back to life by the words of the poet or
orator. . ... This is the power to speak for the dead, who have no voice of
their own. Without prosopopoeia no poetry, no narrative, no literature.[7]

Miller traces the ways in which all forms of literature are acts of speaking for the dead. In *The Century's Daughter*, prosopopoeia, of the kinds
practised by Liza and Frank especially, are understood to stem from
the trauma of silence, of loss and absence. It is the disappearance of
community in the post-industrial dereliction of northern, working-
class England which spurs Liza to find her voice, and to tell stories
about the England to which she belongs. It is the tragic slaughter of
his generation of men, the rendering of a generation into silence,
which gives Frank the imperative to raise the voices of the dead. This
is made apparent to him when he has visions of the dead, and they call
upon him to speak for them:

> The first week after he came out of hospital, he'd gone into the town
> centre and seen people treading on dead faces, prosperous men with
> moustaches and cigars, girls with parasols to protect their skin from the
> sun, treading on dead faces. They couldn't see the corpses that sprawled
> there. But Frank had walked among them, recognizing faces, naming
> names, remembering voices. And the voices had packed together in his
> throat, a hard lump pressing on his damaged vocal cords, hardly distin-
> guishable from the pain of his wound. *Speak for us*, they said. *We cannot
> speak*. (84)

The trauma of survival has given Frank an awareness others don't
possess of the invisible dead. For Frank, the war dead continue to
sprawl and speak amidst the grotesque ordinariness of the town
centre. They clog his throat and demand to be voiced. Or perhaps the
gathering of voices in his throat is the manifestation of survivor's
guilt, the pain of his wound a constant reminder of the burden of his
responsibility to the dead. Barker frequently blurs the boundaries
between the spectral and the psychological, but in any case the
appearance of such spectres are signs of psychic and cultural disturbance. The ghosts may be real or they may be projections of his own
making, but Frank is nonetheless burdened to carry on the litany
of names, the chorus of voices, to keep the dead alive. This is his

irrefutable responsibility to the generation butchered in war, and abandoned in peace. It is not presented as an ethical decision, but, Christlike, as the sacrifice he is compelled to make in the name of the dead.

Frank's glut of voices is, of course, a consequence of the war and, whether understood as impersonation or possession, is a manifestation of trauma and disquiet about the war. Barker's fascination with trauma reaches its apotheosis in the *Regeneration* trilogy, obviously, but it is equally present in the three weeks of silence which follow the rape of Kelly Brown in *Union Street*. In each case, and especially in *The Century's Daughter*, the representation of trauma centres on the imagery of the mouth, the tongue and the throat, and wavers between too much speech and too little, between the unstoppable flow of voices and profound and disquieting silence. Frank is exemplary of this oscillation, wallowing in moody silence with Liza and his children, and pouring out the voices of the dead in his seances and hall meetings. In particular, the image of a mouth blocked or unblocked serves throughout the novel to register the experience of trauma. Frank feels the voices of his dead friends packing into his throat, an image which suggests that silence is not the sound of emptiness but of asphyxiating congestion. There is a constitutive paradox in Barker's representation of the relationship between speech and presence. Silence is always an indication of presence, such as the presence Liza experiences in the heckles on her neck in the silence of the hall. Speech in the novel is often the parroted or parodied speech of the dead, best exemplified by the parrot who recites the bawdy language of the sailors killed at sea, and by Frank, who articulates through his wounded throat the voices of absence.

Speech is also thwarted, or blocked, however. The novel is not just concerned with silence, the absence of speech or noise, but also failed speech. Early in the novel, Liza peculiarly associates the '*flap-flap*' of the torn sole of her mother's shoe with the '*b-b-b-b-b* of a blocked tongue' (14). In part, the image of a blocked tongue is an arresting symbol of the unspoken feelings between mother and daughter, for Liza waits to hear her mother say that she loves her, but the words never come, until, when Liza is a mother herself, she breaks the silence and demands to know, 'You never loved me, did you?' (181). Louise's admission that she did not love her own daughter unblocks her tongue, however, and she pours out the story of her own life. Some such catalyst prompts Liza's own story, for the story of her own life can only be unblocked at the point at which her home and sense of belonging are threatened with destruction. Only by telling her own story can she unblock the story of her street and her community, and counter the silence descending on the world she grew up in.

The blocked tongue is the predominant image in the relationship between Stephen and his father, Walter, too. Walter conceals the truth of Stephen's homosexuality, chastening Stephen into silence whenever the subject of girls or marriage is mentioned in family gatherings. The tongue that might confess Stephen's true sexual identity is blocked at every turn, but Walter has his own sexual confession to make on his death-bed, when he confides in Stephen that he has taken to watching schoolgirls in the wasted years of his retirement. But Stephen feels that his father has manipulated the embarrassed silence about Stephen's sexuality in order to confess what Walter equates as similarly deviant desires, since 'running through the entire conversation, had been one unspoken sentence: *You can't afford to judge me*' (119). The distasteful implications of this conversation manifest themselves in Stephen's mouth, immediately in a sour taste, and later, when he collects Walter's possessions from the hospital, in the feeling of a blocked tongue:

> He reached the car and put the parcel on the roof while he dug in his pocket for the key. It slid towards him down the slope, and he put up a hand to stop it from falling. As he did so, one of his father's slippers fell out. The sole had come loose, and as he bent to pick it up, it flapped like a tongue.
>
> He remembered the clenched mouth, the pact with silence, and found himself gripping the edge of the roof. He let his head hang down between his outstretched arms. The pain in his throat had become unbearable. There was a sense of enormous pressure, as if his father's silence had somehow got in and impacted there, a lump he could neither cough up nor swallow. He thought of Liza's husband, of the bullet in his throat, the dead voices packed inside, and he thought that after all Frank Wright had been sane, or if not sane, that it was a madness he might come to share.
>
> He put both hands to his throat like a surgical collar, and coughed. (123)

If *The Century's Daughter* is especially concerned with figures of prosopopoeia, as I have been arguing, this is one of many instances of a kind of anti- or reverse prosopopoeia in the novel. Prosopopoeia is the gift of the blood and speech of the living to the dead. What happens in the above passage, however, is that the dead block the tongues of the living, paralysing the living, not because the dead appropriate the speech of the living, but because the silence of the dead continues insidiously into the present. Barker's fiction constantly maintains the possibility that the communication between the living and the dead is dialogic, that the dead are not merely raised to speak at the behest and convenience of the living. 'Haunting' is partly a psychosomatic manifestation of grief or a sense of loss, but not every instance of haunting in the novel can be explained rationally or scientifically. The flour discovered on the carpet of Liza's room after her death, for example, should remind us of Mrs Dobbin, Liza's long-dead neighbour, who repeatedly appears caked in flour earlier in the novel. The flour on the carpet could be an accidental spillage caused by Liza's robbers, but the repetition of flour as a signifier (particularly associated with birth earlier in the novel) suggests that a kind of haunting has taken place which has no rational explanation.

We might call this effect on Stephen's throat an instance of haunting, then, and Stephen himself worries that his father's death will mean that he will *'never be able to shut him up again'* (102). The gorge in Stephen's throat is perhaps the manifestation of his desire to repress his father's voice, to refuse the gift of speech to his dead father. It is more properly situated in the novel as an instance of trauma, however, which repeats the dramatic convulsions in the throat which precipitated his father's death:

> He burst into the room and there was Walter, his eyes frenzied and rolling above a black hole, blood spreading over his neck and chest. He stretched out his hand to Stephen. The glugging had stopped, but only because a clot of blood, like a lump of black liver, was stuck in his mouth. Stephen got his finger behind it and hoicked it out. It came away with a dreadful sound, like the plop of an unblocked sink, and red blood gushed out after it. Stephen put his fingers to his father's lips and pressed, as if he could keep the blood in. (120)

Stephen has longed to shut his father up, to silence him when, for example, Walter disguises his son's sexual identity, and at the moment when Walter is choking on his own blood, Stephen both unblocks his throat and closes his lips. He is caught between allowing his father's mouth to gush, and sealing it up, and he finds this drama repeated in the pain in his own throat after his father's death. He can neither swallow nor cough, gush nor contain. This is a pattern which

Shoshana Felman and Dori Laub argue is a central feature of the experience of trauma, 'the uncanny reoccurrence of an event that, in effect, *does not end*'.[8] Stephen's throat pains are the physical embodiments of a mental ambivalence about his father's oscillation between shamed silence and shameful confession, in both of which Stephen's sexual identity was represented as deviant. Moreover, it is the manifestation of a profound anxiety about parental and historical legacy, the anxiety that history repeats itself, that the child inherits and becomes the legacy of the father or mother.

This theme is part of the extension of Barker's vision in this novel, beyond the immediate social and psychological landscape of the present, to the passing of generations through the century. Just as Stephen is concerned about the lodging of his father's voice in his throat, Liza too must work with the legacy of a mother whose silence still resonates in the lives of her children and grandchildren. This anxiety centres on the death of two young men in war, Liza's brother Edward in the first war, and her own son, Tom, in the second. The two world wars occasioned obvious concerns about the repetition of history, but Barker's novel specifically dwells upon the repetition of family history, the reoccurrence of the traumatic loss of children. The childhood song about a mother murdering her own children, which Liza remembers hearing as a child, fades indistinctly into Liza's perception of her own mother, and this has obvious resonances with Liza's suspicions that her mother doesn't love her:

> Mary Ann Cotton had murdered her children, all twelve of them, and her step-children, too, nobody really knew how many, and she did it by making them drink arsenic from a teapot. She pretended it was medicine and made them drink it, but the more they drank the worse they got. They were in awful pain, but she didn't care, she just wanted them out of the way, she didn't love them.
>
> Liza screwed her eyes up tight. She could hear Mary Ann Cotton climbing the stairs, the rustle of her skirt, then the creak of the banisters as she leant on them. She was turning the corner, past the clock, coming up the last few stairs. You could hear her breathing . . .
>
> Liza forced herself to open her eyes. A woman's shadow was growing on the wall. She came into the room, holding her hand up to shield the candle. You could see the dark shadows of bones in the red skin. Her face was candle-gold and smooth, but the black eyes stared.
>
> Liza whimpered and tried to wriggle away.
>
> 'Why, Liza, what on earth's the matter?'
>
> A hand, grave cold, came down and felt her head. (26–7)

Barker's depiction of a child's fear of her mother becoming a child-murderer builds upon the conventions of Gothic fiction. The rustle of Mary Ann Cotton's skirt, the creak of the banisters, the shadows on the wall – these are the stock in trade of Gothic suspense narratives, but the role they play for Barker in this scene is to inform us of Liza's equation of her mother with this figure of monstrous motherhood, the mother who kills her own children. Mary Ann Cotton kills her children by pretending to treat them as sick children, passing off poison as medicine, pretending to care for them when really 'she didn't love them'. Liza fears the same of her own mother, a fear confirmed later when Louise admits to have never loved Liza, and consolidated throughout her childhood by Louise's resentful and sometimes violent treatment of her own daughter. It is also possible to connect this song about Mary Ann Cotton to Liza's mother in another way, because Louise buried her first four children within a week, all of them dying from diphtheria (183). Liza hears children singing a song about infanticide which might well be a taunt about her mother, implying a reputation Liza can't quite dismiss, and fearing her mother's 'grave cold' hand. But the story of child-murder finds its clearest resonance not in Liza's relationship with her mother, but in the deaths of Edward and Tom, and in the recurrent waste of human life through poverty and war.

Barker's novel reports the deaths of Edward and Tom, in the First and Second World Wars respectively, in the same terse, matter-of-fact vein as Virginia Woolf's *To the Lighthouse* records the death of Andrew Ramsay, but also like Woolf's novel, the impact of the war dead is more extensive than this concision implies.[9] For one thing, most of the men in Barker's novel come to be connected through a series of displacements. When Edward dies, Louise latches on to Frank as a surrogate son, as he has served in the same platoon as Edward, and is welcomed for his ability to tell Louise and Liza stories of Edward's time in the war. Liza marries Frank, the last living contact with Edward, and a vessel for communication with the dead, and together they bring up a son, Tom, who is given 'Edward' as his middle name, and whom Louise persistently confuses with Edward. Tom's death leaves an absence which Liza knows she is filling with Stephen, in whom she sees the resemblance of her own son. Each man seems to function as a surrogate for another, and to exist on some level as a ghost in the eyes of the women who have lost sons or brothers. This process of grafting presence on to absence, filling the loss of the dead with substitutes and surrogates, is obviously experienced in acute ways by Frank, for whom the pervasive presence of the dead never ceases to be a reality. This is a novel in which the death of generations of young men in war continues to haunt the lives of the living, not as an honourable sacrifice but as a tragic waste. Liza visits Tom's grave, and refuses to accept 'that he should fade, gently, into the soil'. Instead, Tom's death is 'a wound that wouldn't heal. Nothing was worth it, she thought. She would never be brought to say that his death had been worthwhile' (199). The century has butchered its sons, and maimed its daughters, like the children's song about Mary Ann Cotton, just because 'she didn't love them'.

The historical implications of the war dead resound through the novel, and are central to Barker's vision of England in the twentieth century.[10] The squandering of men's lives in two world wars is echoed in the wasted lives of the young men and women terminally unemployed on the Clagg Lane estate, or men like Frank who trudge from deserted wharf to empty factory looking for work, nightmares of the trenches never far from their minds. One such survivor scoffs ironically at the 'land fit for heroes to live in' promised by Lloyd George, while picking his living from the slag heaps (159). The women who lost their sons in war were asked to believe in the defence of a way of life, the fate of their communities, only to witness the economic decimation of those communities. There is little sentiment or nostalgia for the industrial vibrancy of the past; Barker's fiction abounds with stories of men killed in furnaces, down mines, or wheezing through lungs peppered with coal and iron dust, and women with swollen ankles or yellow-tinged skin from working in factories. But much of Barker's critique of the waste of humanity in class-riven England focuses upon post-industrial England, an England in which working-class communities are abandoned to turn to wasteland. *The Century's Daughter* extends the historical scope beyond Barker's first two novels, but its social concerns remain rooted in the same derelict landscapes and abandoned peoples as those depicted in *Union Street* and *Blow Your House Down*.

Barker's representation of twentieth-century England is of a society dependent on the economic exploitation of the poor, and fractured by bitter class divisions. This is made clear, for example, in the First World War when the daughter of the local industrialist, Elizabeth Wynyard, volunteers for factory work, and becomes embroiled in arguments about class and privilege. The working-class women who have been servants in her house resent her presence, and one accuses her of 'playing' at working in a factory, while the other women are compelled from hunger and poverty to work:

> 'Of course I have to do it,' said Elizabeth. 'All you think about is money. I've got three brothers at the front. Or perhaps you think they're playing, too?'
>
> 'No,' said Ellen. 'I don't think they're playing. But I do think that what they're fighting for, what they really mean when they say *England*, is your little playground.' (55)

Liza's England, which is the revised title of the novel,[11] is no playground. As Ellen points out to Liza, at stake in this divided England is a cruel dichotomy not just between 'people who give orders and people who take them', but also 'people who eat and people who starve', 'people who work their guts out and people who get the profit' (56). To be working class or upper class might be an accident of birth, but it hardens into the shape of a life-story, the force of historical circumstance determining the subjectivity of each class. Even Liza's childhood fantasy of being the girl in the Wynyard house must come to the crashing realisation of an unreconcilable gulf between the classes, and therefore between what Liza is and what she might have become. As she pretends to be the girl of the house, she dances towards her own reflection in a big mirror, 'but the sight of her pale face and deeply shadowed eyes brought her back to earth again' (31). Liza is marked visibly with the pale, sickly stamp of her working-class upbringing.

Visibility is a key marker of class difference in the novel. Not only do the classes look differently from each other, they also *see* differently, as Ellen observes of Elizabeth Wynyard:

> 'But she doesn't *see* us. Haven't you noticed? She looks at you, but her eyes never quite focus. She's used to not seeing people. You know, up there. I don't know whether you remember, you had to wear these caps pulled down right low, so that you all looked alike, and you all looked gormless. Didn't matter how much you'd got on top, you still looked gormless. And you always had to make sure your cap was pulled right down before you went in to see the Missus. You used to stop by the mirror at the foot of the stairs and pull it down. Well, one day . . .' Ellen paused and made an odd little sound in her throat that might have been a laugh. 'One day, I looked in that mirror and there was nothing there. Nothing. Not a bloody thing. I could see the wall behind me. I ran like hell back in the kitchen and Mrs Hayes said, "Don't be so soft, you're imagining things." But I knew I wasn't. That was an awful moment. It was like I didn't exist at all.' (56)

As elsewhere in the novel, psychological reality manifests itself in uncanny effects in the real, so that the invisibility which Ellen is expected to perform as a servant before the eyes of her master becomes her own way of seeing. In the act of not seeing herself in the mirror, she interpellates herself as a working-class subject. In post-industrial England, the working-class subjects are no longer required even to perform invisibility; they are ghosts in the derelict landscapes of the urban unemployed. Frank and Walter are exemplary of this new condition of working-class existence, with no jobs to go to, and neither their labour nor time of any value even to be exploited. Frank notes this change, as does Walter, in the experience of time, in particular: 'He remembered something he'd read in one of Liza's books, something about the working class selling the carcase of time. . . . Time was not a carcase for him now. It roared in his ears and threatened to devour him. Or slowly, day by day, picked the flesh off his bones' (152). Frank experiences this new subjectivity as the feeling of being devoured into nothing, and when Liza mourns his death she longs to shout his name against the awful silence and invisibility of uselessness in which he had been consumed (167).

It is perhaps one of the understated ironies of the novel that the Wynyard house in which Liza's mother worked as a cleaner, the house of a prosperous industrialist, is now occupied by Stephen, a social worker, whose job is not to help the unemployed find jobs, but to help the unemployed pass the time. The shift of power from industry to the management of idleness is bitterly sardonic. One of the boys Stephen is charged with helping bemoans the fact that social work, helping the unemployed to chase nonexistent jobs, is 'the only growth industry there is' (14). While striving to help a generation who can find neither use nor value in a society which has abandoned them, Stephen does find himself defending his occupation as 'work', ironically to his father who is dying from the ill effects of his own working life (41). 'Work', and consequently the meaning of working-class life, are in the process of redefinition in the post-industrial community in which Barker's fiction is set, and the landscape and character of working-class communities are altered as a result. Stephen's first visit to the Clagg Lane estate is hindered, for example, by the formidable and hostile architecture of the streets, every entrance 'blocked by concrete bollards', all the road signs 'uprooted or turned back to front, as if the inhabitants of Clagg Lane expected an invasion' (11). The town itself has been re-territorialised into insular, defensive pockets of bitter rivalries and hostile streets:

Nobody came to the town looking for work now. Grass grew in the ship-yards, and even the steelworks had started to lay men off. And so the streets that had welcomed Scottish, Irish, Welsh, Germans and Swedes, as well as workers from all other parts of England, became closed and clannish communities, suspicious of outsiders. Invisible boundaries lay between apparently identical streets, boundaries that were fiercely defended, by ostracism of those who tried to move in, if you were an adult, or by unrelenting gang warfare, if you were a child. (133)

Barker's narrative may appear overtly sociological at such moments, but the landscape described here is not just an indifferent back-ground against which her characters live and die. Barker is consis-tently focused in this novel not on the individual life-story, but of the interconnectedness of lives and communities, the resonances and coincidences between people and places, and the landscape the novel depicts is a form of metonymy for the complex field of relations between the characters and the environment in which they live. The narrative impulse behind such descriptions of the insular, embittered landscape in which this abandoned community live has little to do with setting the context, but rather the landscape is shown to be in a dialectic relationship with the community which it environs. It is shaped by, and in turn shapes, the class-bound subjectivities of the people who inhabit it.

The Century's Daughter does not just tell the life-story of Liza Jarrett and her individual struggle to survive, then, but, like Liza's own method of storytelling, weaves her story in and out of others, weaves between the past and the present, weaves between the voices of the living and the dead, and weaves between the actual and the dream. Barker's narrative traces the interconnections between the lives of her characters, and this is a familiar characteristic from her previous two novels. What she develops further in *The Century's Daughter*, how-ever, is the historical stratification of such interconnections, the expo-sure of each subject, each community, as densely layered through time. Like Liza's memory box covered in a film of dust, the characters and relationships which Barker depicts in the novel are shown to have accumulated layers of meaning and layers of mystification through time. The narrative method used to penetrate these layers is not akin to archaeology, but photography, as Barker repeatedly returns to the image of X-ray exposure to symbolise the process of recovering his-torical memory. The X-ray penetrates skin to expose the structures of bone beneath, an image which recurs in various forms through the novel, but always at moments in which characters become aware of their own past as layered:

> The flames flickered and played tricks with their faces. In Louise's face a skull could be seen, rising closer to the surface night by night. Liza's face, too, was transformed by the flames, seeming sometimes, in the warm steady glow, to be a child again, but then a ridge of cinders would crash and in the blue bleakness of the flare a woman sat, as stripped of youth and beauty as her mother was, and whenever this happened each was aware of resemblances they didn't see by daylight, or welcome now.
>
> On one of those nights when the surface truths of skin and mind were being stripped away, Liza heard herself ask her mother, 'You never loved me, did you?' (181)

In this uncanny moment, Liza is glimpsed as a multitude of selves and resemblances, and the vision of a multi-layered self prompts her to discover the truth of the relationship with her mother. A similar moment of seeing through the skin to the bones of genealogy and history occurs when Liza's daughter, Eileen, is giving birth:

> As the hours passed, Liza felt herself merge into the girl on the bed. *She* had laboured to give birth like this, in this room, this bed. She became afraid of the vanishing boundaries and turned to the fire, only to feel it strip the flesh from her face and reveal her mother's bones. Eileen was not Eileen, Liza was not Liza, but both were links in a chain of women stretching back through the centuries, into the wombs of women whose names they didn't know. (211)

The light from the fire again occasions a moment of exposure, in this instance exposing the specific moment of identification between mother and daughter, of history repeating itself 'in this room, this bed', as integral to the timelessness of women giving birth. Each link derives from and constitutes the historical chain of women bringing new generations into the world. If history is seen through much of the novel to be a destructive force, repeating the tragic waste of life from one generation to the next, in this moment of resemblance, history is also seen as the history of regeneration. Like her first two novels, Barker here allows just a chink of light into the darkness.

Liza dies from the shock of being robbed and beaten by a gang of desperate youths, whose actions are contextualised in the novel as the product of the social and economic despair of a de-industrialised and abandoned working-class community. Her words and her story will survive, however, for her memory box is passed on within her family, her parrot passed on to Stephen, who recalls the myth voiced in Skelton's verse that 'when parrot is dead he doth not putrify' (282). The parrot symbolises throughout the novel, not just the mocking parody of humanity, but also the gift of continuing to tell the stories of those absent, the gift of prosopopoeia. The dead continue to exist as long as we continue to voice their words, their stories and, more particularly in Barker's novel, as long as we learn from them the lesson that the present is built upon and indebted to the deeds and words of the dead. Finally, then, *The Century's Daughter* is neither a nostalgic nor commemorative novel, but an heuristic one that serves to bring out the interconnectedness of past and present, the living and the dead, self and other, and to remind us that the apparently anarchic dissolution of working-class community is intimately connected with, and in the process of repeating, earlier forms of working-class history in twentieth-century England.[12] The novel concludes not with despair, but with a characteristic motif of regeneration, the small hope that from the wasteland where Liza once lived and told stories of her life something might grow: 'The wind blew, bending the dead flowers, and from one or two of them seeds began to disperse, drifting down across the wasteland, like wisps of white hair' (284).

Notes

1 Lyn Pykett argues that *The Century's Daughter* might even be considered a 'condition of England' novel in the manner of nineteenth-century predecessors. See Lyn Pykett, 'The Century's Daughters: Recent Women's Fiction and History', *Critical Quarterly*, 29:3 (1987), 71–7.

2 The shift between the present and the past in *The Century's Daughter* leads Sue Anderson to argue that readers are encouraged to consider the novel more objectively, and 'to consider the societal implications of the lives of the characters represented there', which makes the novel more overtly a 'social novel' that criticises 'the unfairness of a society that tyrannises the weak'. See Sue Anderson, 'Life on the Street: Pat Barker's Realist Fictions', *It's My Party: Reading Twentieth-Century Women's Writing*, ed. Gina Wisker (London, Pluto Press, 1994), 186, 189.

3 Walter Benjamin, *Illuminations*, trans. Harry Zohn (London: Fontana, 1992), 87. Sharon Monteith also takes this approach in her chapter on *Liza's England* in *Pat Barker* (Tavistock, Northcote House, 2002), 28–41.

4 Barker acknowledges her interest in creating a communal voice in her work, as well as the individual voices of her characters as quoted in 'Pat Barker', *Contemporary Authors*, 122 (New York, Gale, 1987), 40.

5 David Carr, *Time, Narrative, and History* (Indianapolis, Indiana University Press, 1991), 78.

6 James Olney, *Memory and Narrative: The Weave of Life-Writing* (Chicago, University of Chicago Press, 1998), 20.

7 J. Hillis Miller, *Topographies* (Stanford, Stanford University Press, 1995), 71–2.

8 Shoshana Felman and Dori Laub, *Testimony: Crises of Witnessing in Literature, Psychoanalysis, and History* (London, Routledge, 1992), 62.

9 Jenny Newman also traces the influence of T.S. Eliot's 'Little Gidding' and 'East Coker' on Barker's representation of the voices of the dead in the novel. See Jenny Newman, 'Souls and Arseholes: The Double Vision of *The Century's Daughter*', *Critical Survey*, 13:1 (2001), 32.

10 Newman argues that although Liza is the obvious 'descendant' of the women of *Union Street* and *Blow Your House Down*, 'it is the character of Frank . . . who points the way forward to Barker's later fiction'. See Newman, 'Souls and Arseholes', 29. Barker's exploration of the traumas of war memories in Frank's life does seem to be a forerunner to her fuller treatment of 'shell-shock' and the legacies of the First World War in the *Regeneration* trilogy.

11 When Virago reissued the novel in 1996 in the 'Modern Classics' series, it was retitled *Liza's England*, which was Barker's original preference.

12 An alternative argument, however, is articulated by John Kirk. What he describes as Barker's most ambitious novel of the 1980s, *The Century's Daughter*, fails, he says, because it indulges in a sentimentalised nostalgia for lost forms of working-class community, which belies the more astute social realism of her first two novels. Kirk's argument, however, gives too much credence to Liza as the spokesperson for Barker's vision of working-class community. Liza's nostalgia is always offset dialogically by Stephen's job as a social worker in contemporary working-class communities, and by the memories of Frank's sense of dispossession. See John Kirk, 'Recovered Perspectives: Gender, Class and Memory in Pat Barker's Writing', *Contemporary Literature*, 40:4 (1999), 603–26.

5

Searching for heroes:
The Man Who Wasn't There

'I. . . I. . . I had no father; I didn't know who my father was. I was told he was dead. He may. . . he may have been dead – I don't know. He may have been killed in the war.'[1] For much of her life, Pat Barker did not know who her father was, or why he had been absent from her life. It explains to some extent Barker's preoccupation with father figures. There are many fatherless children in Pat Barker's fiction, and the absence of a father is usually significant. In *Union Street*, for example, Kelly Brown might not have been so vulnerable to the strange man who befriends her in the park and who later rapes her, had she not identified him with her absent father. The absent father is a blank space in Kelly's life, which she tries to fill by projecting on to the man who stalks her the story of a father returning to care for his daughter. It is only in her fourth novel, *The Man Who Wasn't There*, however, that Barker explores this theme of the fatherless child more fully. Sharon Monteith has already traced the roots of this novel, and especially its central character, Colin Harper, to Barker's early drafts of *Union Street*, and Barker acknowledges that Colin was planned as a 'viewpoint character' for her first novel.[2] The correspondences between the 'Kelly Brown' chapter of *Union Street* and *The Man Who Wasn't There* are striking. Both children are without fathers, and believe that the dark, spectral men who follow them could be their fathers. Both experience eerie encounters with distorted self-images and spectral fathers in scenes set in fairgrounds and parks. Both skirt around forms of misdemeanour, and seek out derelict landscapes in which to hide out. In both novels, the children exemplify the notorious phenomenon of 'latchkey kids', who lack stable family lives, and are consequently shown to be vulnerable to the predatory shadows who lurk in the dark streets which they inhabit. As Kelly Brown sees a projection of her future self in the women who emerge from the cake factory, so too Colin Harper meets the apparition of his return- ing older self. Of course, Kelly and Colin are set on different paths, and Kelly's awakening into adulthood is more traumatic and violent than Colin's, but the similarities between the two stories should alert us to the continuities in Barker's oeuvre.

This is a point worth considering, given that *The Man Who Wasn't There* has sometimes appeared to mark a break in her work from the woman-centred fictions of her first three novels, to her celebrated explorations of masculinity in the *Regeneration* trilogy, and from the social realism of the first three novels to the historical settings and treatment of war themes in the next five novels.[3] Barker herself refers to the novel as 'an intermediate book', which represents a departure from the contemporary settings of her earlier work.[4] *The Man Who Wasn't There* also marks a transition of a more mundane yet often telling kind, since it is the first of Barker's novels to be published in paperback by Penguin. The decision thereafter to cease publishing with Virago seemed to mark a break from the feminist realism of the early novels, yet my argument throughout this book is that this notion of a turning point in Barker's oeuvre is not borne out by the continu- ities we find throughout her work. Colin is a version of Kelly Brown, and both are precursors of the themes Barker will continue to explore in Billy Prior in the *Regeneration* trilogy, Gareth in *Another World*, and even Danny Miller in *Border Crossing*. Ghosts haunt all of Barker's novels or, perhaps more accurately, there are forms of psychic distur- bance which recur through her work. And there is no retreat from the feminist cultural politics of the early novels, since the vicissitudes of modern gender relations are traced relentlessly through the social and cultural history of twentieth-century Britain in Barker's subse- quent novels. She never ceases to be feminist, just as her work has never adequately been described by the term 'realism'.

In some respects, *The Man Who Wasn't There* is Barker's most autobiographical novel. Like Barker, Colin was born in 1943, and has been told stories that his father was killed in the war, even though it becomes clear to him, as it did to Pat Barker, that his mother didn't know who his father was.[5] But it is typical of Barker's oeuvre that this autobiographical correspondence is just the base for a fiction which encapsulates interlocking themes of the search for the meanings of gendered identity, the predominance of myths of heroism in the aftermath of war, the projection of the self into imaginary forms, the intangible sense that the real is haunted by spectral emanations, and the problem of distinguishing memory and imagination. The figure of the fatherless child in Barker's novels has obvious auto-biographical resonances, but the fact that Barker tells the story of a fatherless *boy* in *The Man Who Wasn't There* is an indication of the fictional and speculative purpose of this figure as a vehicle for exploring wider themes. Autobiography might be the foundation for much of her fiction, but she makes clear in interview that it is by asking the question 'what if . . .?' that the fictional narrative begins.[6]

The Man Who Wasn't There is not only Barker's most autobiographical novel, then, where she uses experiences of her own life in self-consciously fictional form, but it is also a novel about autobiography, about the process of selecting fictional narratives of the self. Colin is searching for a sense of his own identity, but more particularly he is searching for ways of constructing narratives about himself. From the beginning of the novel, Colin is inventing fictional personae, inserting them into stock narratives and dramatic scenes, shifting between differing points of view, and exploring in the process the making of self-identity. He is engaging in what Paul John Eakin describes as the 'autobiographical enterprise, reaching back into the past not merely to recapture but to repeat the psychological rhythms of identity formation, and reaching forward into the future to fix the structure of his identity in a permanent self-made existence as literary text', or, in Colin's case, cinematic text.[7] In that reaching forward, as I will argue towards the end of the chapter, Barker's novel projects the figure of Colin as the returning adult, revisiting the scenes of childhood memory, but it is not this future self but Colin who is shown to be in the process of giving meaning to his own life as a story, and using this process to search through the narratives available to him for the course of his life.

Central to these narratives of identity-formation in the novel is its experimentation with points of view, and in particular, cinematic perspectives. Film dominates not just the imagination of the novel's central character, and permeates the stories other characters tell, but it is embraced in the screenplay form of the fantasy scenes, and in the narrative perspectives established in the novel. Colin sees the world through the cinematic lens, but Barker also moulds the novel through cinematic tropes and forms, and for that reason it is Barker's most cohesive novel formally. Characters tell the stories of their lives through the tropes and tales of the cinema.[8] Colin's fantasy of a life of espionage is not only written as a screenplay, but also constructs his perspective on the world as that of a spy or voyeur. His initiation into the adult world of sexuality happens through forms of voyeurism – spying through the lens of a 'magic lantern' at a vaguely pornographic film, peering through his curtains at his mother and her boyfriend on the street below, eavesdropping on the furtive rustlings from his mother's bedroom. The novel is also preoccupied with the shifting perspectives of the camera, returning repeatedly to tropes of magnification and miniaturisation, distortion and focus, close-ups and long shots. Colin's world is thoroughly shaped and constructed through the icons and lexicons of the cinema:

> At the top, in a glass display case, was a poster advertising that week's film. A man in flying helmet and goggles straddled the scene. Between his legs, blazing planes plunged out of the sky, men in parachutes floated down. Underneath the billowing white, their bodies looked soft and squishy, like moths. (29)

Colin's father is projected as the heroic pilot, individuated against the backdrop of toy war. The pilot is magnified to reflect the elevation of one individual's story to heroic status, while the other pilots, plunging to their necessary, insignificant deaths, are merely part of the skyscape which the hero occupies. For Colin, of course, such films as the poster represents function iconographically not just as forms of identification with his father, but as forms of substitution for an absent father. Other boys might look to cinematic war heroes as analogous with their fathers, but Colin's war heroes mark the absence of analogy, and the rupture of patrilinear identity. Other boys might see their fathers' experiences mirrored and magnified in the war films, but Colin must project the cinematic hero as his father.

This is a pattern not just repeated by Colin, but also by his mother and by other characters. Films come to replace the absent father himself, and permeate the stories which Colin hears about his father:

> Once, a couple of years ago, Viv had talked to him about his father. She'd described how, one night, she and her friend had waited outside the aerodrome, but only her friend's boyfriend came striding across the tarmac to meet them. Colin's father had been killed in a bombing raid the night before. Viv, not wanting to spoil her friend's pleasure, had walked home alone.
>
> It was a moving story, the way Viv told it. Colin was moved. He was moved again a few nights later when he saw the same story on the

screen of the Gaumont. A plane exploded, violins swelled, tears glis-
tened, a young woman walked home, alone. (32)

Viv habitually grafts the films she watches at the picture house on to
the narratives of her own life, problematising the distinction between
fact and fiction. That Viv borrows a story from a war film to substitute
for the story of Colin's father indicates to Colin that he is not only failing to discover the true story of his father, but in fact that there is no
true story or, rather, it is impossible to see behind his mother's fictive
projections. His father is a void – for Viv as much as for Colin –
and can be filled only by fiction, by invention. For Colin, then, the
cinematic representation of the masculine war hero is not so much an
issue, as it is for boys who know their fathers, of how closely the representation resembles the reality, but of there being no reality beneath
the representation. There is only representation, only the simulation
of war, and heroism, and only the fiction of paternity.

The absence of the father is not just a gap in Colin's identity, but is
understood as a rupture, with potentially pathological consequences.
The effects of an absent father are signalled in the novel by ellipses,
in a series of incidents in which men are understood to be the products of men. In the first instance, it is the 'short' birth certificate, with
gaps left where there should be a father's name and occupation,
which alerts Colin to the problems of a masculine identity with no
discernible paternal origin:

> Very slowly, he unfolded the thick paper and smoothed the creases out.
> His own name and sex, Viv's name and occupation, and then:
>
> *Name and surname of father:* _____
> *Rank or Profession of father:* _____
>
> Colin stared at the lines of black ink, even ran his finger across them, as
> if willing them to disgorge words.
> He thought: *It doesn't matter.* After all, whoever his father had been,
> *he* was still the same person, it made no difference to *him*. And all the
> while he thought this, he knew it did matter. (17)

The anxiety about paternal identity is understood here as a linguistic
or nomenclatural problem; hence Colin's desire to will the words of
his father's identity into existence. A man is understood as a name
and a job, and the product of a man with a name and a job, and hence
the gaps in his birth certificate mean that it is not only Colin's father
who is 'the man who wasn't there', but Colin, too, is an absence

waiting to be filled in. This makes him vulnerable to the dangers of being rootless, genderless and anonymous, which of course is one reason why Colin imagines himself not as a war hero whose identity is stable and fixed, one of the 'thoroughly decent chaps' (151), but as the anomic, treacherous master of disguise, Gaston. Without the father, there is only the performance of masculine identity, and, as Colin discovers in the figure of Bernard, performances of gender can be illusory.[9]

The sinuous nature of gender identity is the anxiety behind Mr Sawdon's attempt to encourage Colin to see him as a father figure. Mr Sawdon explains that Colin's mother '"can never do for a boy what a man can do. It needs a man to . . " Mr Sawdon took a deep breath, perhaps remembering Colin's age, "to ensure that a boy's development is . . . healthy. *Normal*."' (68). The ellipses signal that Colin's growth into masculine adulthood is by no means assured, and gesture towards what Colin might become if he is not 'normal' and 'healthy'. Normality must be cultivated, in order for gender to find 'healthy' expression, rather than the fear of effeminacy and homosexuality, which lurk behind the gaps in Mr Sawdon's speech. This idea clearly troubles Colin, for the same anxieties recur in his imaginative transformation of this scene into a fictional interrogation, with Bernard being questioned by the Gestapo:

> I've been like it all my life. Ever since I was twelve years old . . . You see, I never had a father. There was no *male* influence. Nothing *healthy*. Nothing *normal*. I never even joined the boy scouts. And I used to . . .
> *He struggles to hold back the final degradation, but it's no use.*
> I used to wear my sister's knickers.
> *Bernard is now a snivelling wreck, cheeks streaked with mascara, courage, pride, manhood gone.* (71)

Here, the ellipses function not to gesture towards something unspoken, but as points of suspension before the confession of 'deviant' gender behaviour. They signal the difficulty of overcoming normative discourses of gender and sexual identity in the act of confessing transgressive practices. But the scene is also partly comic. It conflates, as in a dream, the Gestapo interrogation with a psychopathological interview, and the signs of the spy which the Gestapo agents think they have identified turn out to be the signs of a remorseful cross-dresser. The conflation of the two genres of confessional interview serve to advert the reader's attention to the fact that Colin's adolescent imagination is using the fictions of espionage he constructs as a vehicle to explore his own growth into adulthood.

Through his fictional projection of Bernard, Colin imagines that the absence of a father figure would account for gender and sexual deviancy, and a proclivity for cross-dressing. The problem for Colin with the models of gendered behaviour which he finds in films and in a figure like Bernard is that they hyperbolise gender identity in the act of performance. The men in the war films, like the man Colin admires in the poster, are abnormal giants, who straddle the landscape, and make masculinity seem an impossibly heroic stature to which to aspire. In contrast to this is Bernard's performance of femininity, which Colin remembers vividly when he tries to sleep:

> He was afraid that when he tried to sleep he would see the man in black, but he needn't have worried. The moment he closed his eyes, Bernie's face appeared. Blue eyelids, lashes gobby with mascara, the mouth red, shockingly red, Colin remembered, like a horse's arsehole just before it shits.
>
> He opened his eyes again, wondering why it should be Bernie's face he saw. (48)

Bernard's performance of femininity is notable by its obscene exaggeration, by its display of gender through metonyms. In this case, the shocking make-up functions as the signs of femininity, but in its excessive production of these signs the make-up also serves to undermine the performance. The difference between a woman and a man imitating a woman is only discernible to Colin when he encounters this obscene over-determination of the signs of gender, and Barker uses the shocking image of the horse's arsehole to make clear that the effects of Bernard's make-up are obscene, not comic. Like the gross magnification of masculinity as hyperbolised performance of courage in war films, Bernard's performance of femininity is excessive to the point of exposing itself as fiction, and thus threatening to expose for Colin that gender is a fictional construct rather than a predetermined 'healthy' or 'normal' reality. The absence of a father figure, and the anxieties surrounding what happens to boys without fathers, reveals the process of gender definition and gender identification as indeterminate and accidental.

Barker's novel develops this theme of the fiction substituting for the real not just in relation to Colin's search for his paternal and masculine ancestry, but more generally in relation to the war in English culture in the 1950s. This is clear, for example, in the case of the real 'dads' who Colin meets in his friends' houses:

> For Colin, the mystery of his father's identity was bound up with the war, the war he'd been born into, but couldn't remember. The war whose relics he saw around him everywhere. Photographs. On mantel-pieces, in friends' houses, dads with more hair than they had now sat astride guns, or smiled against the backdrop of ruined cities. A little coaxing, and they'd show you the things they'd brought back. Guns, knives, a swastika ring, gold teeth sawn from a Japanese corpse.
>
> At school, too, the endless war between British and Germans was re-fought at every break, and the leaders of the opposing armies were always boys whose fathers had been in the war. Who could produce, when need arose, the ultimate authority: *My dad says.*
>
> Everything *Colin* knew about the war came from films. (33)

Colin can turn only to films as an authority on the meanings of the war, while other boys have the frequent testimony of their fathers, and the artefactual archives of war relics collected by their fathers. But, while the narrative emphasises this gap between 'real' archival objects and 'fictive' films as sources of cultural authority, there is in fact con-tinuity between the objects and the films in terms of their function in postwar culture, for the war is now less real than its narration, whether that narration is conducted through relics, testimonies, pho-tographs, films or, indeed, the 'endless war' of representation which takes place in the schoolyard. The war is an integral part of Colin's identity, as much so as his paternal identity, but both can only be imagined. In this sense, it is not just Colin's imagination which is depicted in the novel as heavily indebted to cinematic and dramatic forms of representation. Others share this obsession with telling sto-ries about the war, with inventing the war through its relics and images, with replaying the war as a movie (or as a succession of movies – the war proved a popular subject for British and Hollywood films in the postwar decades). Indeed, Adam Piette argues that the necessary fictions of wartime – 'the hopeless role-playing forced upon minds during the war . . . [and] the way the island dreamt itself through the war' – had a lasting impact on postwar representations of the war as a theatrical and fictional construction.[10]

In 1955, the year in which the novel is set, the most significant British war films on release were *Above Us the Waves, Cockleshell Heroes* and *The Colditz Story*, each of which told the story of brave, self-sacrificing individuals who are pitted against impossible odds,

but, interestingly for the novel, each of which also feature acts of heroism which depend on subterfuge and stealth as much as open
combat. In this sense, it is possible to argue that the films, and
Barker's novel, are registering the shift from the imagery of bravery
in open combat associated with the Second World War, typified by the
iconography of the RAF fighter pilot, to the imagery of cunning and
bravado in espionage associated with the Cold War, typified by Ian
Fleming's emergent fictional hero, James Bond. It is not clear that
Colin alludes to any of these films or novels in particular. Instead, his
mind jumbles together lots of films, and indeed conflates genres of
films, but the significance for Colin is a sort of generic masculine
hero, the 'tough guy' who embodies independence, command and
courage.

But the heroic mythology of the war hero which Colin finds in the
cinema, and with which he identifies his father, is perhaps deflated
from the beginning of the novel. Barker begins the novel with Colin
turning into his road, 'one eye open for snipers', cautious because he
had recently come close to being knocked down by Mr Blenkinsop in
his car. The scene prompts Colin to imagine himself as the fictive persona of Gaston, the resistance agent fighting the Germans in France:

> Gaston jerks himself awake. A sniper is crawling across Blenkinsop's
> roof, but Gaston has seen him. He spins round, levels the gun, and *fires*.
> The sniper – slow motion now – clutches his chest, buckles at the
> knee, crashes in an endlessly unfurling fountain of glass through the
> roof of Mr Blenkinsop's greenhouse, where he lands face down, his fin-
> gers clutching the damp earth – and his chest squashing Mr Blenkin-
> sop's prize tomatoes.
> Gaston blows nonchalantly across the smoking metal of his gun, and,
> with never a backward glance, strides up the garden path and into the
> house. (10)

Gaston's war is already more furtive and murky than the war which
Colin knows from the cinema. This is not the heroic scene of men
pitted against each other in feats of courage and open combat, but of
secretive, treacherous warfare, a war of snipers and spies, of double
agents and disguises. The scene Colin imagines is cinematic in its
perspectives. It consists of classic, stereotypical 'shots' – the hero's
quick awareness of lurking danger, his alert and decisive reaction,
and the slow-motion, hammed-up death-fall of the sniper. These are
the stock-in-trade images of the heroic thriller, but what is also clear

about Colin's debt to cinema is the mixing of genres, for surely the nonchalant blowing 'across the smoking metal of his gun' is an image borrowed from the Western, not the thriller or the war film. Gaston is a cowboy, here, as well as a spy or resistance fighter. Across the three genres of popular cinema in evidence in this scene – war, Western and thriller – masculine heroism is identified with decisiveness, confidence, and a professional indifference to the death of others. But there is obviously another genre at play right from the beginning of the novel, the comic, which deflates the stereotypes of masculine heroism. Colin's pleasure in imagining himself as Gaston killing the lurking sniper turns out not only to be the pleasure of borrowing the mask of the manly hero, but also the pleasure of imagining Mr Blenkinsop's prize tomatoes squashed (Blenkinsop is, after all, Colin's real nemesis in this opening scene). So, Gaston serves as the vehicle for a schoolboy's imagined revenge on a grumpy neighbour. But what is also taking place in this scene is a kind of ironic narration, akin to the way Philippe Lejeune talks about the doubling of narrative forms in autobiographical texts, in which we cannot read Colin's interior cinematic fantasies without being conscious of the ways in which these fantasies are already robbed of their illusory power.[11]

Barker makes clear from the beginning of the novel that the myths of heroism and masculinity perpetuated by the cinema are illusory constructions, and that Colin's borrowings from the cinema are aware of this illusion, and to a certain extent are self-conscious and ironic appropriations of such myths. The comic deflation of the heroism imagined in the first Gaston scene shows that Colin masters these illusions for his own pleasure rather than absorbing them passively. The illusory nature of the cinema is asserted more emphatically later in the novel:

> But he couldn't sleep. For a while, he tried to look at the pictures in his film annuals, but all the films were jumbled together in his head. He was tired of them anyway: the clipped, courageous voices, the thoroughly decent chaps, the British bombs that always landed on target, the British bombers that always managed to limp home. They told lies, he thought. They said it was easy to be brave. (151)

Films have served to provide Colin with possible models of behaviour and identity, but he has never been a passive consumer of their images. He has decided when to succumb to the dream-vision of himself as war hero, when to believe the fictions of film, and when to refuse their illusions. Moreover, his knowledge of films enables him to recognise instantly when Viv, and later Mrs Stroud, attempt to pass off the stories they have seen at the cinema as real. He is, in this sense and others, empowered by the cinema as a storehouse of fictions, memories and myths, rather than subject to its lies.

The particular lie which tires Colin is the lie of masculinity. The 'tough-guy' image of the war film, and the other genres Colin draws upon, is constructed around the repression of sensitivity, fear, weakness and passivity, all of which are associated with femininity. It advertises a hyper-masculinity, painful to imitate in reality, and one which Colin ultimately decides is impossible. Theodor Adorno argues that such models of men 'all have about them a latent violence', which appears to be violence directed against others, but is in fact 'past violence against himself', the laceration of subjectivity into a self-wounding image of 'pure' masculinity:

> He-men are thus, in their own constitution, what film-plots usually present them to be, masochists. At the root of their sadism is a lie, and only as liars do they truly become sadists, agents of repression. This lie, however, is nothing other than repressed homosexuality presenting itself as the only approved form of heterosexuality. . . .. In the end the tough guys are the truly effeminate ones, who need the weaklings as their victims in order not to admit that they are like them. . . .. In its downfall the subject negates everything which is not of its own kind.[12]

Colin acts out this role model of the tough guy in the fictional persona of Gaston, who begins as the conventional courageous, decisive hero, shooting down the sniper, but gradually becomes, as the novel progresses, a more treacherous and sinister figure. He is not the hero fighting for freedom, as in the war films, but the collaborator, who is in league with the Gestapo, in much the same way that Adorno equates such a model of masculinity with fascism and sadism. Likewise, Gaston's masculinity increasingly comes to depend upon killing any signs of femininity, be that signs of cowardice, weakness or passivity, or, when it is clear that he is in league with the Gestapo, he literally kills the feminine by murdering Vivienne. His virility as a man is only asserted by eliminating femininity, and thus the heterosexual male hero of the war films can only project himself as manly by renouncing femininity, which of course is to approach the signs of repressed homosexuality. The threat of homosexuality is, as mentioned above, glimpsed in the ellipses which pass over what Colin might become if he is not led into manly behaviour.

When Colin masturbates in emulation of the masculine display of virility, modelling himself on the man he has seen having sex with a 'right old ratbag' in a bombed-out house, he finds that he is not thinking about that couple at all, but his mother and her boyfriend in the next room (129). This coincides with the screenplay in which Gaston has killed Vivienne, the fictional projection of Colin's mum, mistaking her for Bernard, the cross-dresser (130). This complicated mapping of murder on to simulated virility, treachery on to imagined incest, duplicitous politics on to ambivalent gender, appears to equate Colin's attempted emulation of heroic or virile masculinity with sadistic and also masochistic desires. Colin is defeated by this attempt, left 'feeling small, grubby and alone' (129). The signs of his masculinity are inseparable from what is associated with femininity, and the emulation of hyper-masculinity seems to require the negation of the feminine. As Lynne Segal argues, the 'archetypal male hero' thus becomes 'haunted by the sheer impossibility of actualising the myth in a manner free from deception and pretence'.[13] Colin recognises that the myth of masculinity as it is depicted in the cinema is impossible to act out without the pretence becoming a grotesque parody, much like Bernard's pretence of femininity, or indeed the role that his mother is forced to perform as a waitress in a bunny costume. Colin's attempt to unravel the codes of his identity necessarily involves acting out possible identities, but constantly he sets up a pretence only to examine that pretence.

This accounts in part for the structure of the novel, which incorporates the dramatisation of pretences and fictions of identity into the narrative of Colin's search for his identity. Colin's sense of identity is always ghosted by the absence of a paternal role model, and the consequent availability of many different models of what he might become. Kelly in *Union Street* is troubled by a different quest in relation to her absent father, which is the search for affection and love, but for Colin the search for his father is always inseparable from the issue of what Colin will become. In this sense, Barker highlights Colin's anxiety about the fictional personae of films, as well as the spectral presence of the man in black who seems to haunt him, as an anxiety about becoming. As so often in Barker's work, the character sees himself only through the mirrored reflection of doubles and others:

As he turned from the bathroom cabinet, he caught sight of himself in the mirror. A flaw ran the whole length of the glass, and, for a moment,

he played with it, bobbing from side to side, making his forehead first
bulge and then recede.

Even when he stopped doing that, his face didn't look normal. It'd
changed quite a lot in the last few months, and that wasn't just his imagination, because other people had noticed, too. All the bones jutted out
more. It felt almost as if another face was pushing its way to the surface,
somebody else's face, and he didn't know whose. (92)

Flawed mirrors are a recurrent trope in Barker's fiction, and signify
the difficulty of representing identity, of fixing the image of the self.
Here, Colin's image is not just doubled, but magnified and minia-
turised by turn in the flawed glass. The face he sees in the mirror
when he ceases to play with its distortions is also unrecognisable,
because it at once conceals and begins to project the other, adult face
emerging through his boyish face. Colin senses the emergence of
his older self, but experiences this older self not as a continuity with
his own self, or a likeness, but as an alien other pushing through.
This is the significance, of course, of the 'man' who is glimpsed following Colin throughout the novel, who appears to be at various
points a prowler, a character in Colin's imagined life of espionage,
his father, or the ghost of his dead father, and finally turns out to be
Colin's older self, returning to look mournfully at the home of his
childhood.

Barker plays this out as a thriller narrative, and it takes a chilling
form when Colin fears that the man in the gas mask chasing him is
not his friend, Adrian, 'but something else, something terrible, something so entirely alien that its face, revealed, would be more dreadful
than the mask' (141). This is the alien other of his own identity, the
fear of which has haunted him through the novel:

Colin started to walk towards him. The man couldn't see, he couldn't
hear, there was no way of challenging him, that Colin could think of,
except to stand where he stood, to occupy the space he claimed as his. It
would be all right, Colin thought, as long as his nerve didn't break, as
long as he didn't let the horror of looking into his own face overpower
him. A few inches away, he stopped.

Only one of them would walk away, and Colin realized, at the last
moment, that he didn't know which. He stepped forward. He didn't
know what he'd expected, perhaps a slight chill, a jolt, a shock even, but
he felt none of these things. Just the faint brush of air against his skin,
and then he was alone, in the blanched silence of his mother's room,
with all the furniture back. (153)

As with many of Barker's ghosts, it is not clear how 'real' this ghost of his older self is, and how much imagined. But Colin might not be the only one to see the spectral figure who haunts him. Mrs Stroud, the psychic, is made speechless and collapses by the sight of the ghost who lurks behind Colin, and she recognises in Colin the gift of seeing and communicating with the dead. Colin is unwilling to admit that he has seen the ghost Mrs Stroud saw behind him, because 'any admission would give the thing – whatever it was – greater reality' (119). That the dead are as real as the living is a disturbing thought for Colin, just as the fantasy world he inhabits sometimes takes real form, such as the stigmatic marks which begin to appear on Colin's arm after he has imagined one of his fictional characters suffering Gestapo torture (81).

What Colin discovers, however, is that the man he is seeing is not like the dead young pilots Mrs Stroud once saw returning as ghosts, but instead is the spectral emanation of his future self. This future self has returned to mourn the passing of his mother, Vivienne, and to look over the scene of his childhood, from which he is now removed. In this sense, Barker represents Colin's future self as the 'revisitor', the scholarship boy who escapes from the class into which he was born (the man has a 'thin, oversensitive mouth' and pronounces 'Mam' as if in a foreign language), and is never able to return to his home without the feeling of being an outsider.[14] But Colin is, as I've argued above, already that outsider, already constructing narratives of himself in the third person, as if he was his older self narrating the story of his childhood. The spectral character, then, might be plausibly read as the figure of an imagined adult autobiographer, who promises to make sense of Colin's possible roles and identities in a coherent narrative, written in a future time in which the self has become as whole and singular as the fictional and cinematic heroes Colin searches for. The encounter with himself as the older revisitor enables Colin to dispel the fear of becoming, or rather to defer the anxiety of becoming, and this forms the 'happy ending' of the novel, in which Colin acknowledges that 'the blank space would remain blank. . . . Well, he could live with that. People had survived far worse' (157). The homophobic fear of those other selves – effeminate, cross-dressing, homosexual – which a fatherless boy is thought vulnerable of becoming, is finally dispelled by the exposure of myths of 'normal' masculinity as cultural constructs which are at once unattainable and false. Hence, by the end of the novel, the 'tough-guy' persona of

Gaston is dead, the victim of his own treachery, and Colin seems now to identify with Bernard:

> *Alone in the windswept clearing, Bernard looks up and waves. He watches as the Lysander banks steeply, and heads towards the Channel, dwindling, in a matter of seconds, to the size of a toy plane.*
> *Then he turns up the collar of his coat and slips away into the darkness.*
> Colin, staring straight ahead, waiting for the drone of the Lysander to fade. Then he gave a sharp, decisive little nod, and said, 'The End'. (158)

As he has been throughout the novel, Colin is shown here to be the author of his imagined film, deciding when it ends, and closing with a shot of the new hero, Bernard, surviving and slipping into the darkness. Bernard has always been a contrast to Gaston, and the surviving hero of Colin's film is not the hyper-masculine hero, who turns out to be more treacherous than heroic, but the 'master of disguise', a hero because he signifies the fluidity and multiplicity of identity. Colin's film ultimately implies that the motif of cross-dressing is a more truthful representation of identity than the lies of 1950s war films. What he discovers in his search through autobiographical representation (and Bernard stands as the ultimate figure of this discovery), is, to use the words of Paul de Man, 'not that it reveals reliable self-knowledge – it does not – but that it demonstrates in a striking way the impossibility of closure and of totalization (that is the impossibility of coming into being) of all textual systems made up of tropological substitutions'.[15]

Notes

1 Pat Barker in interview with Robert McCrum, 'It's a disaster for a novel to be topical', *Observer*, 1 April 2001.
2 Sharon Monteith, *Pat Barker* (Tavistock, Northcote House, 2002), 43.
3 See, for examples, Philip Hensher, *Guardian*, 26 November 1993; Blake Morrison, 'War Stories', *New Yorker*, 22 January 1996, 78–82; Sharon Carson, 'Pat Barker', *British Writers: Supplement IV*, ed. George Stade and Carol Howard (New York, Simon and Schuster/Prentice Hall, 1997), 45–63; Geoff Sammon, 'Pat Barker: A Modern British Woman Writer', *Neusprachliche-Mitteilungen aus Wissenschaft und Praxis*, 49:1 (1996), 42–4. All argue to various degrees that a dramatic shift takes place between the first three 'realist' novels and the more 'historical' novels since *The Man Who Wasn't There*.
4 Donna Perry, 'Pat Barker', *Backtalk: Women Writers Speak Out* (New Brunswick, Rutgers University Press, 1993), 44.

5 Barker describes Colin's situation in the novel as 'very autobiographical' in Perry, 'Pat Barker', 46.

6 Ibid., 45.

7 Paul John Eakin, *Fictions in Autobiography: Studies in the Art of Self-Invention* (Princeton, Princeton University Press, 1985), 226.

8 Sharon Monteith traces the possible film intertexts of the novel in her essay, 'Screening *The Man Who Wasn't There*: The Second World War and 1950s Cinema', *Critical Perspectives on Pat Barker*, ed. Sharon Monteith, Margaretta Jolly, Nahem Yousaf and Ronald Paul (Columbia, University of South Carolina Press, 2005), 115–27.

9 Pat Wheeler discusses the performative in gender in her essay, 'Transgressing Masculinities: *The Man Who Wasn't There*', *Critical Perspectives on Pat Barker*, ed. Monteith, Jolly, Yousaf and Paul, 128–43.

10 Adam Piette, *Imagination at War: British Fiction and Poetry 1939–1945* (London, Papermac, 1995), 2.

11 Philippe Lejeune, *On Autobiography*, ed. Paul John Eakin, trans. Katherine Leary (Minneapolis, University of Minnesota Press, 1989), 61. My thanks to Sharon Monteith for pointing out the similarities between my argument about point of view and Lejeune's thinking on ironic narratives of childhood.

12 Theodor Adorno, *Minima Moralia: Reflections from Damaged Life*, trans. E.F.N. Jephcott (London, Verso, 1978), 46.

13 Lynne Segal, *Slow Motion: Changing Masculinities, Changing Men* (London, Virago, 1990), 114.

14 An argument Pat Wheeler develops fully in 'Trangressing Masculinities', 132–4.

15 Paul de Man, 'Autobiography as De-Facement', *Modern Language Notes*, 94:5 (December 1979), 922.

6

History and haunting:
the *Regeneration* trilogy

The *Regeneration* trilogy has attracted more critical attention and acclaim than any of Pat Barker's previous work. *Regeneration* (1991), *The Eye in the Door* (1993) and *The Ghost Road* (1995) were widely praised both individually and as a trilogy. *Regeneration* was nominated as one of the four best novels of 1991 in the *New York Review of Books*, and spawned a film version directed by Gillies MacKinnon and starring Jonathan Pryce in 1997. *The Eye in the Door* won the *Guardian* Fiction Prize, and *The Ghost Road* was the Booker Prize winner in 1995. Sharon Carson observes that 'it was only with these [novels] that she claimed international attention'.[1] It is not my intention here to account for the reasons why Barker achieved greater success with the trilogy, although there are a number of factors which are worth considering besides Barker's talent and vision as a writer. Historical fiction was certainly a popular genre, perhaps for some even too popular, as the chair of the Booker Prize judges in 1995, George Walden, complained about the lack of writers tackling contemporary settings. The First World War also remained a popular subject with the British public, its famous poets still taught to schoolchildren and widely anthologised, its stories and imagery still abundant in literary fiction, popular histories, and even television comedy, in *Blackadder Goes Forth* (1989). Perhaps, too, the fact that few of its combatants survived into the 1990s, that there was a sense marked at each Remembrance Day service that the living witnesses of the war were disappearing, meant that the subject was ripe for valedictory fictional representation.

The trilogy builds on the popularity of the subject and form of First World War representations, then, and according to Blake Morrison it also filters the war through a 'very nineteen-nineties preoccupation with gender, emasculation, bisexuality, and role reversals', and even her officer characters speak 'not in their adopted "mock-medieval facetious humour," but in current idiom'.[2] Barker's trilogy is a work of historical fiction, but it is also, perhaps inevitably, a contemporary revisionist fiction of the war, which uses the story of the war as an index of contemporary social, cultural, sexual and political debates. But lest she is criticised of bringing a revisionist agenda to the war, Barker shows that the war was replete with its own mythologising and revisionist tendencies. Through the conversations of Owen and Sassoon, for example, Barker traces the revision of perhaps the most famous poem of the war, Owen's 'Anthem for Doomed Youth', revealing at an early point in the trilogy that what we take to be the monumental visions of the war were themselves finely honed, carefully reworked, and styled towards their epic forms.

The *Regeneration* trilogy is not, therefore, a slick appropriation of the war for contemporary purposes. It is Barker's most meticulously researched and historically based writing to date. Of her previous novels, Barker told an interviewer, 'I wrote about what I saw happening in depressed regions',[3] although, as I argue in other chapters in this book, Barker's novels were always densely allusive and multi-accentual representations of historical situations. But whereas the early novels can sometimes mask their learning behind the veneer of sharply observed realism, and privilege the voices of the unrepresented and silenced communities of post-industrial England, in contrast the *Regeneration* trilogy tackles a well-mined subject, and stays close to familiar accounts of the war by some of its participants, as well as to the writings of its principal character, Dr W.H.R. Rivers, a distinguished anthropologist and psychoanalyst. The scope of the trilogy enables Barker to range across various, underexplored dimensions of the war, however. *Regeneration* (1991) constructs a fictional version of the true story of Rivers's treatment of the poet, Siegfried Sassoon. Sassoon is sent to Rivers to be 'cured', because of his supposedly irrational protest against the war. Rivers is certain that Sassoon's protest is a great deal more rational than the war, but it is nevertheless his duty to restore Sassoon to psychological fitness so that he can return to the front. *The Eye in the Door* (1993) takes up the story of a fictional patient of Rivers, Billy Prior, who develops a dangerous split in his psychic life, which magnifies Freud's experience of his uncanny 'double' to 'Jekyll and Hyde' proportions. The novel also focuses on the true story of a woman convicted of conspiring to assassinate Lloyd George in 1917. The final volume of the trilogy, *The Ghost Road* (1995), shifts between Prior's account of his fateful return to the war in France, and Rivers's own psychological crisis, as he wrestles with his own demons and ghosts. Prior's diary in this novel takes us directly, for the first time in the trilogy, to the familiar, iconic terrain of First World War representations – the trench, no-man's-land, and the futile charge 'over the top'. In the same novel, Barker turns to Rivers's accounts of his experiences as an anthropologist in Melanesia to engage a cross-cultural dimension to the meanings of war. Each novel in the trilogy has its own preoccupations and distinctive tropes, and brings to the fore a particular dialogue – Rivers and Sassoon in *Regeneration*, Rivers and Prior in *The Eye in the Door*, and Rivers and Njiru in *The Ghost Road* – but it is on Barker's achievement across the coherent and cohesive whole of the trilogy that this chapter will focus.

The trilogy is populated for the most part with actual historical figures, usually drawn extensively from sources, as Barker's 'Author's note' at the back of each of the novels acknowledges and explains. If her previous novels had earned Barker the reputation of 'an uncompromising, working-class regionalist', in Blake Morrison's words,[4] the trilogy found Barker engaging with the very public, national history and mythology of the 'Great War', and that she did so with a potentially hazardous fusion of well-known historical accounts, contemporary interests in gender and sexual identities, and fictive characters, is a sign of the confidence and ambition of her work. In her most successful and substantial writing to date, Barker the historian and Barker the novelist are thoroughly interfused, and it is the seamless blending of historical fact with the literary vitality of fictional characters like Prior and fictionally expanded dialogue, thoughts and dreams of Rivers and his patients that accounts for the popularity and acclaim of the trilogy. On the other hand, this fusion of history and fiction has also led to criticism of her work. Ben Shephard criticised the novel for failing 'to re-create the past in its own terms' in the *Times Literary Supplement*,[5] and Martin Löschnigg follows Shephard's lead in chiding Barker for her preoccupation with Elaine Showalter's 'gender-oriented studies of shell-shock', the result of which for Löschnigg is that Barker 'provides a somewhat one-sided representation of the phenomenon of "shellshock" which neglects the medical, military and social implications' and 'continues a mythification of shellshock victims'.[6] Barker herself drew upon these criticisms in her next novel, *Another World*, in the insistence of her character, the

historian Helen, on imposing a series of 'late twentieth-century preoccupations. Gender. Definitions of masculinity. Homoeroticism' on
the 'raw' memories of a First World War veteran.[7] This is testimony,
if it were needed, that Barker not only reads reviews of her work, but
is engaged in a continual dialogue with the ethical issues of representation raised by her work, and that her oeuvre can be read as a continual process of expanding, revisiting and revising her concerns with
representation (particularly representations of trauma) since *Union
Street*.

It is as an experimental work of historical fiction that the *Regeneration* trilogy will be considered here. Barker experiments firstly with
telling the story of the war from less familiar perspectives: the home
front, the psychoanalyst charged with getting traumatised soldiers
back to military duty, the secret war against dissenters and rebels, the
social and sexual politics of the war, and the meanings of the relationship between civilisation and war (which Barker examines through the
binocular perspectives of Britain and Melanesia). She experiments further, however, and I think to more significant purposes, with the war
as an analogy for wider trends in modern history and culture. In one
sense, the war represents a watershed in historical consciousness for
Barker, an horrific vortex in which the Victorian sense of progress and
civilisation is thrown into crisis, and the (post)modern age of scepticism and irony emerges. However, as Peter Hitchcock argues, Barker's
vista is also wider than simply reiterating the mythology of the war as
an epistemic break with all that went before: 'Not surprisingly for a
social realist, Barker makes connections between the mutism, hysteria
and nightmares precipitated by the experience of the war and the social
values and culture that pre-exist yet are foregrounded by this extreme
situation'.[8] Hitchcock rightly argues that the process of social change
prior to and after the war is the focus of Barker's representations,
rather than the war itself. Prior is the principal means through which
we can see the conflicts of class and gender, which pre-exist the war,
coming into intense focus during the war. As a 'temporary gentleman',
raised from the ranks of the working class to his 'temporary' officer
status because of the extreme conditions of the war, Barker uses Prior
as a device to mark the social, sexual and cultural boundaries of Edwardian England, much as she uses Sarah Lumb, Prior's girlfriend, to
mark the peculiar but temporary shift of women's experiences from
the domestic enslavement of prewar society to the potentially transformative 'adventures' of factory work during the war.

Rivers himself is ideally placed to suggest such an analysis of the war as an intensification of the symptoms of social change, for we know that as an anthropologist he has studied the signs of social transformation (and decay), and he remarks to Prior about the socially divided ways in which soldiers experience the traumas of war: '"All the physical symptoms: paralysis, blindness, deafness. They're all common in private soldiers and rare in officers. It's almost as if for . . . the labouring classes illness *has* to be physical"' (*Regeneration* 96). Rivers's hesitation in naming 'the labouring classes' perhaps itself identifies the social conflicts taking place between Rivers and Prior, suggested by the occasional snobbery of Rivers, relentlessly rebutted by Prior. Later, Rivers observes the differences between how he treats the officers for 'shellshock' symptoms with the gentle 'talking cure', and the way the 'men' are treated brutally and physically by Yealland. So, too, the dialogues between Rivers and Prior (and Barker's predilection for the psychoanalytic exchange as a means of narrative commentary is particularly striking here) enable Prior to 'report' on the social implications of the war, telling Rivers, for example, that class is as deeply marked in the trenches as in prewar streets: 'What you wear, what you eat. Where you sleep. What you carry. The men are pack animals' (*R* 67). The visual signifiers of class continue to be effective in the supposed maelstrom of the war, and this is perhaps where Barker is at her most effective in demythologising the war, which, like the Second World War, has continued to be mythologised as a time of class unity and the dissolution of social differences. 'People at home say there are no class distinctions at the front', Prior tells Rivers, to which he adds: 'Ball-*ocks*' (*R* 67).

This focus on the war as a continuation of pre-existing social processes is also apparent in relation to gender and sexuality, although here Rivers is compelled to challenge, if not overturn, the prevailing myths of Edwardian England:

In leading his patients to understand that breakdown was nothing to be ashamed of, that horror and fear were inevitable responses to the trauma of war, that feelings of tenderness for other men were natural and right, that tears were an acceptable and helpful part of grieving, he was setting himself against the whole tenor of their upbringing. They'd been trained to identify emotional repression as the essence of manliness. Men who broke down, or cried, or admitted to feeling fear, were sissies, weaklings, failures. Not *men*. And yet he himself was a product of the same system, even perhaps a rather extreme product. Certainly the rigorous repression of emotion and desire had been the constant theme of his adult life. In advising his young patients to abandon the attempt at repression and to let themselves *feel* the pity and terror their war experience inevitably evoked, he was excavating the ground he stood on. (*R* 48)

In part this passage remarks upon the dangers of Rivers's psycho-analytic method – which is analogous to the medical experiment on regenerating nerves from which the novel and trilogy title is partly taken – of deliberately severing and suturing the nerves, and exposing the injured subject to carefully administered but extreme pain. Rivers recalls his moral distress about inflicting pain on his colleague in the experiment, even though his colleague has volunteered for the task, but his scientific sense of detachment enables him to continue with the experiment (*R* 46). Similarly, the mental lives of Rivers's patients must be stripped down, and exposed to the rawness of their emotions, in order for them to rebuild themselves. But the exposure of emotions runs counter to everything they have been taught to experience as men. Manliness is about repressing emotions, of doing your duty without thinking about feelings. As with the case of social class, Barker's trilogy traces the traumatisation of masculine subjectivity in the war back to the construction of that subjectivity in the first place:

> Mobilization. The Great Adventure. They'd been *mobilized* into holes in the ground so constricted they could hardly move. And the Great Adven-ture – the real life equivalent of all the adventure stories they'd devoured as boys – consisted of crouching in a dugout, waiting to be killed. The war that had promised so much in the way of 'manly' activity had actu-ally delivered 'feminine' passivity, and on a scale that their mothers and sisters had scarcely known. No wonder they broke down. (*R* 108)

Consequently, for Barker, the symptoms which Rivers encounters in the trilogy known as 'shellshock' are not the products of the trauma-tising experiences of the war, although they are of course triggered by those experiences, but are the products of a longer process of con-structing particularly restrictive and repressive ideologies of mas-culinity. Greg Harris argues that Barker 'strategically separates men from masculinity' in the trilogy, by examining how the 'gender per-formativity' of the soldiers is brought into crisis by the 'feminising' experiences of the war.[9] Peter Hitchcock takes this critique further, however, by arguing that Barker shows that the war, although born out of the gender ideologies of the Edwardian period, actually delivers a contradictory situation, in which 'men go off to war but the war itself undermines every formula of masculinity and class', and 'working-class women prove to themselves and their communities that they can labor just as productively in the factory as they can in the house-hold, and that this contradicts labor and sexual divisions deemed natural before the war'.[10]

In this sense, the trilogy represents the war as functioning as a kind of ideological chiasmus, at least in terms of gender ideologies, in which the masculine is feminised, and the feminine masculinised, but Barker's novels are too canny politically to allow this transforma-tion to appear in any sense emancipatory or ideal. The transgression of gender and sexual codes is usually shown to be debilitating rather than emancipatory. Women might enjoy the temporary relaxation of gendered labour divisions, but working in hazardous, exhausting con-ditions in munitions factories is hardly presented as a liberating transgression either, even if it contradicts and problematises prewar gender stereotypes. The idea that the factory for women or the trenches for men provided some kind of temporary hiatus in social structures, or enabled transgression of social codes, is contradicted by Barker's representation of working-class identity, as we have seen in previous novels, as a cyborgian subjectivity. Sarah Lumb's yellow skin and shock of copper hair, the effects of working in a munitions fac-tory, prompt her reflection that she and the other women 'don't look human. . . . They looked like machines, whose sole function was to make other machines' (*R* 201). So, too, Prior observes that the war is an extension of the reified subjectivity of working-class men:

> One of the ways in which he felt different from his brother officers, one of the many, was that *their* England was a pastoral place: fields, streams, wooded valleys, medieval churches surrounded by ancient elms. They couldn't grasp that for him, and for the vast majority of the men, the Front, with its mechanization, its reduction of the individual to a cog in a machine, its blasted landscape, was not a contrast with the life they'd known at home, in Birmingham or Manchester or Glasgow or the Welsh pit villages, but a nightmarish culmination. (*The Eye in the Door* 115–16)

The point strikes Prior as he clambers across an urban wasteland near his home, which quickly and disturbingly reminds him in every detail of the jagged, metal-strewn, cratered landscape of the battlefields. Coming home provides no relief from the mechanised slaughter of the war, because Barker reminds us of how these men were already reduced to cogs in a machine long before they went to war.[11] Prior may be emblematic of sexual transgression, passing between same-class heterosexual relations with Sarah and cross-class homosexual relations with Charles Manning, and Prior's bisexuality is partly understood by Rivers as a factor in the feisty vitality of their relationship, but it is the relationship with Sarah which comes closest to representing a future possibility for Prior, a conventional heterosexual marriage. Manning is only ever a sex toy for Prior. And, of course, Prior's transgressive potential is pathetically levelled when he dies with so many others at the front line. The possibilities of transgression, then, of sex, class or gender, are shown to be temporarily intensified by the war, but they have a longer history, and an uncertain future. Whatever other changes the war might effect, it is a continuation and intensification of prewar social processes and conflicts, and yet what Barker holds in tension throughout the trilogy is a contradictory sense of the war as one episode in a larger process of historical change, and the war as a singular event.

The 'Great War' is surely a large enough canvas in itself for Barker's palimpsestic rewriting of history, but Barker also draws our attention to the wider discursive and ideological conflicts of modernity. A central device of the trilogy is to funnel the effect of the social changes associated with the war through Rivers's perspective as an analyst. Rivers is the principal viewpoint character, obviously, while at the same time he is also a symbolic figure for wider questions. Is the pre-eminent science of enlightenment modernity, psychoanalysis, capable of explaining and rationalising all forms of psychic disturbance? Or are there events and experiences so unique, so intense, so powerful, that they remain unrepresentable or ineffable? And if the psychological problem is the failure to distinguish between real and imagined, as appears to be the case with many of Rivers's patients, what happens when the 'clear sight' of psychoanalysis is itself problematised? Is war entirely a political and social issue, or is it rooted deeper in psychology? Can men decide to turn to and from war, or is there some instinctual, human need for a generational purge through violence? Is war regenerative, or is it wholly, inescapably traumatic? Is war historical or mythological, a matter of will or ritual? Many of such questions raised in Barker's trilogy indicate a broader range of interest than in her previous novels, and suggest philosophical as well as historical and social themes, many of them deriving from the early twentieth-century energies invested in psychoanalysis and anthropology. It is not just the attempt to find an unusual niche in the story of the war that leads Barker to the figure of Rivers. As a psychoanalyst and anthropologist, Rivers is representative of the new sciences which emerged at the end of the nineteenth century to expand knowledge into new territories.[12]

Anthropology and psychoanalysis were the great extensions of modernity's claim to master nature, to subject nature to the knowledge and power of human beings, into the hitherto 'dark' and 'mysterious' terrains of other cultures and the unconscious. Both the psychoanalyst and the anthropologist were breaching the frontiers of modern knowledge, exploring and explaining what remained unknown, but what the high modernity of the Victorian era believed to be knowable. If these archetypal nineteenth-century sciences could explain the strangeness of other cultures and the irrationality of the unconscious, and read the unreadable signs of otherness, human civilisation would continue to expand and know itself. Freud's work is paramount in the directions the sciences of the mind and of culture took at the beginning of the twentieth century, and the difference Barker charts between Rivers's methods and his contemporaries in psychoanalysis appears to derive from the influence of Freud. Likewise, Rivers's doubts about the claim to be a civilised society, repeatedly prompted by the traumas of his patients and the memories of his time in Melanesia, find their echoes in Freud's work.

Freud's essay on 'The Uncanny' is revealing in this respect, for Freud contemplates the founding precept of psychoanalysis – that the other is the familiar returning, the *heimlich* which has become *unheimlich* – and finds a troubling doubt about the capacity of the analyst to distinguish the familiar from the other. In a footnote, Freud offers an anecdote of his own encounter with the deceptive elision of the real and the imagined, of the living and the dead, which might illustrate the experience of the uncanny:

> I was sitting alone in my *wagon-lit* compartment when a more than usually violent jolt of the train swung back the door of the adjoining washing-cabinet, and an elderly gentleman in a dressing-gown and a travelling cap came in. I assumed that in leaving the washing-cabinet, which lay between the two compartments, he had taken the wrong direction and come into my compartment by mistake. Jumping up with the intention of putting him right, I at once realized to my dismay that the intruder was nothing but my own reflection in the looking-glass on the open door. I can still recollect that I thoroughly disliked his appearance.[13]

Freud insists that this incident did not *frighten* him, but served merely to register his failure to recognise his own image. The anecdote is offered in the context of a distinction between 'primitive' beliefs in the return of the dead, or the power to translate thoughts and wishes into reality, and the 'modern' incredulity to such superstition and myth. Freud's lack of fear, confronted with the ghostly reflection of himself, certifies his modernity, his rational distrust of 'animistic beliefs'. There is some room for doubt in Freud's mind, however. Is it not possible, he asks, that his dislike of his double 'was a vestigial trace of the archaic reaction which feels the "double" to be something uncanny?'

Freud's concern is that the archaic might seep into the modern, that the boundaries between primitive superstition and modern rationality are more permeable than he imagines. He insists that 'anyone who has completely and finally rid himself of animalistic beliefs will be insensible to this type of the uncanny', and yet, for a moment, disoriented by the jolt of the train, perhaps, Freud too has *seen* the fiction of another being, 'an elderly gentleman'. The 'double', experienced as a kind of ghostly apparition, threatens to undermine the teleological distinction between superstition and rationality, primitive and civilised, reality and fiction, and so, as Avery Gordon argues, it is inevitable that Freud 'simply refutes the reality of haunting by treating it as a matter of lingering superstition'.[14] The primitive belief in the 'uncanny' or ghostly appearance of the double, for Freud, then, is the anachronistic trace of a different mode of knowing, a different way of seeing the world, which he experiences, if only briefly.

Like Freud, Rivers seems certain that the ghosts who haunt his patients are not 'real', but he is nevertheless compelled to acknowledge that his patients are haunted. Haunting, in this sense, as Gordon argues, 'describes how that which appears to be not there is often a seething presence, acting on and often meddling with taken-for-granted realities'.[15] Sassoon in *Regeneration* sees corpses lying all around the streets of London (*R* 12) and, in Craiglockhart hospital, he wakes to find the ghosts of dead soldiers in his room (*R* 188). Burns, another of Rivers's patients in the same novel, continually relives the smells and tastes of finding his nose and mouth filled with the decomposing flesh of a German corpse (*R* 19). So, too, in *The Ghost Road*, Wansbeck is visited in hospital by the ghost of the German prisoner he murdered, who becomes, visibly and olfactorily, more and more decomposed with every visit (*The Ghost Road* 26). Prior in *The Eye in the Door* becomes his own ghost, by splitting into two opposing personalities, one of whom, as Prior's demonic alter ego, commits the betrayals and deceptions which the 'real' Prior finds unpalatable. Prior's demon even visits Rivers, where he demonstrates, by his oblivion to pain, that he has a physiological reality distinct from his double (*ED* 242). Rivers is left in no doubt of the 'reality' of Prior's demonic other, which is to say that he knows that Prior is not just pretending, but lives, remembers, feels and thinks differently from his alter ego. These examples from the novels are all manifestations of things which are verifiably 'not there', and yet which exercise a disturbing, sometimes dangerous, effect on Rivers's patients.

Rivers responds to these ghostly manifestations with an impressive array of psychoanalytic and rational explanations. In part, Rivers functions as a kind of surrogate rational reader, solving the mystery of his patients' ghosts, hallucinations and nightmares, explaining away the signs of psychic disturbance, as well as of protest. He is the detective charged with finding the cause of the symptoms presented to him. Sassoon's ghosts are simple – his guilt for being absent from the front takes the form of hallucinated images of his dead comrades come to beckon him to return. Wansbeck's apparitions perform the same function, in exercising his feelings of guilt and regret. In both these cases, ghosts appear as the visible forms of feelings which both Sassoon and Wansbeck think they should have, or indeed desire to have. Burns is a more difficult case, and Rivers entertains the simple notion that Burns's experience of finding his mouth and nostrils filled with rotting human flesh might just be so disgusting and vile to warrant his traumatic recurrences of nausea, and the 'complete disintegration of personality' which such recurrences have produced. However, when Burns begins to put his experience into perspective, the first stage of recovery, Rivers finds that 'his own sense of the horror of the event seemed actually to have increased' (*R* 184). A persistent theme of the trilogy is the effect that the war is having on Rivers, as the psychoanalyst who must encounter and make sense of the horrific experiences of his patients. Burns, like Sassoon, Prior and others, serves to transform Rivers's sense of himself, and his conception of the war, science, psychology and modernity.

Prior's demonic double is, for Rivers, an all-too-transparent manifestation of the dissociation of self required under the disciplinary structures of modern society. Prior works for the intelligence services of the Ministry for Munitions, and finds himself tasked with destroying a group of anti-war protestors with whom he is already familiar from childhood friendships. While Prior works subtly to help the pro-testors, his demonic alter ego carries out the acts of subterfuge required to ensure their destruction. Rivers suggests, in other words, that Prior is generating his own monster, precisely to conduct the tasks he finds himself unable to do. Thus, his alter ego appears as a kind of exaggerated parody of an arch-villain, the self-conscious prod-uct of Prior's imagination, whom Prior even describes as his 'Hyde' figure.

Prior experiences the 'uncanny' effect of an alienated self, the sub-stance of Freud's anecdote, in a violent, magnified form, then. But *The Eye in the Door* seems at the same time to represent continually the scene which Freud describes. When Prior is 'puzzled by some-thing unfamiliar' in his office, he realises 'that the change was in him-self' (*ED* 44). Later, when his train enters a tunnel, Prior 'turned to face his doubled reflection in the window and thought he didn't like himself very much' (*ED* 88). And again, on a boat, Prior sees himself going up to a man and tapping him on the shoulder, 'and the face that turned towards him . . . was his own' (*ED* 185). Like Freud, Prior *sees* himself as an other, as an alien self, and constantly encounters him-self as a stranger. Rivers finds that Prior invents this dissociated self, or (rather) hypnotises himself into a dissociated state, in order to escape from traumatic situations. The originary childhood scene which Rivers helps Prior to remember is of domestic violence, in which the child Prior was torn between obedience to and fear of his father and empathy with and fear for his mother. In order to resolve the conflict, Prior would sit on the staircase and hypnotise himself into the reflection on the glass of a barometer (*ED* 248). Prior's invented other is thus a kind of psychic safety valve, which enables him to cope with conflicting demands or situations.

Here again, Rivers solves the mysterious appearance of a psychic double, or a troublesome ghost, with skilful rational examination. Prior turns out not to have a monstrous alter ego, after all, just a rather mischievous coping mechanism. Prior is cured of his split personality and, in *The Ghost Road*, is sufficiently stable to return to the front line, where, with tragic but inevitable irony, he joins the ranks of the dead in one last senseless assault. Rivers, in the same novel, is forced to con-front his own ghosts. He can explain the ghosts of his patients away, but his own return to haunt him. In *Regeneration*, in order to assuage Sassoon's anxieties about confessing to seeing apparitions, Rivers con-fesses to his own encounter with ghosts on an anthropological mission in the Melanesian islands. At a wake, at which the mourners await the sound of the spirits coming in canoes to collect the soul of the dead, Rivers hears not the paddles which he has been told he might hear, but instead a sudden gust of 'whistling sounds':

> Nobody was making those sounds, and yet we all heard them. You see, the *rational* explanation for that is that we'd allowed ourselves to be dragged into an experience of mass hypnosis, and I don't for a moment deny that that's possible. But what we'd been told to expect was the swish of paddles. Nobody'd said anything about whistling. That doesn't mean there *isn't* a rational explanation. Only I don't think that particular rational explanation fits all the facts. (*R* 188)

In *The Ghost Road*, Rivers becomes obsessed by this scene, and the events surrounding it, and the novel concludes with Rivers being visited in hospital by the 'not in any way ghostly' apparition of Njiru, the witch doctor in Melanesia (*GR* 276). Rivers must distinguish between the irrational visions and healthy realities of his patients constantly and unequivocally. Yet his own experiences of the hauntological in Melanesia defy his attempts at rational explanation, and serve to disturb the stability of his distinctions between appearance and reality, illness and sanity, superstition and reason. If he must deal with the effects of his patients' haunted memories routinely, Rivers cannot finally dismiss the reality of ghosts either.

Barker's trilogy represents the crisis for modern rationality principally through conflicting modes of visibility and vocality. Rivers's patients suffer from a variety of speech impediments and hallucinations, which it is his duty to observe and cure. Rivers must teach his patients to see or to speak again, by encouraging them to put their repressed experiences into perspective, and to recover absent, traumatic memories through introspection. As Anne Whitehead argues, *Regeneration* shifts from 'a series of ghost stories, in which Rivers's patients are haunted by their pasts and by the recent dead, to a detective story', in which Rivers must uncover the missing fragments of memory which will enable his patients to see or speak clearly again.[16] In this sense, Rivers is cast as the agent of salvation for his patients, the medium through which they will achieve sanity and perspective, but he is also perceived, chiefly in his treatments of Prior and Sassoon, as an agent of social discipline.

Regeneration begins with Sassoon being sent to Rivers for 'speaking out' against the war, and for seeing corpses in the streets of central

London. Rivers 'can't pretend to be neutral', and must induce Sassoon to change his view (R 15). Rivers concedes that Sassoon's protest against the war is far from irrational and, through his increasing despair at the severity of some of his patients' mental traumas, comes to share Sassoon's belief that 'Nothing justifies this' (R 180). Rivers can explain away Sassoon's visions of corpses and ghosts. They are simply the return of his repressed feelings of horror and guilt. But Sassoon's protest provokes a crisis for Rivers in his conception of the function of psychoanalysis. Towards the end of Regeneration, Rivers has a nightmare, which fuses his recent experiences of observing Dr Yealland using electric shocks to 'cure' a patient's silence with his own influence on Sassoon's decision to return to the front. When he analyses the nightmare, he comes to recognise that both he and Yealland 'were both in the business of controlling people' and, more disturbingly, in silencing them:

> Just as Yealland silenced the unconscious protest of *his* patients by removing the paralysis, the deafness, the blindness, the muteness that stood between them and the war, so, in an infinitely more gentle way, *he* silenced *his* patients; for the stammerings, the nightmares, the tremors, the memory lapses, of officers were just as much unwitting protest as the grosser maladies of the men. (R 238)

The image of an open mouth recurs throughout Barker's trilogy (and indeed many of her other novels), but has particular significance in *Regeneration* for notions of protest and control. Rivers's nightmare revolves around 'the tortured mouth' of Yealland's patient, and figures his treatment of Sassoon as 'uncomfortably like an oral rape' (R 236). Rivers thus reconsiders his relationship with Sassoon, who has 'spoken out', and with Prior, who has been unable to speak, as a form of domination rather than healing. His methods may be 'infinitely more gentle' than Yealland's, but he has still functioned effectively as an instrument of control and authority over his patients.

Rivers's moral anxieties about his role in silencing protest are effectively the means by which the reader's attention is shifted from the soldier-poet figure, Sassoon, at the beginning of the novel, to Rivers as a more complex figure of ambivalent authority by the end. Moreover, the very moral questions which Rivers raises compel us to read the signs of disturbance with which he is presented as signs of protest. Mutism, paralysis, stammering, blindness, deafness, nightmares, insomnia – these are the involuntary expressions of dissension from the war and,

Barker implies, the social structures and ideological forces which precede the war. Sassoon's letter of protest is only the most public and visible form of his expressions of dissent, and it makes him only the most articulate and perhaps even the least damaged of Rivers's patients to protest. For equally, Burns's repetitive, violent vomiting, or Prior's silence, or later Moffet's paralysed legs, constitute what Showalter calls the 'body language of masculine complaint' against the demands placed upon them in the war.[17]

The war is a continuation of social processes already at work in England prior to 1914, but it is also experienced intensely, apocalyptically, as a traumatic event by many of its combatants. Rivers considers this trauma as he gazes at the stained-glass images of the crucifixion and the altar on which Abraham prepares to sacrifice Isaac:

> The two bloody bargains on which a civilization claims to be based. *The* bargain, Rivers thought, looking at Abraham and Isaac. The one on which all patriarchal societies are founded. If you, who are young and strong, will obey me, who am old and weak, even to the extent of being prepared to sacrifice your life, then in the course of time you will peacefully inherit, and be able to exact the same obedience from your sons. Only we're breaking the bargain, Rivers thought. All over northern France, at this very moment, in trenches and dugouts and flooded shellholes, the inheritors were dying, not one by one, while old men, and women of all ages, gathered together and sang hymns. (*R* 149)

Like many of the war poets, Barker draws out here an analogy of the war with a long tradition of the Christian mythology of sacrifice.[18] The father sacrifices the son, or is prepared to sacrifice the son, in order to achieve new life, the resurrection. God promises Abraham that his people have inherited the earth, once he recognises Abraham's fearful willingness to sacrifice his own son. But Isaac is spared, a tethered ram sacrificed in his place, supposedly symbolising the end of human sacrifice. So, too, God sacrifices his own son, Jesus, so that his followers are redeemed from sin, but Jesus rises again from the dead. This is the sacrificial gift promised in the Christian tradition, but, while Rivers gathers with the old men and women celebrating and calling upon that tradition, its very codes appear to be broken. There is no substitute or resurrection for the dead rotting in the blasted mud of the battlefields, and a generation is being sacrificed like animals, with nothing to inherit. The Christian tradition of sacrifice seems bankrupt. Even the stained-glass representation of Abraham and Isaac appears self-ironic, showing that 'Abraham, if he regretted having to sacrifice his son at all, was certainly hiding it well and Isaac, bound on a makeshift altar, positively smirked' (R 149).[19] Rivers can only associate such imagery with failure, with the tragic irony of the men being sacrificed for no purpose or meaning whatsoever in France. And yet, at the same time, the symptoms of illness and trauma which Rivers's patients present to him can also be read as unmistakable echoes of that sacrificial tradition. The involuntary bodily signs of trauma are the marks of the 'mysterium tremendum', the 'fear and trembling' by which Paul reports that the Christian body must work out its own salvation, and acknowledge the awesome power of divine will.[20] 'This trembling seizes one at the moment of becoming a person', writes Jacques Derrida, 'and the person can become what it is only in being paralyzed, in its very singularity, by the gaze of God. Then it sees itself seen by the gaze of another, "a supreme, absolute and inaccessible being who holds us in his hand not by exterior but by interior force".'[21] Fear and trembling before the face of God is thus the very foundation of Judaeo-Christian subjectivity, the physiological manifestation not just of believing but of becoming. Abraham's paralysed arm, his silence before the voice of God, his fearful obedience, testify to his interpellation as a faithful subject. Fear is the sign of his obedient subjectivity, the sign that God has sought in order to confirm Abraham's inheritance.

In Barker's trilogy, however, the physiological signs of fear and trembling witness not the power of God, but the indefatigable force of history and, more pointedly, the existence of 'supreme, absolute and inaccessible' historical forces which have neither ethical purpose nor ethical bounds. No angel appears to silence the guns. The trilogy abounds with moments of 'becoming', of being born in fear and trembling into a new subjectivity. Prior's alter ego confesses to Rivers that he was 'born two years ago. In a shell-hole in France' (ED 240). Sassoon also, to a lesser extent, gives birth to an alter ego, the efficient company commander who leads his men in war, a dissociated personality born in and through the war (ED 229). And Rivers dreams of soldiers rising from their mud graves, 'creatures composed of Flanders mud and nothing else, moving their grotesque limbs in the direction of home' (ED 244). What these born-anew subjectivities have in common is the extreme dissociation of feeling. Rivers's nightmare mud-men are made of 'nothing else', zombies mechanically marching home. Prior's new self burns a cigarette into his hand, unflinching, while Sassoon's battlefield persona cuts off his feelings of anguish, of protest. They share with Abraham the apparent ability to do their duty without feeling, pain, or thought, to raise the knife without complaint. They share also with Abraham the trembling which is the sign of their becoming subjects, but whereas Abraham shows himself subject to God, Barker's characters tremble their subjectivity to the social forces and processes we call 'the war'.

And yet something fails. The nightmares, the stammerings, the mutism and paralysis, are all registering protest against Abraham's bargain. In the climactic final scenes of *The Ghost Road*, the rosy-pink dawn light which passes over the dead in French fields is the same light which begins to seep through the tall windows of Rivers's ward, appearing perhaps as a new stained-glass icon of sacrifice. But tellingly, Rivers's ward still echoes with the garbled dying shouts of Hallet, '*Shotvarfet. Shotfarvet*', murmured also from the 'damaged brains and drooping mouths' of other patients, and translated by Rivers as 'It's not worth it' (*GR* 274). As Catherine Lanone argues, Barker's trilogy 'draws much of its strength from the rewriting of Christian motifs, to suggest the horrible mystery of a world full of abandoned meanings'.[22] The 'mysterium tremendum' of Rivers's patients testify, then, to a world awful in its loss of meaning and of purpose, in which the men tremble not from absolute faith but from absolute terror.

If *Regeneration* is a novel about violence and protest, figured through tropes of speech and silence, *The Eye in the Door*, as its title suggests, is a novel about visibility as a mode of knowing. The novel's dominant image is the panopticon, the ideal architectural technology for correctional surveillance, which Foucault studies as a model of modern authority and control.[23] The panopticon prison appears just briefly in the novel, when Prior visits an old friend who is incarcerated for plotting to kill Lloyd George (*ED* 29). In the prison, Prior is disturbed by the 'eye' hole in the cell door, particularly as it reminds him of his traumatic experience of finding nothing of his dead comrade but an eyeball in a trench in France. The recovered eyeball (which Prior thinks of as a 'gob-stopper', thus prompting him to 'stop' his 'gob', to become silent) is the source of Prior's psychological breakdown in *Regeneration*. In *The Eye in the Door*, the 'eye' replaces the 'mouth' as the instrument of control and resistance.

Panopticism pervades the novel as a mode of social control. Prior is aware of the scrutinising gaze of others from the beginning of the novel, when he considers self-consciously how he must look to passing strangers (*ED* 3). His suspicion that he is watched intensifies considerably in the prison, and thereafter the novel shows Prior encountering his own uncanny image repeatedly as the object of scrutiny. This develops into his extreme dissociated state, in which he lapses out of consciousness for hours at a time, during which his double conducts the tasks to which Prior remains blind. In this schema, Rivers is just one 'eye' in the surveillance net in which Prior is caught, observed and monitored constantly, not least by his demonic double. Rivers, as a psychoanalyst, must subject Prior to observation and objectification, and so becomes part of the disciplinary apparatus which defines and controls Prior.

The trouble for Rivers is that Prior is capable of subjecting *him* to the same objective gaze. Rivers reveals to Prior during one of their sessions that he has no visual memory after the age of five, which is too tempting a 'blind spot' in Rivers's psyche for Prior to leave unexamined. Rivers and Prior change places, and Prior probes Rivers's memory of a childhood experience in which something so terrible happened that his mind 'suppressed not just the *one* memory, but the capacity to remember things visually at all' (*ED* 137). Prior's diagnosis is emphatic, and troubles Rivers afterwards: '*Whatever it was, you blinded yourself so you wouldn't have to go on seeing it . . . You put your mind's eye out*' (*ED* 140–1). Rivers is sufficiently self-conscious to realise that he has his own psychological problems and repressed memories, but that he might be the victim of what Prior suggests was a monstrous rape or beating when he was five shocks and disturbs the analyst. The realisation that his own lack of visual memory may conceal as dark a repressed past as he has encountered in his patients triggers a crisis of authority in Rivers and, in the final novel of the trilogy, he is immersed in his own anamnestic efforts to trace the source of his ghosts. Rivers, in one sense, becomes his own patient in *The Ghost Road*, as haunted by spectres as Prior or Sassoon. Here, his own divisions are especially manifest, since his rational self – what he calls the 'epicritic' mind – must analyse and exorcise the demons of his emotional self – what he calls the 'protopathic'. This division between the epicritic and the protopathic occupies much of Rivers's thinking throughout the trilogy, but it becomes especially significant in the final volume, in which it appears to take the form of a split personality. Rivers in *The Ghost Road*, then, is both the capable analyst, who unravels his patients' anxieties and repressions, and the haunted, frightened patient, vulnerable to his own nightmares and hallucinations.

Neither Rivers's ghostly visions nor his paralytic stammer undermine his authority as a psychoanalyst, however. In fact, Rivers's vulnerability appears to earn him greater credit with Prior. The return of Rivers's spectres and repressed memories illustrates instead the inseparability of the epicritic and the protopathic, or, to put it another way, it shows that the rational is thoroughly infiltrated by the irrational. This is an argument which Michel de Certeau makes in relation to haunting more generally:

> There is an 'uncanniness' about this past that a present occupant has expelled (or thinks it has) in an effort to take its place. The dead haunt the living. . .. [Any] autonomous order is founded upon what it eliminates; it produces a 'residue' condemned to be forgotten. But what was excluded re-infiltrates the place of its origin – now the present's 'clean' place. It resurfaces, it troubles, it turns the present's feeling of being 'at home' into an illusion – this 'wild', this 'obscene', this 'filth', this 'resistance' of 'superstition' – within the walls of the residence, and, behind the back of the owner (the *ego*), or over its objections, it inscribes there the law of the other.[24]

De Certeau here counters Freud's notion that the modern rational mind can 'rid himself' of primitive beliefs in the ghostly and the uncanny, and argues that the present is perpetually haunted by the dead. In psychoanalytic terms, de Certeau seems to be addressing the return of the repressed, but he is also implicitly critiquing the conceit of psychoanalysis that it can make the ghosts go away. If, as de Certeau argues, haunting is the figurative return of the 'residue' or excluded others of the past to the 'present occupants', then the attempt to exorcise these ghosts is merely an attempt to prolong the repression of voices of protest or difference. Rivers recognises that this might be the case when he worries about whether he has, in 'curing' his patients, merely silenced their intuitive expressions of protest.

There is a larger question behind this concern, about the relationship between ethics and science, a question which lurks behind the mnemonics of twentieth-century history. 'Mons, Loos, the Somme, Arras, Verdun, Ypres', Prior lists (*GR* 257), to which we might also add names such as Auschwitz, Hiroshima, Dresden, and too many more. Modern science delivers the awesome power of technological warfare, for which there are only ethical bounds. Is Rivers, in silencing the protests of his patients, simply delivering up efficient machines of war? Is psychoanalysis merely being used to suppress ethical imperatives for the demands of technological efficiency? Could any of these twentieth-century atrocities have been stopped by a proper dialogue between ethics and science? What Barker's trilogy shows is that such contests between ethics and science, between complicity and protest, are not so easily suppressed, however, and it does so precisely by fictionalising history as a minefield of protests against what is often presented in historical narratives as the inevitable course of events. Against the dreadful silence around those mnemonics, Prior realises 'there's another group of words that still mean something':

> Little words that trip through sentences unregarded: us, them, we, they, here, there. These are the words of power, and long after we've gone, they'll lie about in the language, like the unexploded grenades in these fields, and any one of them'll take your hand off. (*GR* 257)

Quite properly, Barker's trilogy is ultimately attuned not to the course of historical events, but to the latent potential in language and silence for alternative histories. This is why I disagree with Martin Löschnigg's argument that 'Barker's novels are not postmodernist novels at all. Indeed, the trilogy seems to rest upon the transparency of its discourse with regard to an objectifiable historical reality'.[25] The trilogy might well continue to testify, often from testimonial sources, to the historical reality of the war, but it simultaneously and relentlessly opens up for critique the representation of the war, and specifically how we read that latent potential in language. Prior's thoughts form a warning – the 'us, them' of the First World War will reverberate through more twentieth-century events, and cause millions of deaths and countless more injured. But words which lie about in the language, the silences which remain hidden in the gaps between language (and Barker literalises those gaps in the typology of stammered speech, for example), also contain the potential for protest, and ultimately then for imagining history otherwise.

Barker's trilogy is obviously not postmodern in the kind of self-reflexive or metafictional modes characterised by Linda Hutcheon, but it is certainly postmodern in its critical attention to discourses of modernity, and the haunting of historical representation by its others. History is never allowed to appear transparent, for ultimately our surrogate rational reader Rivers's vision (like his visual memory) is opaque. History is still the minefield of language and silence Prior believes it to be. And the past never seems to stay still in Barker's trilogy long enough to be objectifiable. Barker shows that the return of the dead to haunt the living, whether in the form of ghostly apparitions or uncanny experiences, functions to unsettle the conceit of the present. The teleological narratives of historical progress, cultural superiority and technological prowess, which underpinned notions of European civilisation, and which ultimately led to the 'Great War', produced the most savage, regressive and irrational conflict the world had yet known. The dead lying on the battlefields of France are material testimony to the gaps and contradictions in such narratives and, hence, they are witnessed by Rivers's patients in the trilogy as the spectres haunting Europe. The uncanny experiences represented in the *Regeneration* trilogy, then, are disturbing not just in their meanings for scientific and psychoanalytic claims to knowledge, but also in their implications for the chrono- and geopolitics of modernity.

Barker represents this crisis in European modernity through tropes of displacement and temporal disjunction. Throughout the trilogy, everywhere – the hospital corridors of Craiglockhart, the landings of a prison, the hollows of an urban wasteland, the labyrinthine streets of a city – comes to resemble the topographical features of the trench or no-man's-land. The streets of London and the fields around Craiglockhart seem to resemble the battlefields of France, so that Rivers's patients sometimes behave, mentally and physiologically, as if they are still at the front. They listen for the whine of incoming shells, and see the corpses of their comrades lying all around them. Rivers experiences his own version of this, when his memories of life with a 'primitive' tribe in Melanesia become confused with his waking life in England. Here, the geographical 'otherness' of Melanesia refuses to remain in its place – it continually appears to haunt and disrupt Rivers's sense of 'home'.

Moreover, even the modern disdain for war, which has recurrently been represented through the twentieth century by iconic images of the slaughter and destruction of the First World War, is subverted by the novel's representation of cultural otherness. Melanesia is the site for Rivers of troubling questions not only about the cultural boasts of European modernity, but also about the supposed moral certainties of

European liberalism, for here Barker depicts a tribe whose rituals and ways of life depended upon war: 'Head-hunting had to be banned, and yet the effects of banning it were everywhere apparent in the list-lessness and lethargy of the people's lives. Head-hunting was what they had lived for. . . . This was a people perishing from the absence of war' (GR 207). Barker's novel places the tragedy of the war slaying a generation of young men in Europe in dialogic tension with the tragedy of the absence of war in Melanesia. The war is never allowed to become the subject of pathos, and Barker's project in the trilogy is larger than simply re-enlisting our sense of sympathy for the wastes of war. In Melanesia, Rivers discovers that war, however morally decrepit, appears to have a regenerative function, and this serves to question whether the same ghastly idea might be true of the 'Great War'. This is to recognise, I think, that Barker's moral landscape in the trilogy is as complex as her earlier probing of poverty, rape, dereliction and prostitution in previous novels.

The temporal logic of modernity, too, is continually disrupted in Barker's trilogy. The very notion of anamnesis, as Freud explained it in 'Beyond the Pleasure Principle', involves a radical disturbance in the patient's sense of time: 'He is obliged to *repeat* the repressed mate-rial as a contemporary experience instead of, as the physician would prefer to see, *remembering* it as something belonging to the past'.[26] Rivers's patients are, for the most part, stuck in time, in reliving one particular moment of experience or trauma, which continues to exer-cise a grip on their consciousness. The effect of the severe disjunction of time undergone by the war veterans, Middleton and Woods explain, is that they 'find that the ordinary realism of memory is no longer adequate and must re-imagine the space-time of the past'.[27]

In Barker's *Regeneration* trilogy, then, history is experienced always as untimely, as anachronistic. It is not just that her characters fail to grasp the significance of the events of their own time, but rather that time itself seems to become profoundly discontinuous and unstable. Barker must have been aware of this when writing *Regeneration*, as the outbreak of the Gulf War of 1991 was reported through images of soldiers waiting in trenches, scrambling for gas masks and huddling from artillery barrages. It should be no surprise, then, that in Barker's trilogy the war repeats the time of other wars, churns up the dead of other centuries, and refuses to be contained in its present time. For Barker's characters, to use Paul Fussell's terms, 'war detaches itself from its normal location in chronology and its accepted set of causes and effects to become Great in another sense – all-encompassing, all-pervading, both internal and external at once, the essential condition of consciousness in the twentieth century'.[28] This is experienced in the trilogy as a chronic disturbance in the function of memory.

Rivers's patients suffer either from amnesia or anamnesia, too little or too much memory. Both amnesia and anamnesia are forms of representation (especially after Freud), open to psychoanalytic interpretation, and mark out by presence or absence the reappearance of the past in the present. It becomes apparent to Rivers that the memory crises of his patients are not just indications of psychological failure – not just the signs of mental disorder – but instead are registering a more general, social and cultural, crisis. Memory appears, in the words of Richard Terdiman, as 'a problem, as a site and source of cultural disquiet'.[29] It emerges as the involuntary counter-narrative of modernity, bearing witness to that which modernity forgets or fails to see. But memory functions not just as the *repetition* of the past, not just as a kind of video replay of the event, but rather, as Derrida indicates, as the deferred past. The recovered memory of the past is, for Derrida, 'the *supplementary delay* . . . the reconstitution of meaning through deferral, after a mole-like progression, after the subterranean toil of an impression':

> This impression has left behind a laborious trace which has never been *perceived*, whose meaning has never been lived in the present, i.e. has never been lived consciously. The postscript which constitutes the past present as such is not satisfied . . . with reawakening or revealing the present past in its truth. It produces the present past.[30]

Not surprisingly, Derrida describes this eruption of the past into present consciousness in ghostly or hauntological terms – trace, delay, deferral, the present past. The past as such is a perpetual palimpsest, continually rewritten, and in continual dialogue with its present enunciation. Derrida's conception of the time of memory is structured by absence, in which the possibility of the past revealing its truth is endlessly deferred. In this sense, as Jean-Luc Nancy argues, to represent the past 'is not to re-present some past or present presence. It is to trace the otherness of existence within its own present and presence.'[31]

Barker's trilogy concludes on this theme of the encounter with the 'otherness of existence'. Rivers envisions his cultural other, the Melanesian witch doctor Njiru, dancing an invocation to the gods to 'go down and depart'. The dance repeats a scene he has witnessed often in Melanesia, but appears now dislocated from its normal time and place, in Rivers's hospital ward. Njiru sees the 'end of men', and his dance is performed for the *mate*, the living dead. Rivers now belongs, the scene implies, to the land of the living dead, like all his patients. Just as the final scene signifies the dramatic return of Rivers's powers of visualisation, it indicates, too, a traumatic shift in historical consciousness, from one in which time unfolded progressively towards healing, to one in which time is structured around loss, absence and otherness. History, after the Great War, Barker's trilogy suggests, is continually haunted by the memory of loss, and is constantly striving and failing to regenerate the past.

Rivers functions, then, as a test case for the wider conflict between rationalism and trauma, enlightenment and ineffability, science and seance. His ambivalence about the capacity of science to explain all manifestations of trauma and abnormal behaviour back to a rational source becomes particularly acute in Prior's reciprocal diagnosis of Rivers's own 'blind spots'. But Rivers is also the moral conscience and often provides the controlling viewpoint of the trilogy: his diagnosis of the gender dynamics of the war ('shellshock' as the hysterical response of men to a situation in which to be heroic and masculine is to passively await death in a mud hole, for example), and his doubts about both the validity of the war and the validity of psychotherapeutic treatments of its victims, are rarely contradicted or problematised. Although he is shown to have weaknesses of his own, in his explanations and reservations about the war, he is a reliable viewpoint character. He is the voice of modern rationality and science, but is also sufficiently sceptical, and sufficiently open to questions of social, political, sexual and cultural difference, to command late twentieth-century sympathy. More importantly, Rivers is the focal point through which the trilogy examines how science, rationality and psychoanalysis attempt to reason away the signs and voices of difference, but frequently fail to do so. Sassoon's objections to the war, stated in the opening page of the trilogy, remain forceful and legitimate by the end of the novel, and it is Rivers who is compelled to change his views, to acknowledge the force of his own ghosts, by the end of the trilogy.

In the *Regeneration* trilogy, then, history is represented as trauma, the effects of which tend to manifest themselves in figures and tropes of haunting. The recurrent figures of haunting in the trilogy serve to underline the potency of history experienced as traumatic event, but they also compel us to see the war as both haunted by and haunting other social processes. Haunting signifies the repetition of time, the refusal of the past to stay in its place. This is, in many respects, what Rivers must confront in each of his patients – the excess of memory, of history, the disturbing eruption of the past into the present. But, more broadly, the excess of memory and history experienced by Rivers's patients is also, Barker's novels suggest, the prototypical temporal condition of the twentieth century. Barker traces our contemporary concerns with recovered memory, hidden subjectivities, forgotten stories – the exclusions and elisions of history – to the 'Great War'. The effects on memory and consciousness of the war is so great as to induce a re-imagination of the experience of time and space. In one memorable scene, the traumatised Burns finds refuge from a violent storm in the ruins of a moat, reliving the security of the trench against the battery and thunderous noise of war. The medieval moat and the modern trench are here collapsed into one image of the attempt to burrow into some security in the face of war. This folding of one historical image into another, and folding of one time into another, is a recurrent feature in Barker's work. It also appears in a conversation between Owen and Sassoon in *Regeneration* about their experiences of time as ghostly:

> [Owen:] 'Sometimes when you're alone, in the trenches, I mean, at night you get the sense of something *ancient*. As if the trenches had always been there. You know one trench we held, it had skulls in the side. You looked back along and . . . Like mushrooms. And do you know, it was actually *easier* to believe they were men from Marlborough's army than to to to think they'd been alive two years ago. It's as if all other wars had somehow . . . distilled themselves into this war, and that makes it something you . . . almost can't challenge.'

> [. . .]

> [Sassoon:] 'I had a similar experience. Well, I don't know whether it is similar. I was going up with the rations one night and I saw the limbers against the skyline, and the flares going up. What you see every night. Only I seemed to be seeing it from the future. A hundred years from now they'll still be ploughing up skulls. And I seemed to be in that time and looking back. I think I saw our ghosts.' (*R* 83–4)

Both Owen and Sassoon articulate here the sense of history transforming into myth, of a war which is the distillation of all wars, of a war which is already the ghostly imitation of itself. Owen's experience of the war is filtered through its historical resonances, through notions of cyclical recurrence and repetition, while Sassoon sees the war through the postmodern lens of the future anterior.[32] For both, it is necessary to see the present through images of its otherness, of its double, or, more pertinently, of its ghostly resemblances through time. What is not possible is for Owen and Sassoon to see their own time in its modernity, to see the present as a homogenous self-present identity. Instead, they, like other characters in the novel, such as Burns who can only find solace in a medieval moat, or Manning's soldiers billeted in a graveyard, achieve some understanding of their situation only by radically dislocating their 'place' in historical chronology. To situate themselves, it is necessary, in other words, to conceive of the radical heterogeneity – the hauntedness – of their own time. Barker is here drawing our attention to the displaced temporality of the war, the sense that the time of the war is never self-present, but must always be filtered through its mythic resonances or its future significance. The war is, at one and the same time, the repetition of the 'timeless' mythic story of Abraham and Isaac, and the decisive moment of epochal shift from the Victorian faith in progress and civilisation to the postmodern scepticism of the twentieth century.

Barker's trilogy, in this sense, registers the displaced chrono-consciousness of the late twentieth century, for one paradoxical consequence of living in an age which defines itself as post-historical is that we are both free to be 'timeless', and we are condemned to live in everyone else's past. All of Barker's novels are set in belated time, her characters living in the ruins of someone else's time or civilisation. The problem for Barker's characters is that time is constantly displaced, the past endlessly invading the present, usually with disturbing consequences. In such a condition, the trilogy suggests, the very possibility of rational analysis, and therefore the possibility of scientific or historical knowledge, is thrown into crisis in the disturbed and unstable temporalities of our postmodern, post-historical sensibility.

This sense of living in post-history is present in all of Barker's novels, however, not just the *Regeneration* trilogy. The blighted, derelict landscapes of her early novels suggest the same sense of post-industrial, post-historical decay, of living on after time has stopped. History is over, then, according to Barker's fiction, which is a hyperbolic way of saying that the twentieth century has witnessed a profound shift in our sense of historical consciousness and belonging, that the means and forms of our connections with the past have altered radically. The heightened attention in contemporary literature to problems of memory, to the disturbing meanings which lie buried in the past awaiting present discovery, to the malleability and equivocation of history, are all manifestations, of one form or another, of this crisis in our sense of history. The effects of such attention are not simply to be found in the variety of historical settings and themes in contemporary literature, but also in the ways in which contemporary writers interrogate the framing axioms of historical narrative and representation, and we might find common ground for Barker here among such contemporaries as Peter Ackroyd, Iain Sinclair, Jim Crace and Michèle Roberts. The *Regeneration* trilogy rewrites the historical novel as historiographic novel, interrogates the very frames and forms of the genre, and presents historical reality as a narrative construct haunted by the ghosts of historical becoming. The risk of the trilogy is that it might contribute to the valedictory monumentalisation of the war, but Barker's achievement is that instead the trilogy shows the war and its social contexts to remain alive with troubling questions about the relationships between reality and representation, language and silence, science and ethics, and history and haunting.

Notes

1 Sharon Carson, 'Pat Barker', *British Writers: Supplement IV*, ed. George Stade and Carol Howard (New York, Simon and Schuster and Prentice Hall, 1997), 45.
2 Blake Morrison, 'War Stories', *New Yorker*, 22 January 1996, 78–82.
3 Donna Perry, 'Pat Barker', *Backtalk: Women Writers Speak Out* (New Brunswick, Rutgers University Press, 1993), 45.
4 Morrison, 'War Stories', 78.
5 Ben Shephard, 'Digging Up the Past', *Times Literary Supplement*, 22 March 1996, 12.
6 Martin Löschnigg, '". . .the novelist's responsibility to the past": History, Myth, and the Narratives of Crisis in Pat Barker's *Regeneration* Trilogy (1991–1995)', *Zeitschrift für Anglistik und Amerikanistik*, 47:3 (1999), 222, 215. Löschnigg's title is borrowed from Shephard's review, and he fleshes out Shephard's argument that Barker's responsibility towards representing the past as a novelist is problematic.
7 See Barker's *Another World*, 83.
8 Peter Hitchcock, 'What is Prior? Working-Class Masculinity in Pat

Barker's Trilogy', *Genders* 35 (2002): http://genders.org/g35/g35_
hitchcock.txt

9 Greg Harris, 'Compulsory Masculinity, Britain, and the Great War: The
Literary-Historical Work of Pat Barker', *Critique* 39:4 (1998), 303.

10 Hitchcock, 'What is Prior?', 11.

11 Anne Whitehead suggests one reason why Rivers might fit so neatly into
Barker's vision, in this respect. Rivers, she argues, was primarily interested in the 'frequent development of neurotic symptomatology *after* the
soldier had been removed from the distressing scenes that had (supposedly) occasioned his illness. Rivers argued that the pathology of war orig-
inated not in a specific disturbing event, but in the subsequent efforts on
the part of the soldier to banish from his mind unpleasant thoughts of
war'. See Anne Whitehead, 'Open to Suggestion: Hypnosis and History
in Pat Barker's *Regeneration*', *Modern Fiction Studies*, 44:3 (1998), 679.

12 Anne M. Wyatt-Brown briefly surveys Rivers's distinguished and cross-
disciplinary career, and argues that Barker over-plays the significance of
father–child relationships in her representation of Rivers, in 'Headhunters and Victims of War: W.H.R. Rivers and Pat Barker', *Literature
and Psychoanalysis: Proceedings of the 13th International Conference on
Literature and Psychoanalysis (Boston, July 1996)*, ed. Frederico Pereira
(Lisbon, Instituto Superior de Psicologia Aplicada, 1997), 53–9.

13 Sigmund Freud, 'The Uncanny', *The Penguin Freud Library, vol. 14, Art
and Literature*, ed. Albert Dickson (London, Penguin, 1985), 371.

14 Avery F. Gordon, *Ghostly Matters: Haunting and the Sociological Imagination* (Minneapolis, University of Minnesota Press, 1997), 53.

15 Ibid., 8.

16 Anne Whitehead, 'Open to Suggestion', 688.

17 Elaine Showalter, *The Female Malady: Women, Madness, and English Culture, 1830–1980* (London, Penguin, 1985), 172.

18 Owen's 'Parable of the Old Man and the Young' appears especially rele-
vant here, in which the 'old man . . . slew his son, And half the seed of
Europe, one by one'; *The Poems of Wilfred Owen* (London, Chatto and
Windus, 1985), 151.

19 Catherine Lanone observes that more significant for Barker's rewriting of
the Abraham and Isaac myth, however, is Rembrandt's sketch, showing
Abraham covering Isaac's face and silencing him (264). See Catherine
Lanone, 'Scattering the Seed of Abraham: The Motif of Sacrifice in Pat
Barker's *Regeneration* and *The Ghost Road*', *Literature and Theology*, 13:3
(1999), 259–68.

20 'The Epistle of Paul the Apostle to the Philippians', 2:12, *The New Testa-
ment (King James* version).

21 Jacques Derrida, *The Gift of Death*, trans. David Wills (Chicago, University of Chicago Press, 1995), 6.

22 Lanone, 'Scattering the Seed of Abraham', 267.
23 Michel Foucault, *Discipline and Punish: The Birth of the Prison*, trans. A.M. Sheridan Smith (London, Penguin, 1979). See also Jeremy Bentham, *The Panopticon Writings*, ed. Miran Božovič (London, Verso, 1995).
24 Michel de Certeau, *Heterologies: Discourse on the Other*, trans. Brian Massumi (Manchester, Manchester University Press, 1986), 3–4.
25 Löschnigg, '". . .the novelist's responsibility"', 227.
26 Sigmund Freud, 'Beyond the Pleasure Principle', *The Penguin Freud Library, vol. 11, On Metapsychology: The Theory of Psychoanalysis*, ed. Angela Richards (London, Penguin, 1991), 288.
27 Peter Middleton and Tim Woods, *Literatures of Memory: History, Time and Space in Postwar Writing* (Manchester, Manchester University Press, 2000), 88.
28 Paul Fussell, *The Great War and Modern Memory* (Oxford, Oxford University Press, 2000), 321.
29 Richard Terdiman, *Present Past: Modernity and the Memory Crisis* (Ithaca, Cornell University Press, 1993), vii.
30 Jacques Derrida, 'Freud and the Scene of Writing', *Writing and Difference*, trans. Alan Bass (London, Routledge, 1978), 214.
31 Jean-Luc Nancy, 'Finite History', *The States of 'Theory': History, Art and Critical Discourse*, ed. David Carroll (Stanford, Stanford University Press, 1990), 165.
32 Jean-François Lyotard argues that the future anterior is the defining tense of the postmodern. See *The Postmodern Condition: A Report on Knowledge*, trans. Geoff Bennington and Brian Massumi (Manchester, Manchester University Press, 1984), 81.

7

The return of history: *Another World*

Another World might almost be described as a supplement to the *Regeneration* trilogy, for it continues to explore the trauma and disturbing memory effects of the First World War on one of its survivors, Geordie, a 101–year-old veteran of the Somme. Through Geordie, Barker revisits the same memory landscape – the rotting, skull-lined trenches, the phosphorous-lit nights crawling across the cratered mud and barbed-wire tangles of no-man's-land, the screaming, bloody carnage of the battlefield. In the trilogy, Barker treats the horrific memories of the combatants as eruptions of protest. In *Another World*, the recurrence of war nightmares and hallucinations in a veteran eighty years after the end of the war signals the continued (and disturbing) eruption of the past into the present. Geordie has made public appearances as a witness to the war, in schools, colleges, museums, in books and on television, driven by a sense of mission to warn about the dangers of repeating history: '*It happened once, therefore it can happen again*' (82). But his private reliving of the horror of the war, and specifically the traumatic memory of the killing of his own brother, Harry, mean that Geordie has not been able to contain the war as something that 'happened once', even when he warns of the dangers of recurrence, for the war is clearly continuing to happen for Geordie. As the epigraph from Joseph Brodsky professes, 'the past won't fit into memory without something left over', and, as in the *Regeneration* novels, Barker's focus in *Another World* is the residual force of the past, its capacity to drag and pull on our attention in the present. Geordie believes, for example, that he is not dying because of cancer, but because his bayonet wound has reopened, and this is a fitting metaphor for Barker's sense of time. It is not that history repeats itself, but that some historical experiences have never gone away in the first place. They simply open up again in the present.

Another World is not as obviously concerned with psychoanalysis as Barker's trilogy had been, and yet the same interest in the repetitive structure of trauma, and the relationship between trauma and representation, remains central to this novel. '*It happened once, therefore it can happen again*' could indeed be the refrain of this novel, as in other Barker novels, because it runs through all of the intertwined stories of the novel, not just Geordie's, which only begins in the fifth chapter of the novel. *Another World* begins with the troubled, haunted lives of the family of Geordie's grandson, Nick, and for them too, as their story interweaves with Geordie's, the past seems to seep disturbingly into the present. The fear that the murder of James Fanshawe, the toddler in the Victorian painting which Nick and his family discover on moving into their new house, might be played out again in the present is the motor for much of the suspense and tension of the novel. Likewise, at the beginning of the novel when Nick arrives late to collect his thirteen-year-old daughter, he is plagued by the terror that events can recur: 'A few months ago a fourteen-year-old girl was thrown from a train by some yob who hadn't got anywhere when he tried to chat her up' (3). Such fears of recurrent horror are superstitious and irrational, perhaps, but Nick cannot dismiss them so easily:

> This is all rubbish, he knows that. But then, like everybody else, he lives in the shadow of monstrosities. Peter Sutcliffe's bearded face, the number plate of a house in Cromwell Street, three figures smudged on a video surveillance screen, an older boy taking a toddler by the hand while his companion strides ahead, eager for the atrocity to come. (3)

Barker plays upon the contemporary iconography of evil in this passage, recalling the television images associated with each of the atrocities instead of the names. Such events exist primarily, she recognises, as symbols, iconic images, which resist narrative, which resist our attempts at representation. This relationship between traumatic events and representation has been a persistent concern in Barker's work. Kelly Brown stays silent for three weeks after she was raped, and then 'suddenly she set on screaming' (37). Maggie in *Blow Your House Down* survives an attempt to murder her, but struggles to understand her experience of terror. *Blow Your House Down* is based on the case of the Yorkshire Ripper, Peter Sutcliffe, of course.

Barker's characters are frequently the victims, survivors or uncomprehending subjects of terror, and a survey of this theme across her
writings finds her connecting, in specific and critical ways, the traumatic effects of combat experience with the unspeakable experiences
of rape, murder and violence in more domestic and quotidian
settings.

Both *Another World* and *Border Crossing* have as a subtext the
murder of toddler, James Bulger, by two children.[1] The Bulger
murder, more than many other recent instances of a child killed by
children, caught the public imagination and, as Barker suggests in
her allusion to the 'smudged' figures on a surveillance video, is
remembered primarily through iconography. That the murder is
remembered through the symbolic image of terror, rather than
through a narrative of its specificities as a family and social tragedy,
suggests both a resistance to understand it as an event, and its cen-
trality to the process of understanding terror. The public and media
reaction to the murder of James Bulger raised many questions, as
David James Smith reports:

> If the boys were guilty, what had possessed them to commit such a ter-
> rible crime? Were they evil, born bad, led on by adults, influenced by vio-
> lence on television, desensitising computer games, video nasties? Were
> they playing a game that went wrong, were they lords of the flies acting
> out the wickedness of children (the latent cruelty in us all), or were they
> just plain possessed? These theories were offered less as speculation
> than as statements of fact. Many people, it seemed, needed to explain
> James Bulger's death to themselves and to others. And if there was no
> ready explanation, what then?[2]

In *Another World*, Nick and Fran's toddler, Jasper, is almost murdered
by his older, jealous brother, Gareth, a boy obsessed with violent films
and computer games. In the central traumatic scene of the novel,
Gareth throws rocks from a cliff ledge down on Jasper. It begins as a
game, but becomes deadly serious when Gareth tries to kill Jasper. In
this scene, Barker takes her readers part of the way down the chilling
road that James Bulger walked to his death, and explores many of the
possibilities suggested by the above questions.[3] The fear of such
seemingly inexplicable horrors are the monstrous shadows which
loom over everyday life, and Barker's novel explores the way in which
the fear of recurrence, and specifically the fear of underlying forces
driving such recurrence, resonates through the mundane experiences

of Nick's family. In the midst of the most ordinary, even stereotypical, settings – the traffic jam, the train station, the shopping mall, the seaside, at home – the images and icons of terror are also present.

The novel begins with Nick's own version of hell – the centre of Newcastle on a Friday night, stuck in a traffic jam surrounded by violent, yelling gangs of lads, and tortured by fears of what might happen to his daughter waiting alone at the train station. But it ends by asserting that the fears of contemporary social life are not yet analogous to the hell experienced by Geordie and his brother in France. In this sense, *Another World* functions as an afterword to the *Regeneration* trilogy, bringing into parallel the contemporary fascination with terror and the historical experience of war, and drawing conclusions on the viability of such analogies. I argue in this chapter that *Another World* plays with the generic conventions of several fictional forms – the social realist novel, historiographic fiction (of which I argued in the previous chapter that the *Regeneration* trilogy was an exemplary instance) and Gothic fiction – in order to bring the reader to a reflexive and ultimately elegiac resolution. In particular, this novel plays games with readers, inviting analogies, which it then dismisses (although never wholly satisfactorily).

The interplay of styles, genres and points of view is distinctive to and characteristic of Barker's fictional method. *Another World* begins as an exemplary social realist novel of an extended middle-class family. Indeed, one of the extraordinary achievements of the novel's opening is that Barker introduces the complicated network of relations which constitutes Nick's family in the first chapter. We learn very quickly (within thirteen pages) about Nick's previous marriage to Barbara, their daughter Miranda, Nick's current relationship with Fran, who has a son, Gareth, from a previous relationship with Mark, about Nick and Fran's son, Jasper, and that Fran is pregnant with another child, about Nick's grandfather, Geordie, and Geordie's daughter (Nick's aunt), Frieda. Moreover, we learn details of the history of many of these relations – that Fran considered aborting Gareth, for example, or that Nick's former wife, Barbara, is experiencing mental illness – which are quietly significant indications of the nature of some of the relationships, and have small roles to play in providing contexts for how some characters behave. The number of characters introduced here, even characters like Barbara and Mark, who play no further part in the story, and the complicated history of family relations, give the opening of the novel a fairly full and dense sense of social realism. Barker is establishing a familiar, credible modern family setting, which will mirror but also refract the painted image of the Victorian family which Nick uncovers, and which raises a connection with contemporary debates about what constitutes 'family', particularly conservative tendencies to contrast the modern 'broken' family with a Victorian ideal of the family unit.[4] So, too, the opening chapter introduces a number of familiar social realist themes: alcohol-induced violence, abortion, absent fathers, the increased sense of children's vulnerability, the passage from childhood to adulthood, and the burden of childcare. And it begins to suggest some of the emotional life of the family, the tensions between Nick and Fran about parental responsibilities, that Nick's role as 'father' is not much more than 'a bipedal sperm bank' (5), the perpetual moodiness of Gareth, which Fran tries to decipher, and Gareth's resentment of Miranda, Jasper, and Fran's pregnancy. The density of the social and emotional fabric of Nick's family which Barker achieves in the first chapter, then, is a signal that the novel is grounded in this knowable, realist terrain.

By the end of the first chapter, however, Barker has also introduced various levels of symbolism. There is the symbolism of terror – the icons of monstrosity Nick fears on his way to collect his daughter from the train station – but there is also the Lawrentian symbolism which Barker has deployed frequently in earlier novels.[5] The chapter ends with Nick retrieving a blackbird's nest of dead fledglings as he clears out the garden, and the novel frequently returns to similar images of death in the natural world, including dead puppies and kittens, all of which prefigure the theme of infanticide, but which also mark the contrast between the unremarkable, habitual occurrence of death in nature and the unspeakable terror of human death. The body, and specific forms of bodily interaction, also function as symbols of identity and change. Nick recognises that Miranda is no longer a child from a new awkwardness in the poise and movement of her body, in the way her childish 'boisterous hug' has been replaced with 'a grown-up peck delivered across the divide of her consciously hollowed chest' (4). Fran finds herself recoiling from physical contact with her older son, Gareth, a symbol of strained relations between them not just in the present because of her pregnancy and his moodiness, but going back to her decision when he was in her womb not to have him aborted, a decision which symbolised the loss of her own independence and identity (7). Her reluctance to embrace him is symbolic of her sense of alienation from her own body, signified also in her adoption of a particular tone of voice which she doesn't recognise as her own, 'a Joyce Grenfell comic-nanny sort of voice [which] she can't believe [is] coming out of her mouth' (7). Perhaps the most significant representation of the body as symbolic signifier in the novel, however, is the juxtaposition of Geordie's bayonet scar with the various attempts to narrate the stories of his life. Doctors tell Geordie that he is dying of cancer, but Geordie feels the pain in his bayonet wound, which he believes is opening up again. Nick and others want Geordie to talk about his war experiences, yet for most of Geordie's life 'his body with its ancient wound, as hard to decipher as the carving on a rune stone, had been left to speak for him' (163). Geordie's wound is figured in the novel as an irreducible, unnarratable mark of the violence of history, a signifier of the indelibility of history as event, which contrasts with the historian Helen's theory that Geordie remoulds his memories of the war according to changing public perceptions. Barker focuses on the body as a signifier which resists the fictionalising or self-styling properties of verbal signification, and thus the body symbolises the monumental against the shifting fashions of what stories we tell about ourselves.

Barker's early reputation as a realist novelist has always been somewhat complicated by her abundant use of symbolism. *Union Street* abounds with symbolic images of birds and broken shells, for example. Her fictional method is frequently closer to the styles of early modernist fiction, such as Kate Chopin or Joseph Conrad, in whose work the familiar forms of nineteenth-century realism have been adapted to include both greater access to introspective consciousness and an abstractive use of symbolist devices. If, as Raymond Williams argues, modernist writing consisted of 'taking nothing as it appeared but looking for deep forms, deep structures with the eyes of a stranger',[6] then it could be argued that Barker's search for deep forms and deep structures is modernist in its combination of an intensive realism which explores the minutiae of everyday life and an explosive symbolism which seizes on icons and symbols as expressive of underlying forms and forces. The two modes of fictional narration work in productive tension, pulling the reader into the detail of daily life and simultaneously down to the shaping structures and recurrent patterns of life, so that the specific social circumstances in which Jasper's young life is endangered are clearly related to a more esoteric and occult theme concerning child murder, social taboos and dark spectral forces at a more abstract level.

On the one hand, Barker is a sharp observer of the fine details of everyday domestic and family life. The texture and tincture of ordinary, almost ritual existence, such as the following scene on a summer day-trip, is described and represented precisely:

> Two hours later, after Sunday lunch in a pub, they're trudging across a car-park with the sun of their backs.
>
> 'Are we going home now?' Gareth asks.
>
> 'No,' Fran says. 'We're going to the seaside.'
>
> Fran's got prickly heat on the backs of her thighs, Nick's shirt has sweat moons in the armpits. It takes them ten minutes to get Jasper into his seat. Gareth walks up and down the car-park, kicking an ice-cream carton. They're always so patient – it never seems to occur to them to give the little bugger a good slap. When he's finally strapped in, wailing, miserable, red in the face, pulling at his ears, Gareth slides in beside him. The plastic glues itself to the backs of his thighs. He winds the window further down and looks out, wincing at the glitter of sunlight on bumpers and windscreens. (178–9)

The daily life of the family is represented almost always in the novel as disjointed and uncomfortable, and this scene is exemplary of how this impression is forcibly conveyed. The words 'trudging', 'prickly', 'wailing', 'miserable' and 'wincing' obviously signal discomfort and unhappiness, as do the recurring images of sweat, heat and physical unease, which is a leitmotif running right through the novel (Geordie's bowel movements being only the most obvious example). That the physical discomfort of the characters manifests itself in different ways also conveys a sense of disunity. They don't even experience the pervasive sticky heat in the same manner, although interestingly Barker shows that the two characters who speak and signal disagreement about what they want to do, Fran and Gareth, both feel the heat on the backs of their thighs. Any discomfort Miranda might feel in the heat isn't described, which reinforces the sense that Miranda remains (or tries to remain) aloof from family activities. Gareth, however, actively resents these enforced family outings, and his resentment is signalled by violent images of kicking and slapping. Gareth's perspective is allowed to intrude into the third-person narration, suggesting that his reaction against the pressures of belonging to a family is the focus of the narrative, as indeed it needs to be, given that he will soon attempt to murder his younger brother when they reach the seaside. In passages such as this, then, Barker employs a broadly realist style of narration and descriptive representation, not only to depict the credible behaviour and feelings of a family involved in everyday life, but also to suggest the social and environmental causal factors in their existence. Moreover, the omniscient capacity of the realist text to generate the impression of a fully knowable, comprehensible world is indicated by the manner in which the narrative focus shifts from one character's consciousness to another, revealing motivations and causes for seemingly inexplicable behaviour.

On the other hand, the novel is punctuated with neo-modernist symbols and devices. The dead animals symbolise degeneration, much like the wasteland imagery of desolation and decay which pervades Barker's depiction of urban landscape in this and previous novels. The body images and scars symbolise the painful impact of history, or more particularly that the body is the material signifier of the traumatic passage of human living – Fran's episiotomy scar is as significant in this respect as Geordie's war wound. So, too, paintings, photographs and ghostly apparitions recur through the novel, and usually have a symbolic function, registering psychic disturbances in the daily lives of the characters. But Barker also generates in this novel a potentially disruptive tension in the relationship between the realist narrative and modernist devices. This is a point worth emphasising and explaining in detail, because in other Barker novels symbolism tends to augment the realist narrative. The chickens about to be slaughtered in *Blow Your House Down*, for example, are symbolic of the 'passive uncomprehending terror' experienced by the characters in the face of the threat of random, vicious, urban violence.[7] In *Another World*, however, Barker becomes more interested in the failure of symbolic exchange, the failure of one thing to stand in for another, the failure of narrative to represent the world adequately. Barker draws our attention instead towards the aporia of representation, the gaps in the stories that people tell about themselves, the silences around which no narratives can heal or provide a comforting sense of presence. The realism of Barker's novel allows readers to know everything about the domestic strains and intimacies of Nick's family, and yet by the end of the novel the silence in Geordie's story about the death of his brother Harry remains. The central mystery the plot has to offer remains unresolved, for the most part. Geordie killed Harry, but whether it was a mercy killing, or a jealous murder, we are not told. Narrative cannot fill the gap, a somewhat surprising admission for a supposedly realist novel to make.

Another World is especially good at yielding meaning from a paucity
of expression, too. Nick, for example, is able to chart the rift between
Geordie and his mother over the death of Harry from the severely cur-
tailed telegrams Geordie has sent from the front, on which soldiers
crossed out the least appropriate phrases from a short list of possible
expressions (229–31). Here, Barker shows the possibility of forming
meaningful narratives about the emotional currents between a grieving mother and a guilty son from meagre utterances. Geordie's
telegram reporting, 'I am quite well', just ten days after Harry's death,
suggests that something is wrong. The succession of telegrams thereafter stating, 'I have received no letter from you for a long time',
records his mother's silent resentment that 'the wrong one died'
(231). But that wealth of meaning generated from minimalist
telegrams is contrasted with the crucial gap in Geordie's memorial
narratives: 'All Geordie's words, Nick realizes suddenly – and there
are thousands of them in this interview alone – orbit round a central
silence, a dark star' (158). Geordie has begun to talk voraciously about
the war, to make public appearances as a veteran and do interviews
recalling his experiences, but at the centre of his narratives is the
aporetic kernel, a silence he cannot fill with words. This is the key link
between Geordie's war memories and the subtext of the James Bulger
murder, for in both cases what *Another World* draws upon is the
critical contradiction between an event which is the subject of
intense public interest and representation, and yet at the same time
is effectively unrepresented.

In the mid-1990s, when Barker was working on *Another World*,
there was an abundance of public narratives about the history of war.
The fiftieth anniversary of the end of the Second World War had occasioned many books and television documentaries. Terrestrial and
cable television channels devoted substantial portions of broadcast
time to history programmes, and in particular to those concerned
with the two world wars. In witnessing such commemorations, it was
possible to believe that the truth of history was available in the narrative testimonies of its survivors. Barker registers a very different sense
of history, history as a catalogue of unspeakable traumas, before
which witnesses are reduced to silence. Nick feels this when he visits
the Somme cemeteries in Thiépval:

> The monument towered over the landscape, but it didn't soar as a cathe-
> dral does. The arches found the sky empty and returned to earth; they
> opened on to emptiness. It reminded Nick, appropriately enough, of a

warrior's helmet with no head inside. No, worse than that: Golgotha, the place of a skull. If, as Nick believed, you should go to the past, looking not for messages or warnings, but simply to be humbled by the weight of human experience that has preceded the brief flicker of your own few days, then Thiepval succeeded brilliantly. . .. Out there were the graves of men whose bodies had become separated from their names; inside the monument thousands of names that had become separated from anything at all. A scrap of blue or khaki cloth. A splinter of charred bone. Nothing else remained. Echoing footsteps, lists of names, arches opening on to emptiness. It seemed to Nick that this place represented not a triumph *over* death, but the triumph *of* death. (73–4)

This passage is a key representation of the failure of narrative, as figured in many of the recurring symbols of emptiness, silence and death which recur through the novel. The visit to Thiépval finds Nick and Geordie awed into silence. It should be an occasion for the exchange or transfer of experiences and memories, for Geordie telling the story of his past to his grandson, another of Geordie's warnings from history. Instead, it registers the impossibility of narrative, the failure of stories and language to represent the experiences commemorated in the cemetery adequately. Only the aporetic architecture of a monument reaching to and from emptiness can begin to record the weight of human history, a history which has violently dehumanised its agents, separating bodies from names, matter from meaning. In lines which echo Shelley's famous 'Ozymandias' sonnet, Barker depicts a scene of commemorative architecture which, instead of marking human presence, testifies to absence and emptiness.

The novel deploys a series of opposed images and symbols to reflect on the significance of contemporary commemorations of war. The humbling silence and emptiness of Thiépval contrasts with the pomposity and self-conscious worthiness of the televised annual cenotaph memorials, which Geordie does not attend. The conventional platitudes of the procession of mourners who attend Geordie's funeral prompt Nick to remember, in contrast, Geordie's final, agonising words: 'I am in hell'. Likewise, language can be consoling and ritualistic, as in the Doctor's last advice to Geordie that 'we'll soon have you up and about again' (227), when both know that he is going to die within days; or language can be horrific and unbearable, and Harry's screaming mouth is the recurring image of that horror. The contrasting notions of language and representation implied in these examples indicate that part of Barker's focus in this novel is the problem of representation, and specifically how to represent the past without resorting to nostalgia or believing that commemorative narratives can fill the gaps left by loss, grief and past wrongs. There is always, as Brodsky's epigraph to the novel suggests, 'something left over' when we attempt to achieve this, an excess, in this case the painful silence at the heart of Geordie's testimonies.

My argument here is that *Another World* addresses representation as both an aesthetical and ethical problem to a degree which is neither so evident nor so central to previous novels. To begin with, the novel is concerned with commemorative representation, and the extent to which any attempt to represent and commemorate the experience of loss or trauma can be successful. The memorial architecture of Thiépval clearly gestures towards this problem. Secondly, the contrasting accounts of how Geordie and Helen attempt to interpret Geordie's experiences show that the representation of the past is always subject to contest and contradiction. Geordie's memories may be 'carved in granite', as Nick believes (86), but crucial aspects of what he remembers, centred obviously around what happened to Harry, cannot be admitted in his public representations of the war. Helen believes that Geordie reshapes his memories to accord with public perceptions, and in one sense both Helen and Geordie are right. Geordie's memories remain unchanged, but what he can represent of those memories in public is constantly changing. Moreover, what troubles Nick increasingly in the novel is the question of whether Geordie is 'remembering' the darkest moments of his past, for he realises in reading the transcripts of Geordie's interviews that 'Geordie's past isn't over. It isn't even the past' (241). Partly, Barker is returning to the problems of psychoanalysis which were addressed in *Regeneration*. Psychoanalysis is premised upon a separation of the narrating patient from the trauma or illness of the past, so that the past disturbance is smoothed over by the reliable self-narration of the present. But how do you represent the past when it continues to be experienced as the present? How can narratives of memory heal the wounds of the past when the narrator continues to experience those wounds as a perpetual present? The very construction of the verb 'to re-present' requires that passage of time which makes the 'present' available to be brought *back* into view.

One element in the novel's problematising of representation, then, lies in Geordie's story, and the unresolved crisis in his ability to represent the trauma of his war experiences. But *Another World* refuses or fails to resolve other representational issues. How are we to understand the apparent appearance of ghosts and shadowy figures which are part of the pseudo-Gothic apparatus of the novel? To take one example of this, Gareth believes that Miranda appeared above him on the cliff top and urged him on to throw stones at Jasper (190–1). But when Gareth confronts Miranda about this, she denies that she was there. The novel offers one possible rational explanation for this contradiction when Nick discovers that Miranda, like Geordie, sometimes sleepwalks. But this remains an unsatisfactory resolution to the problem. If Miranda sleepwalks, why did Gareth interpret her presence as encouraging him to kill Jasper? Did Miranda, in her sleeping state, take on the form of a sinister other, an evil persona, similar to the Jekyll and Hyde manifestations of Prior in the *Regeneration* trilogy? The novel invites us to think that she might have been possessed in some way by the Fanshawe girl depicted in the Victorian wall painting in Nick's house. And elsewhere in the novel, we are led to believe that spectral presences do exist. Gareth feels a presence behind him in his room, and tells it to go away (96). Miranda herself sees a girl through the window, who vanishes when Miranda chases after her, only for Miranda herself to frighten Jasper when she peers at him through the window to see what the girl might have seen (177). Was the girl in the window a reflection, a real girl who just happened to be passing, the spectral presence of the Fanshawe girl, or a figment of Miranda's overactive imagination? So, too, Nick believes he has hit a girl running across the dark road in his car, but can find no trace of her when he stops, and explains the experience rationally as a hypnogogic hallucination (89). And after Geordie's death, there lingers the smell of the aftershave which Geordie wore on his last day alive, and Nick cannot quite explain why the smell persists so strongly (254). All of these instances are tropes of haunting, of impossible presences, which, because they are multiple, seem to imply the existence of the paranormal.

Barker raises questions about the nature of these experiences – be they hallucinations, ghostly presences or explicable illusions – by having her characters raise questions themselves about what it is they see or experience. But occasionally omniscient narration is used to hint at the possibility that the dead come back to haunt the living, as is the case when Nick's family uncover the portrait of the Fanshawes:

> The moon sails clear. White light falls on the choppy sea of dust sheets covering the living-room floor. The Fanshawes, visible again, though now there's no one to see them, gaze through the French windows over

the lawns, the rose beds, and the rhododendron bushes of the garden
that had once been theirs. (45)

Barker uses the same invisible and omniscient narrative perspective
briefly in other novels, most notably in *Blow Your House Down* after
Kath has been murdered. In the scene quoted above, it is difficult to
establish what is being represented. The uncovered painting of the
Fanshawes makes them 'visible again', but they are not now being
seen, so the narration of this moment is itself spectral. And moreover,
the painted figures are now given life, gazing over the property they
once owned. We might, of course, read this scene metaphorically, that
it is 'as if' the Fanshawes had come back to life and were watching
their former home. But the possibility remains, and is substantiated
by the numerous 'ghost' figures who appear throughout the novel,
that we are invited to believe here that the Fanshawes have returned
in some form from the dead.

Of course, this is where the novel which blends realist and modernist devices draws also upon Gothic conventions, and the novel
abounds with playful allusions to the Gothic as well as to specific
Gothic texts. Thoughts of reading *Jane Eyre* prompt Miranda to feel like
'a prisoner in a tower', and to remember her mother in a mental
hospital. The same image of Miranda pressing her face against the
glass and looking out from a tower is mirrored by Gareth later on, and
appears to be an allusion to *The Turn of the Screw*, Henry James's
Gothic novella which is close to Barker's concerns about notions of
childhood innocence.[8] So too, the idea of a house cursed by an atrocity
committed by its sometime inhabitants is a familiar trope in Gothic fiction and film, and recurs in the fears of Nick in particular, that the
murder of James Fanshawe will be repeated. The analogy between the
Fanshawes and his own family seems too strong to be ignored. Nick's
attempts to dismiss his fears as irrational and superstitious make them
no less powerful, and he acts on those fears instinctively when Jasper
goes missing and is later injured. But again, although the novel builds
up the analogy primarily through Nick's fears, it also suggests that
there are coincidental likenesses between the families which Nick does
not perceive. The report of the murder of James Fanshawe which Nick
reads records that the child's eerie first word was 'sadda', indicating his
prescient fears of the ominous shadows in his bedroom, and so too, the
omniscient narrator in *Another World* tells us of the shadows which
pass with equal forboding over Jasper's face (45). The novel builds up

the expectation that the dreadful history of the Fanshawes will be mysteriously repeated, but the anticipated Gothic climax is then deflated. Gareth is not, it seems, possessed by the evil spirits of the dead, but is, more mundanely, overwhelmed by sibling rivalry. The shadows over Jasper may have forewarned in some supernatural fashion of the violence visited upon him by Gareth, but Jasper's fate is not the same as James Fanshawe.

The conclusion to the novel makes it clear that we have been reading not a Gothic tale of haunting, cursed ground, and vengeance from the grave, but a lesson in the dangers of analogies:

> Six weeks since they'd uncovered the picture. Six weeks since Miranda stepped back and said, in that soft murmur that had raised the hairs on the nape of his neck, 'It's us.' Not true, [Nick] thinks, even as the covered-up figures rise once again to the surface of his mind. He doesn't regret not telling the family about the Fanshawe murder, because even now he doesn't see how the knowledge would have helped them. It's easy to let oneself be dazzled by false analogies – the past never threatens anything as simple, or as avoidable, as repetition. (277–8)

Another World effectively seduces its readers with a model of Jungian synchronicity. The discovery of the painting of the Fanshawes, the circumstances of the family tragedy played out over ninety years earlier, and the novel's depiction of the Fanshawes coming back to life through the painting, sets up the possibility of a meaningful coincidence between the fates of both families. Jung maintained that synchronicity was the meaningful link between events or objects by coincidence in time, which gave rise to an individual being able to access a deeper collective truth.[9] In Barker's novel, the painting of the Fanshawes seems to establish a series of paranormal connections between the two families, and those connections suggest deep mythological forces determining the fate of people down through history. Nick's fear is that even knowledge of these analogies and connections cannot help us to avoid this predestined course of events. But the analogies have turned out to be false – Jasper's fate is not as Nick had feared. Is it Nick's observation, then, or that of the novel's spectral narrator, that 'it's easy to let oneself be dazzled by false analogies'? Is Nick reflecting on his own weakness in being taken in by such analogies, or is it the narrator addressing the reader more directly? Either way, that phrase rebounds on the reader, for we as much as Nick have been dazzled by these analogies, led to expect that Jasper will be victim of the same fate, the same seemingly invisible psychic forces, as James Fanshawe, or the underlying subtext of James Bulger.

If the novel seduces us with the appearance of synchronicity, it concludes that we have been suffering from a kind of apophenia, the psychological condition of finding meaning in coincidences where none exist, and finding connections between unrelated phenomena. The warning against being dazzled by false analogies suggests that the paranormal connections we've been chasing are distractions from the real story. The final scene pulls the reader back from the Gothic narrative of recurrent acts of infanticide to the historical connections between James Fanshawe and Geordie's brother, Harry, and between James's brother, Robert, killed also in the First World War, and Geordie. Nick comes across the Fanshawe memorial in the graveyard which commemorates the deaths of both Robert and James Fanshawe, and finds strange the 'determined linking of the two deaths, the conviction of guilt for both' (277). The Gothic plot of the novel builds suspense around Nick's fears of what might happen to Jasper, but this is the stuff of sensationalist fiction, based on false analogies. Instead, the real horror is not just the fates of the murder victims, James and Harry, but the traumatic and tortured lives of the murderers, Robert and Geordie.

This is not to trivialise how close Jasper came to death, nor to minimise the novel's examination of the potentially dangerous undercurrents of rivalry and jealousy in domestic life, but the conclusion redirects our attention to historical rather than potential tragedy. It is in the mode of the serious historical (and historiographic) novel that Barker concludes, with Nick in the final scene contemplating the lessons of the graveyard:

> He wanders off down the path that leads round the outer perimeter of the churchyard, taking the long route back to Geordie. Some of the graves, here under the trees, are so old the names are hidden by moss. They're forgotten, and the people who stood beside their graves and mourned for them are dead and forgotten in their turn. He remembers the trip to France with Geordie, the rows upon rows of white headstones, ageless graves for those who were never permitted to grow old. He'd walked round them with Geordie, marvelling at the carefully tended grass, the devotion that kept the graves young. But now, looking round this churchyard, at the gently decaying stones that line the path, he sees that there's wisdom too in this: to let the innocent and the guilty, the murderers and the victims, lie together beneath their half-erased names, side by side, under the obliterating grass. (278)

The idea that Geordie's memories, specifically those connected with his brother, are carved in granite has served in the novel as an instance of how the past is inseparable from the present, how the past refuses to be moulded or changed. But this scene shows stone decaying, carved names becoming half-erased or hidden by moss. The past does recede. The dead are slowly forgotten, here by the 'obliterating grass', just as earlier in the novel Nick covers over the Fanshawe portrait with what he thinks of as 'alzheimer white' paint (118). The present continuous tense in which the novel is written also becomes more pointed, the 'here' and 'now' indicating the separation of the present time and place from the safely absent past. Nick can affirm the comforting wisdom of the graveyard, and feel secure from the threatening leakage of the past into the present, precisely because he is nowhere made more conscious of the 'here' and 'now'.

This final paragraph of the novel performs a dual function, therefore, in marking an elegy for the dead which is at the same time affirmative for the living. It is affirmative in a very specific and critical way, for it reclaims the proper domain of the historical novel, the agency of human beings acting positively in concrete historical conditions. What makes this novel finally not just a historical novel, but also a markedly anti-Gothic novel, is that it renounces the tantalising idea that murders are the consequence of irrational, ahistorical, evil forces, and pulls our attention back to the specific historical conditions in which the murders of James and Harry are shown to take place. William Fanshawe recoils from the inhuman murder of his son, James, but his profession is an armaments manufacturer, his chosen role to make profit from the inhuman uses of his products, and he has his own share of guilt in the war which kills his other son, Robert. Gareth's attempt to hurt Jasper does not take place in isolation from social conditions, either, for the 'harmless' game of throwing stones at the child is an extension of the contemporary fascination with dehumanising representations of violence and death. The novel provides us with sufficient clues to understand that history is made by human beings, even if it is also prudent enough to recognise that the capacity to change social conditions is limited.

At the end of the novel, therefore, Barker has brought her readers to a reflexive realisation of the role of the historical novel, to show history as the product of human action within a fictional form which can represent the density and complexity of human experience and motivation. The warning against the false analogies proposed by the

Gothic plot of the novel serves as a kind of metafictional commentary, steering the reader back towards the properly historical conclusions of a historical novel. Numerous characters are drawn to the attractions of imagining the 'other world' of the title, usually an unreal or paranormal world, but the novel closes by returning readers peremptorily to 'this world', and its concrete social and historical conditions. As I've been suggesting at various points throughout this chapter, however, there remains something not quite satisfactory about this attempt at closure. We have been led to such false analogies, not just by characters who are shown to be fallible and susceptible to fears, illusions, perhaps even hallucinations, but sometimes too by an invisible and barely questionable omniscient narrator. The ghosts, shadows and supernatural occurrences are not wholly explained away. The coincidences and correspondences between Nick's family and the Fanshawes are not all without meaning or substance. The attempt to restabilise the ground of historical fiction at the end of the novel, therefore, does not completely succeed in casting out the spectres and speculations which have kept the narrative rumbling along. The novel is ultimately more open to the possibility of other worlds than its final scene allows. The graveyard which Nick wanders around is quiet, suggesting closure, suggesting that the dead don't return, that there is no such thing as haunting. The very erasure of the dead in the graveyard defies the logic of what Gothic narratives necessarily ask the reader to believe. But even in this final scene, Barker doesn't fully resolve the question of whether the dead stay dead, of whether the living are solely the sentient agents of this world, for in the final line the novel again personifies the dead, as they 'lie together . . . side by side' (278). Beware of false analogies between one event and another, one war and another, one murder and another, certainly, but what Barker also attests in her refusal to close the question of agency is that the dead are never wholly dead, that history is never fully settled in the grave.

Notes

1   James Bulger, aged two years and eleven months, was murdered on 12 February 1993 by two older boys, Jon Venables and Robert Thompson, both aged ten years. James was led by the boys from a shopping mall, where he had strayed briefly from his mother, to a deserted railway, where he was murdered. The circumstances of the murder are reported extensively in David James Smith's book, *The Sleep of Reason* (London, Century, 1994). Barker uses several details from the case in the novel,

although Gareth's slide from playing at throwing stones to trying to kill Jasper is borrowed from an earlier case, in Liverpool in 1973, and it is important to stress that Barker draws from such instances of child murder generically, as it were, rather than in any sensationalist or graphic manner. In *Border Crossing*, the James Bulger case seems a less obvious subtext, as it concerns a child who killed an elderly woman, but the imminent release of Bulger's killers formed part of the context of the novel's exploration of the psychology of child killers.

2   Smith, *The Sleep of Reason*, 1.

3   Barker suggested in an interview with Robert McCrum that Gareth is almost a prototype character for Danny Miller in *Border Crossing*, who in turn is the basis for Peter Wingrave in *Double Vision*. See Robert McCrum, 'It's a disaster for a novel to be topical', *Observer*, 1 April 2001.

4   Sharon Monteith argues that *Another World* is a subversion of the family romance genre. See Sharon Monteith, *Pat Barker* (Tavistock, Northcote House, 2002), 87–93.

5   Michael Ross explores Lawrentian influences on Barker's work in 'Acts of Revision: Lawrence as Intertext in the Novels of Pat Barker', *D.H. Lawrence Review*, 26:1–3 (1995), 51–63.

6   Raymond Williams, *Writing in Society* (London, Verso, 1983), 223.

7   See Barker's *Blow Your House Down*, 156.

8   Henry James's *The Turn of the Screw* arguably becomes an even more overt intertext in *Border Crossing*.

9   See C.G. Jung, *Synchronicity: An Acausal Connecting Principle* (London, Routledge and Kegan Paul, 1972).

8

Redemption: *Border Crossing* and *Double Vision*

Border Crossing

In her two most recent novels, *Border Crossing* and *Double Vision*, Pat Barker is concerned with ostensibly religious themes of salvation or redemption, the capacity of human beings to turn from evil to good, except that these themes are explored in wholly secular contexts and ways, and good and evil are understood in thoroughly historicist and humanist terms. The transformative capabilities of human beings are figured through the perspectives of characters who are involved in intellectual work. In the course of her literary career, Pat Barker has gradually shifted her attention towards middle-class intellectuals, and especially towards those who are professionally involved in the task of 'rehabilitating' or reorienting other people towards socially constructive behaviour. This is in marked contrast to the focus of her characterisation in her early work. In *Union Street*, middle-class people are seen only from a distance, or are absent altogether, and they are thoroughly alienated from the working-class characters whose stories make up the novel.[1] The social worker who comes to tell Alice Bell that she will be evicted from her house and moved into a care facility for the elderly is seen through Alice's eyes as an anonymous bureaucrat, who even struggles to look at Alice as a fellow human being.[2] Gradually, however, Barker has made such figures as the social worker and the psychologist more and more central to her novels. In *The Century's Daughter*, the social worker Stephen is still of subordinate interest compared to Liza, but in the *Regeneration* trilogy, Rivers the psychologist is the central character, and in each of Barker's three novels since then – *Another World*, *Border Crossing* and *Double Vision*, the central characters are middle-class intellectuals. They are writers, artists, psychologists and social workers, who work in some capacity to record, interpret or analyse, and, more significantly, have been empowered with some form of authority to represent others. That authority was shown under strain in Barker's depiction of the emergence of the 'talking cure' of psychoanalysis in the *Regeneration* trilogy. Prior constantly questions and unsettles the power balance of analyst and patient, sometimes inverting the relationship. In each novel since the trilogy, Barker has continued to examine the ethics and politics of representing others. In *Another World*, Helen's attempts to construct meaningful narratives of Geordie's wartime memories are seen to be incapable of representing his most traumatic and disturbing experiences. *Border Crossing* and *Double Vision* continue to explore the same problematics of representation, but in very different settings and situations.

According to Alan Sinfield, intellectual work (which he also calls cultural production) is the critical agency through which a society is imagined, represented and maintained. 'Intellectuals, cultural producers, are important because they help to maintain or undermine belief in the legitimacy of the prevailing power arrangements. They help to set the boundaries of the thinkable. They confirm or change the stories through which we tell ourselves who we are'.[3] As intellectual work has become a more prominent and numerous form of employment, so too intellectuals have become less significant as arbiters than agents of social processes. Social workers, psychologists, university teachers and journalists do not decide on the fate of the world, but they do exercise degrees of authority in the course of their professional function. They shape the prevailing beliefs and cultural practices of a society, albeit often in subtle and necessarily limited ways. One of the recurrent concerns of Barker's novels about the role of intellectuals is whether their authority is used to maintain or to change the world they live in. Rivers in *Regeneration*, for example, knows that his function as an army psychiatrist is to silence protest, and to return officers to mental health so that they can continue to fight the war. Sassoon, on the other hand, signifies the opposite tendency, the use of intellectual authority to articulate dissent and refusal to serve. Most of Barker's intellectual workers are almost powerless to effect any kind of change in the world, but what her novels increasingly make clear is that intellectuals are critical agents in the contest for meaning and understanding.[4] As Sharon Monteith observes, one of the contexts for Barker's exploration of murderous children in

Border Crossing is former prime minister John Major's remark that 'we must condemn a little more, and understand a little less'.[5]

Border Crossing is concerned from the beginning with the problems of seeing and understanding clearly, with the very difficulty of representation. The first chapter is particularly attuned to an artistic view, paying particularly attention to perspectives, points of view, and uses painterly splashes and washes of colours to depict its derelict riverside setting. The opening scene also makes it clear that truth depends upon perspectives altered by time and space. As Tom Seymour and his wife Lauren walk along the river path in the opening line, we are told that 'as far as they knew they were alone' (1). Already another consciousness is suggested, another perspective which would reveal that they were not alone. When Tom looks up from his walk to watch a gull flying past, the narrative indicates another shift of perspective: 'Perhaps this focus on the bird's flight explained why, in later years, when he looked back on that day, he remembered what he couldn't possibly have seen: a gull's eye view of the path' (2). Here, the memory substitutes Tom's actual experience of the event, with a cinematic, bird's eye view, an impossible memory which provides him with a vision of 'the whole scene', including a third-person view of himself, and Lauren, and the young man about to attempt suicide in the river. It is a more total view than he actually saw, but it is also false, and the narrator corrects his misperceptions: 'In reality, it was Lauren who first noticed the young man' (3). This corrective view serves to stabilise the scene for the reader, acknowledging that there was a single, verifiable reality to be witnessed, but it also makes clear that the reality of the event is subject to the distortions, vagaries, distractions, and gaps of consciousness and memory. Tom cannot rely on his own memory, nor his own perspective, to verify what happened. This proves a crucial starting point for a novel about Tom's attempts to recover the memories and the state of mind of the suicidal young man, Danny Miller, who, as a ten-year-old, killed an old woman. Tom's testimony as a psychologist helped to convict Danny of the crime, and it is for this reason that Danny dramatically re-enters Tom's life, to find out on what basis Tom was able to testify to Danny's state of mind.

A careful reading of the way in which the opening scene of the novel problematises the relationship between memory, consciousness and truth, as indicated above, reveals that the novel is sympathetic to Danny's quest, even if it also plays with the possibility that Danny might have turned up in Tom's life for more sinister purposes.

Barker uses the conventional devices of the horror or thriller genres to figure Danny as the murderer returned to wreak vengeance on those who convicted him. The same kinds of questions about the implications of the Bulger murder which concern *Another World* – about the existence of good and evil, the causes of human action, the struggle between rationality and superstition, and the capacity of human beings to change or to repeat patterns of behaviour – are also addressed in *Border Crossing* through Tom's anxieties about the motives for Danny's return. *Border Crossing* even uses the same scenario of an older boy coming dangerously close to murder by throwing stones at a small child as Barker had used in *Another World*, except that, in *Border Crossing*, importantly, it is Tom Seymour who was the older boy. Tom remembers coming so close to being a murderer himself, to crossing the border between good and evil, to becoming a child-killer, just like Danny Miller. This is just one of the ways in which Barker shows how fine is the line dividing the analyst from the patient, the reliable witness from the convicted murderer, a point which appears to be ultimately the purpose of Danny's return.

Barker is fascinated by such dividing lines, the permeable borders between states of consciousness, or states of existence, and the titles of her three most recent novels reveal this as an abiding concern of her later work. 'Coincidence is the crack in human affairs that lets God or the Devil in', Danny tells Tom (22), and their apparently chance reunion is the subject of speculation in the novel as to whether Tom's salvation of Danny from suicide is the beginning of Danny's redemption from the sins of his past, or the beginning of Tom's damnation at the hands of evil. Barker deploys her familiar, tantalising symbolic imagery to suggest that Tom might be walking into a kind of hell when he admits Danny back into his life, when he is surrounded by flowers known as 'red-hot pokers', which 'seemed to breathe in his horror and incredulity, and exhale them as heat and dust' (26). The imagery gives credence to the suspicion, which Tom attempts to dismiss as 'God-bothering rubbish', that there is a providential meaning to the coincidence of meeting Danny again. Barker juxtaposes the rational explanation with the paranoid suspicion:

> The fact is, that when confronted by a number of disturbing events, the human mind insists on finding a pattern. We can't wait to thread the black beads on to a single string. But some events are, simply, random.
>
> Perhaps. Adjusting the mirror, he caught his own eye in the glass, and stared back at himself, alert, sceptical, unconsoled. (27)

The rational dismissal of providence seems initially to be brushed aside with the force of authoritative statements about the 'fact' of humans imagining meaning where none exists. The image of the rosary beads is used to suggest that religion produces such a false consciousness of human affairs, and pits religion as the enemy of rationality. Tom is sceptical about religious or supernatural explanations of random occurrences, but that he remains unconsoled by his own authoritative statements inverts the order of this opposition. Rationality is not the clear, shining light piercing the darkness of superstition, but is instead a weak, flickering candle which provides scant comfort against the fear of darkness. The premise of enlightenment modernity – that human beings master their own destiny by means of rational control – is shown to be flimsy and fragile, while the fear of recurrent evil and the instinctual suspicion that human destiny is subject to all sorts of supernatural forces seems constantly to pull on even the most sceptical minds.

Tom's confidence in the premise of his own profession is undermined throughout the novel, however. He cannot prevent an irrational physical repulsion from his wife's desire to have a child from ending their marriage, and cannot talk through his own problems in the way that he encourages his patients to do. For all that he is supposed to help others through difficult relationships and divorces, he is no better equipped to deal with his own pains and disappointments. Danny unerringly observes to Tom the failings of his role as a therapist: "'all sorts of people whose jobs actually depend on a belief that people can change, social workers, probation officers, clinical psychologists" – he smiled – "psychiatrists, don't really believe it at all"' (68). The point is not simply that Tom's life as a psychiatrist is a sham, but rather that he lives with an irreconcilable opposition. The ideal of healing, of turning away from crime, of a positive change in human behaviour, must co-exist with the daily disappointment of failure to change. Tom acknowledges that the jobs Danny mentions 'furnish people with a good deal of evidence that [change] doesn't happen' (68), and yet must be guided by the possibility that it does. What Danny understands from this is that 'under all that compassion you don't actually give a toss for anybody' (69), a view partly endorsed by the novel's depiction of how Tom effectively alienates and detaches himself even from those closest to him in order to do his job. The work he is employed to perform necessitates a psychical state in which repetition and difference, damnation and salvation, good and evil, the rational and the irrational, must be tolerated as irreconcilable oppositions.

To live with such contradiction, Tom produces a kind of splitting of the self, the detachment of his rational from his emotional self, 'the clinician's splinter of ice in the heart' (13). Like Nick in *Another World*, and Rivers in the *Regeneration* trilogy, Tom is emblematic of the dissociation of the self which occurs as a result of the pursuit of a rational, clinical subjectivity. Barker is exploring in each case the paradoxical inhumanity or damaged humanity produced in the very people charged in our societies with humanist tasks. The figure of the psychologist or social worker has become central to her work for exactly this reason, that it enables her to examine the fragility of modern society through the prism of those authorised to repair or reform its human discontents. The premise of Tom's occupation is that human civilisation has evolved sophisticated scientific means of coping with eruptions of violence or conflict, ways of engineering social harmony and normativity. But the novel questions the basis of this premise through the figure of Danny and, furthermore, through erasing the distinctions between analyst and analysed. Tom's capacity to detach himself, to produce a split subjectivity, is after all merely the mirror image of Danny's more controversial dissociated personality. Danny's former teacher, Angus, describes him as 'frozen' and 'shut down', 'dealing with only 10 per cent of himself' (204), detached even and perhaps especially from those who try to help him.

Tom's role in Danny's conviction was to provide a psychological assessment of whether or not the boy knew that killing was wrong, and that death was a permanent state. When Danny re-enters his life as an adult dangerously close to mental breakdown and suicide, Tom is compelled to dig deeper into Danny's psychic state, and the novel embarks on a journey to discover the psychological causes of Danny's horrific murder of Lizzie Parks. Danny offers an explanation of his own personality as 'permeable', not always able to distinguish his own feelings from those of others (77). This is confirmed later by another former teacher who describes Danny as a 'bottomless pit' who 'wanted other people to fill him' (164):

> [He] borrowed other people's lives. He . . . it was almost as if he had no shape of his own, so he wrapped himself round other people. And what you got was a . . . sort of composite person. He observed people, he knew a lot about them, and at the same time he didn't know anything because he was always looking at this mirror image. And of course

everybody let him down, because you couldn't *not* let Danny down.
Being a separate person was a betrayal. (171)

Hélène Deutsch calls this form of emotional disturbance the 'as if'
personality, because 'the individual's whole relationship to life has
something about it which is lacking in genuineness and yet outwardly
runs along "as if" it were complete'.[6] Tom is constantly anxious, for
example, that Danny's seemingly most intimate confessions are not
genuine at all, but calculated, imitative and manipulative, while at the
same time it is only when he sees Danny through Lauren's eyes that
he recognises that Danny functions 'as if' he were a perfectly normal
young man. Like Tom, Danny has produced a split personality, a dissociated self, in order to function normally. The normative personality which Danny erects masks a labyrinth of borrowed personalities
and identities, the 'composite person' fabricated from the tissues of
other people's stories, other people's lives. At the core of Danny's personality is the empty mirror, the primal quest for identification, a
vortex which sucks in everyone to whom Danny becomes attached.

In keeping with the precepts of psychoanalytic theory, Danny traces
the roots of his personality disorder, even when he doesn't recognise
it as such, to his mother and father. It is important to recognise that
Danny is the author of his own psychoanalytic enquiry here. Tom is
not the Freudian detective, deciphering the codes hidden in Danny's
symptoms. Danny is the one who provides the psychoanalytic explanations, while Tom is closer to the figure of the sceptical reader, puz-
zling whether these explanations are fully to be trusted and, if so,
what they mean. Danny reports that his mother became depressed
after his birth, and that his father became angry with her inability to
cope: 'Apparently he used to come home, and I'd be screaming in one
room, and she'd be slumped in a chair. More or less in the same position she'd been in when he left. I think she just about fed me and kept
me clean, but that was it' (115). Without any interaction from the
mother, and with his screaming unanswered, Danny is left as an
infant with the impression that the world does not answer to his control, and that the only solution is compliance, or imitation. In his case,
this means imitation of his father, a role model of action and aggressive mastery, and the transfer of his infantile projections, which
Danny is able to pinpoint in 'two photographs of me round four, five.
One's of me sitting on Mum's knee in a Paddington Bear t-shirt. And
the other – this is only two months later – I'm wearing a flak jacket

and carrying a gun' (116). The emulation of the mother's projected image of a child has become the emulation of the father's projected image of a man, shaped to mirror the father's own life as a soldier and killer.[7] Danny imitates his father's expressions, his walk, and repeats his father's opinions as if they were his own, even in telling Tom about his childhood. Danny struggles to live up to his father's ideal masculinity – 'He was tall, he was strong, he had a tattoo that wiggled when he clenched his fist, he had a gun, he'd killed people . . . I thought he was fucking brilliant' (124). Danny is not yet ready to become his father's ideal man, however. He winces at the sight of dead rabbits, baulks at the idea of having to kill the hens who are being pecked by others, and cries when he is hit by a cricket ball, for all of which his father punishes him severely. Danny's upbringing raises a number of questions about the motivations for the murder of Lizzie Parks. Was Danny seeking to prove that he was a man by killing someone? Did Danny learn from his father that masculinity consisted of the propensity to kill? Did his father teach him that life was divided into hunters and the hunted? As he hid in Lizzie's wardrobe, Danny was surrounded by fox fur, presumably a scarf, with a real fox's face and paws. Does Danny identify himself with the fox, or is he the hunted animal who must kill to survive? Lizzie is described as 'just skin and bones', feeding herself on dry cornflakes, so was she the pecked hen which Danny is taught it is kinder to kill?

The animal imagery of *Border Crossing* functions as a metaphorical mode, through which chickens, rabbits and foxes come to represent human consciousness or human society in some form. Tom thinks of the fragility of human existence, its thin façade of civilisation, when after the 'talk, laughter, companionship, lights, warmth, wine [and] food' of a writers' group meeting, these comforts are shattered by the human-like screams of a rabbit, trapped and soon to be killed by a fox (208). This hard world of predators, traps, killing and screams lies just below the surface of human existence, and becomes metaphoric whenever a horrific murder takes place, but it is the world to which Danny's father seems most determined to expose him as real. The court which convicts Danny, it appears, was particularly shocked by the words which Tom quotes from Danny's interview: 'If you wring a chicken's neck, you don't expect to see it running around the yard next morning' (111). What shocks the court in particular, then, appears to be the grafting of the animal world on to the human, the image of the casual, daily brutality of the farm projected on to human life. The court reads Danny's matter-of-fact statement about the routine killing of farmyard animals as a metaphor for his horrific killing of another human being. Both Danny and Tom recognise that a categorical error has occurred in this reading, that Danny's description of the objective world of animals is misinterpreted as metaphoric. Arguably, the same categorical slippage from objective to metaphoric modes is also more pervasive. Danny's father carries over the predatory and brutal world of animal relations into his own life as a soldier and father, for example, and it is also possible to understand what little we are told of Danny's 'playing' with the dead body of Lizzie Parks as the play of a predator with its fallen prey. The animal world functions, then, not as an exterior, objective reality, but in metaphoric relation to human consciousness, as subordinate to human mastery. The fox fur scarf in Lizzie's closet is perhaps the clearest emblem of this, but what Barker is resisting in paying attention to this metaphorical mode is the argument that such murders are the return of the animalistic to human society, for what is evident here is that the animal is always already translated into human signification. The animal is always metaphoric, that is, of something brutal in human affairs. The animal imagery thus serves to remind us that if we want to find out the causes of Lizzie's murder, our categorical error would be to read it as a sign of the return of the animal or primitive. The answer must be found within human relations only.

While Danny's upbringing offers a psychoanalytic explanation of personality disorder, a psychic state bordering on psychosis, his narrative also offers a rational justification of his actions as a 10-year-old child. Tom recognises that the point of Danny's revelations about his mother and father is not to present symptoms of his psychic state, nor excuses for his actions, but to provide a context in which the murder of Lizzie Parks was not wholly irrational. 'He was talking about moral circles, the group of people (and animals) inside the circle, whom it is not permissible to kill, and the others, outside, who enjoy no such immunity. . . .. The question was implicit. You said I had a clear understanding that killing was wrong. *Are you sure?*' (124–5). Barker's question concerning the public response to such killings is also implicit. The fists pounding against the police van, the death threats and media witch-hunts, all seem to say that Danny is evil, that his killing of Lizzie Parks can only be explained by reference to a purely evil force, or at the very least that such a murder is beyond human comprehension. As discussed above, *Border Crossing* is never wholly supportive of the notion that human affairs can be explained by rational means alone, and the incidents of synchronicity and haunting which pervade the novel suggest that there may well be forces at work beyond human comprehension. But 'evil' is shown to be a very limited and contingent concept for what remains difficult to represent or understand, as Tom explains when Danny asks him if he believes in evil:

> 'In the metaphysical sense? No, I don't. But as a word to describe certain kinds of behaviour, I've no problems with it. It's just the word we've agreed to use to describe certain kinds of action. . ... Killing Lizzie was an evil thing to do, but I don't think *you* were evil when you did it, and I certainly don't think you are now. (255)

Danny's question is essentially theological, if evil exists as a permanent and indefatigable state of being in the world, but typically Tom offers a secular understanding of evil instead, which refuses to condone 'certain kinds of action', but which situates 'evil' deeds in their social and psychological contexts. Evil actions undoubtedly occur, but within rationally comprehensible circumstances, and even then what is meant by evil is a matter of social convention, not an authoritative description. The nature of evil, then, is something of a muddle, especially as Danny's introspection about what led him to kill Lizzie (arguably, the motor of the novel's plot) finds him ultimately confessing, 'I don't know why I killed her. I didn't know then, and I don't know now. And I don't know how to live with it' (243).

Danny can finally produce no reason for killing Lizzie. The novel provides a detailed psychological profile of his personality and upbringing, an equally detailed account of his social circumstances, and the 'warrior' mentality of children from poor social backgrounds, but it cannot finally translate these rationalisations of Danny's life into an explanation of why he murdered an old woman. The novel goes through the motions of psychoanalytic interview and confession, but arrives at no clear revelation of the reasons for murder. Similarly, the 'heart of the darkness', the five hours which Danny spent with Lizzie's dead body in which police believe 'he played with her' is a blank in Danny's memory. The reference to Conrad's novel is no accident; Conrad's *Heart of Darkness* is equally shaped around an absent centre, the 'horror' which remains abjectly inexplicable (Barker's novel also begins and ends on the riverside). In both novels, the journey into the heart of darkness produces nothing for the truth-seeker other than the experience of darkness. Indeed, Tom only learns as much as he does about Danny's psychic state at the time of the murder by bringing him close to that state again (254), a repetition of the scene of trauma rather than a critical explanation of it.

Tom becomes disturbed by the fact that Danny experiences his memories of what he did to Lizzie as if they are happening in the present. This he realises is not the stuff of rational enquiry but a dangerous transgression of psychological states. As Danny begins to recall the murder, he seems to slip into his childhood consciousness: 'Under his normal voice, a child's piping treble was faintly audible, growing clearer by the minute. Danny was producing this sound without sign of strain, without a hint of falsetto, and seemed to be unaware that he was doing it. Tom felt a prickling at the back of his neck' (235). Tom is undoubtedly aware of the rational explanation for this apparently paranormal occurrence, which is that Danny has so effectively repressed the traumatic memories of what happened that he is having to lapse into the psychic state of his ten-year-old self in order to recover them. But this doesn't prevent him from feeling fear and alarm, which feelings register the suspicion that there is something dangerous taking place. This suspicion raises a problem for Tom's secular notion of evil, for in Tom's conception 'evil' is thoroughly historicised. Tom can rationalise Danny's murder of Lizzie Parks as a specific and inimitable event, peculiar to certain contextual conditions, and is convinced that Danny is different now and in different circumstances. But that Danny can slip obliviously into the psychic state of his ten-year-old self, and cross the border between his controlled, 'normal' self and his unconscious, psychotic self, suggests that 'evil' might be the product of a particular kind of psychic condition, closer to what Tom dismisses as the metaphysical understanding of evil.

Tom's fear, then, as is often the concern of Barker's novels, is that history can repeat itself, or rather that the wounds of one time may open up in another, with no less effect. The seepage of the past into the present is as much a theme here as in earlier novels. Tom witnesses an exploitative circus act which could belong to any Victorian fairground (139), for example, and senses the 'ghosts of steam trains of the past' haunting the railway station, while Danny explicitly compares his father to the ideal father of Victorian discourses of masculinity, as if his father had been dislodged from his rightful place in the past. Each of those feelings of anachronism register that what would once have been certain and secure in previous ages, has become uncertain and muddled in the contemporary. Tom's more particular fear about the seepage from the past is that Danny's borderline psychotic state may result in more killings, and yet Tom bends the rules, and does not report this fear to anyone who might act on it. He bends the rules not for any rational justification, but out of hope, the hope that Danny might yet be redeemed. For redemption, the possibility of change, is indeed the key concern of the novel.

The words 'redemption' and 'damnation' are repeated several times in the novel, and both are curiously pre-modern, pre-secular terms which jar against Danny's experience of a prison system intent on reforming and rehabilitating him. As mentioned above, Barker plays upon the imagery of damnation, with Tom walking into a metaphorical hell of 'red-hot pokers', and later Danny, in his near-psychotic state, surrounding himself with a flaming fire. But the novel concludes with Danny's redemption, as he makes his way in the world with a new identity, his past concealed even from those closest to him: 'And that's the way it has to be, Tom thought. He was looking at success. Precarious, shadowed, ambiguous, but worth having nevertheless. The only possible good outcome' (281). Nor is Danny the only sign of redemption (or, to use Barker's earlier term, regeneration) in the novel either. The derelict riverside setting of Tom's flat is changing too, 'the crumbling jetties and quays were demolished, paths laid, trees planted' (276), and Tom marvels when he sees otters playing along the river bank. After the novel has charted the collapse of his marriage, the concluding chapter finds Tom also beginning to find love again, this time a relationship with Martha characterised as the comfort of 'pulling on an old, warm, well-trusted sweater' (276). It is hardly a romantic resolution, and there is cautious optimism about each sign of healing and redemption, but it is probably the happiest ending of all Barker's novels. The novel ends with 'the only possible good outcome', which is itself an acknowledgement of its fragility, of the uncertainty with which Tom must still regard Danny's new life as a sign of success.

Border Crossing does not explain Danny's killing of Lizzie Parks, nor is this possible within its own terms, since it stays close to Danny's own confusion about why he did what he did. It cannot provide a rational explanation for what appears beyond reason, nor can it dismiss fully the possibility that 'evil' exists in some supernatural, transhistorical form. In part, it explores the role of social and gender ideals, and the psychology of child-rearing, as possible contexts in which to explain Danny's behaviour, but acknowledges that such contexts do not fully answer cases such as Danny's either. Although Danny initially seems intent on challenging Tom's authority to analyse him, it is Tom to whom Danny turns as a redeemer figure. When Tom saves Danny from drowning, he is compelled ironically to see Danny as his offspring, Danny's 'purple face, wet hair, that drowned look of the newborn, cast up on to its mother's suddenly creased and spongy belly' (8). Tom becomes, then, the same figure as Barker explored in Rivers in the *Regeneration* trilogy, the 'male mother', who finds a way of nurturing Danny into new life. Instead of imitating the father figure, Danny learns from this foster mother to 'keep a safe distance' (281), and to acknowledge rather than run from his past.

The novel concludes not with the fate of Danny, however, but the memory of his victim. On seeing Danny getting on with his new precarious identity, Tom remembers Lizzie Parks, seeing in his mind's eye, 'with almost visionary clarity, a woman with white hair walking down a garden path, five or six cats following her, their tails raised in greeting' (281). This too is a happy memory of Lizzie, not the disturbing and traumatic recollections of her death which pervade much of the novel. It symbolises that Tom and Danny have reached a new understanding of the relationship between the past and the present, one predicated on the proper mourning of the past, rather than a debilitating submission to its losses. *Border Crossing* is a novel firmly rooted in the precepts of modernity, and focused on the ambivalent position of the intellectual worker within an apparently dysfunctional modern society. What it shows, however, is that the cost of a truly secular faith in the powers of human change, of regeneration, is also an abandonment of myths of absolute authority, and the consequent struggle to live with the muddle and uncertainty of postmodernity, or at least a weakened modernity.

Double Vision

11 September 2001 – 9/11, as it has become popularly known. At the time of writing, this date is frequently evoked in US and British political rhetoric as a turning point in world history, and denotes an event so iconic it seems unnecessary even to describe it. The successive images of two passenger aeroplanes smashing into the sides of the twin towers of the World Trade Center in New York, followed by

the collapse of those towers into a billowing mushroom cloud of dust, smoke and debris, have supplanted the details of the event as such. There are other images which have become equally symbolic – the gaping hole in the side of the Pentagon building in Washington, the tiny specks of people escaping from the burning towers by falling to their deaths, or the jagged, twisted metal remains of the towers' supposedly crashproof structures. All these images testified to the vulnerability of the United States, and also to the 'Western' world as such, and were followed by anxiety that similar attacks would occur in other cities associated with globalisation and Western power. As Jean Baudrillard argues, the success of the terrorist attacks on a symbolic level means that 'all other forms of violence and the destabilization of order work in [terrorism's] favour. Internet terrorism, biological terrorism, the terrorism of anthrax and rumour – all are ascribed to Bin Laden'.[8] The images of 9/11, then, denote not just the events in New York, Washington and Pennsylvania on that day, but an apparently new state of mourning, vulnerability and terror which they ushered in. And yet, the imagery of urban disaster and apocalyptic cityscapes, which US movies had fantasised about since *King Kong*, could not be permitted to signal this vulnerability to the world. Just ten days after the 9/11 attacks, President Bush addressed the US Congress and announced that resolute action had to take the place of grief.[9] Judith Butler rightly suggests that what followed in US attacks on Afghanistan and Iraq is the attempt to 'banish [grief] in the name of an action with the power to restore the loss or return the world to a former order, or to reinvigorate a fantasy that the world formerly was orderly'.[10] The process of grieving for the dead, and the shattering of illusions of US domestic impregnability, was substituted with a programme for revenge which was represented as an opportunity to banish vulnerability altogether.

Double Vision is set in the aftermath of 9/11, and I argue here that the novel engages critically and imaginatively with the politics of post-9/11 vulnerability. Two of its central characters, Kate Frobisher and Stephen Sharkey, are grieving for the loss of their husband and colleague respectively, Ben Frobisher, who is killed on assignment as a war photographer in Afghanistan. Kate attempts to get on with her life by continuing to work as a sculptor, but her current commission to create a new sculpture of the risen Christ for a cathedral is an obvious focal point for questions about human vulnerability and the possibility of hope. Stephen, meanwhile, has resigned from his job as a foreign correspondent to write a book about how war is represented, in which he intends to include some of Ben's disturbing photographs. 9/11 is not a starting point for the novel's consideration of human vulnerability and the problems of how to represent trauma and war. Ben and Stephen had also worked in Bosnia together, and the media representation of the brutalities of that war is as important in the novel as 9/11. In fact, if there is a starting point for the novel's concern with the representation of war it is the Gulf War of 1991, 'the first war to appear on TV screens as a kind of *son et lumière* display, the first where the bombardment of enemy forces acquired the bloodless precision of a video game' (241). Stephen's concern about such visual displays of a harmless war is a democratic one, about what happens to public opinion in societies in which 'fear and pain never come home' (242). The attacks on New York and Washington, of course, are understood in that context, as desperate attempts to 'redistribute' fear and pain in a deeply inequitable global economy of violence. Barker stops short of endorsing the view that 9/11 marked an abrupt break between order and disorder, security and vulnerability, or complacency and action. But the imagery of 9/11, and the questions it raises about the ethics of representation, pervade the novel.

Ben and Stephen were working together in New York on the day of the attacks, and so were there to witness what happened. When Stephen remembers the day's events, the day he also discovers that his marriage is over, he thinks of 'images of shocked people covered in plaster dust' (96), images which cannot but resonate with Kate's studio, which is also covered in plaster dust, and in which she had begun to work on plaster figures of 'the young men at the controls who had seized aeroplanes full of people and flown them into the sides of buildings' (66). The images of a dust-filled city are also ghosted in the novel by other images of snow, fog, the whiteness of Kate's studio, and the impenetrable sea mist which endangers Stephen and Justine in their boat trip to Holy Island, images which recurrently figure the problems of seeing.[11] The plaster dust and debris, crunching underfoot, is also a leitmotif which runs from New York, to Kate's studio, to Justine's dream of walking on creaking ice. What 9/11 signifies in the novel is the paradox of representation which forms the epigraph from Goya, 'One cannot look at this. I saw it. This is the truth.' To bear witness to trauma, horror, to war, is to testify to the unspeakable, to see what is too awful to see, but at the same time, it is the truth which must be represented and shown.

Moreover, the spectacles of destruction and carnage which Ben and Stephen are compelled to witness are designed by their perpetrators to be displayed. The attack on the twin towers, the rape and murder of the woman in Bosnia, the execution which Ben photographs, and for that matter the risen Christ which Kate is sculpting, were events designed to be demonstrations of power and vulnerability. 'This was designed to be a photo-opportunity,' says Ben of the twin towers attack, 'and what have I done? I've spent the whole day photographing it' (101).

Art must bear witness to horror, then, even when that responsibility brings its own costs. Ben dies photographing the war in Afghanistan and, more precisely, capturing an artistic image of the ruins of war, a line of wrecked tanks that looked in silhouette like a wave breaking. In Stephen's mind, it is difficult to accept the cost of Ben's sacrifice for art. 'Your life – *for that?*' he exclaims on seeing the image which Ben risked and lost his life to capture, and yet the only difference between Ben's last photograph and the others described in the novel is that here Ben risked his life for an image of ruins transformed into art, an image which acknowledges the despair of war wreckage at the same time as it beholds the energy of a breaking wave. There are no people in the picture, merely the rows of decomposing Soviet tanks from the last war in Afghanistan, and 'a small white sun, no bigger than a golf ball, veiled in mist' (123). It is an apocalyptic image, a 'vision of the world as it would be after the last human being had left', but it is also the product of Ben's capacity to see art in ruins, to find truth in an image of debris. In other photographs, Ben is sacrificing himself in more disturbing ways. To photograph the rape victim, for example, Ben rearranges her body to the state that he and Stephen found her in, which makes Stephen feel, on seeing the photograph, that the woman 'had been violated twice' (121). So, too, when Ben photographs an execution – 'A man on his knees staring up at the men preparing to kill him' – he includes his own shadow in the shot, and in the following shot in which the man lies dead (123). Ben is figuring his own complicity in the shot. The execution is happening for public display, and there he is, the dutiful photographer, putting it on display. But this is what makes his final photograph a redemptive image in some ways, too, for if both Ben and Stephen are sometimes guilty of becoming too complicit in the atrocities and horrors they represent, then their salvation is the capacity to find hope in the representation of terror.

In *Double Vision*, then, the role of the artist in this world of terror and vulnerability is a key focus. Barker sets her novel in a rural community, very different from the more familiar settings of urban dereliction in her previous novels, but it is clear from the beginning that the rural world depicted is not the pastoral antithesis of the urban. It is equally fragile, equally vulnerable to larger social and political forces. This quiet, isolated community is the place to which artists and writers come to escape the speed, claustrophobia and pressure of urban, professional life, but Barker undermines the illusion that it is in any way idyllic or outside of social and political events. That she is playing off the iconography of the pastoral landscape is evident in the novel's representation of Stephen's return to the country:

> A man gets off a train, looks at the sky and the surrounding fields, then shoulders his kitbag and sets off from the station, trudging up half-known roads, unloading hell behind him, step by step.
>
> It's part of English mythology, that image of the soldier returning, but it depends for its power on the existence of an unchanging countryside. Perhaps it had never been true, had only ever been a sentimental urban fantasy, or perhaps something deeper – some memory of the great forest. Sherwood. Arden. Certainly Stephen returned to find a countryside in crisis. Boarded up shops and cafés, empty fields, strips of yellow tape that nobody had bothered to remove even after the paths reopened, just as nobody had bothered to remove the disinfectant mats that now lay at the entrance to every tourist attraction, bleached and baking in the sun. (201)

The myth is that the returning soldier (and it is important to note that war correspondent Stephen is figured as the returning soldier here – in the age of wars waged by representation, the distinction between correspondent and combatant has become blurred[12]) can 'unload hell' behind him, washing off the filth and stench of war in the clean, still waters of the countryside, but Barker's figuration of the rural as the scene of devastation, abandonment and crisis forcibly dispels this illusion. The livestock upon which the farming community depend have been destroyed by government officials after a nationwide outbreak of foot-and-mouth disease. The village handyman, Peter Wingrave, admired by Kate as an image of rugged masculinity as he scythes grass in the churchyard, turns out to be an ex-convict who had committed murder as a child (he is an older version of Danny Miller from *Border Crossing*[13]), and shows disturbing signs of psychopathic behaviour later in the novel. The rural retreat to which Stephen retires to write his book in peace and quiet becomes the scene of a failing marriage (the crisis in his brother's marriage begins to resemble the end of his own, from which of course he is partly escaping), and a burglary in which his young lover, Justine, is violently assaulted. The rural is as much the scene of random violence and pain as the urban has been in previous Barker novels. Ben's photographs of the English landscape, Kate reflects, are as dark as his war photographs: 'Fenland, waterland, brown tarns in gorse-covered hills, snow light, water light – all with the same brooding darkness in them. . . .. You always knew, looking at these empty fields, these miles of white sand with marram grass waving in the wind, that somewhere, close at hand, but outside the frame, a murder had been committed' (65).

The role of artistic representation in *Double Vision*, it seems, is to deliver such epiphanies, to reveal what is 'outside the frame' but inexorably true of what is presented. An image of landscape which contains no human figures can yet testify to the inevitable scars of human presence. Kate's sculpture of the risen Christ paradoxically shows the torture, betrayal and murder which brought him to the point of redemption she depicts. Ben's photographs of war and violence, supposedly distant events recorded to inform us, figure the complicity of the viewer, our consent to the spectacle of murder and destruction. The theme of such art is connectedness, the intangible presence of relations between the local and the global, between the individual and society. Kate's Jesus is a man, and what she figures in her sculpture is that his suffering, his redemption, is real, historical, and mirrors the suffering and redemption of others. He takes his place alongside the Goya paintings and Ben's photographs of the victims of torture, rape and war, as an image of the paradoxical condition of humanity. His gouged chest, scored belly, and bruised, swollen face show him as a victim (180), someone who bears the scars of having been beaten up, like Justine towards the end of the novel. He is a figure of history, in which 'the strong take what they can, the weak endure what they must, and the dead emphatically do not rise' (181). Kate, of course, does not believe in Christ or the resurrection, and yet this makes her version of the risen Christ all the more paradoxically human. Like the faces from Goya's prison scene, which Kate goes to see in the Bowes Museum, her Christ must be truthful to the abject terror of history, and at the same time, impossibly, figure the promise of hope. The Goya, she believes, achieves this impossible double vision: 'These men have no hope, no past, no future, and yet, seeing this scene through Goya's steady and compassionate eye, it was impossible to feel anything as simple or as trivial as despair' (152–3).

In a novel which, like all Barker's novels, floats from one subject of consciousness to another, the problem addressed most persistently in *Double Vision* is how the subject attends to the other as a subject. Goya's art is understood as an achievement in attending to otherness, to seeing desolation, murder, rape, imprisonment through a 'steady and compassionate eye'. The problem is partly understood psychologically. Peter Wingrave, it seems, is unable to distinguish clearly the boundaries between his subjectivity and others, and hence he takes on and mimics the characteristics of those he comes close to. His disturbing night of dressing up as Kate and imitating her movements as a sculptor seems to Kate as if 'he had indeed succeeded in stealing her identity' (179). The novel plays with the possibility that this form of psychopathic behaviour might become dangerous, perhaps even murderous, but Barker refuses to allow Peter to become the easy scapegoat. Stephen's nephew Adam suffers from a different problem, Asperger's disorder, a 'difficulty in seeing other people as people' (83). He sees human beings as objects, and struggles to recognise that other people have their own mental lives. This combines with a grisly fascination with dead animals, and specifically an enthusiasm for collecting the bones of animals. While Adam's father, Robert, proudly extols this as an early sign of interest in orthopaedic surgery, Stephen, who can't help but associate the boy's macabre enthusiasms with some of the most vicious atrocities he has covered as a journalist, cynically thinks that it might just as easily be the early signs of a serial killer (45). Both Peter and Adam serve to illustrate the ethical problems of failing to see others as others, and others as subjects. And they are, then, intimately connected with the ways in which the novel explores the problems of representing war, for Stephen's concern is precisely about when the image of war objectifies the other, and fails to represent the other as human.

This is as much a personal as a professional concern for Stephen, of course, as his work threatens to dehumanise him, to make him incapable of recognising the needs of others. The break-up of his marriage is partly the result of the detachment he has sought in his work, his inability to share the feelings and stresses his work engenders with his wife. His instinctual response on returning home from covering wars abroad is to go 'to ground', to isolate himself from others, while his wife increasingly 'had her own life' (155). Stephen finds it difficult to adjust himself to the emotional demands of 'normal' social life when his work routinely involves emotional extremes. At the same time, his work calls for a human response to human tragedy. The body of the woman raped and murdered in Sarajevo, in particular, he regards as an ethical challenge to his ability to represent the fate of others adequately: 'She was waiting for him, that's the way it felt. She had something to say to him, but he'd never managed to listen, or not in the right way' (55). What Stephen experiences here, and affects him profoundly, is the feeling of having been addressed by the other, and called upon for a response. He cannot contain her as the object of his writing, just as Ben reveals his own image with the image of those he photographs. The subject–object relations of representation are repeatedly undermined. Instead, she claims his attention, and specifically Stephen understands this call as the responsibility to listen, to hear her speak, an ethical demand which he also feels incapable of fulfilling.

Goya's paintings also demand for us to listen, according to how the novel represents them. 'You saw the mouths first in Goya's paintings', Stephen thinks, 'combining to produce that roar that even in the Prado, off season, early in the morning, almost deafens you' (196). Goya is depicted as exemplary of an artist committed to the ethical representation of war and terror, whose paintings do justice to the paradox of the novel's epigraph. The mouths in his paintings cry out to be heard, and produce a roar which cannot be ignored. This is explicitly contrasted with the sanitised television images of war, which Stephen associates with the Gulf War of 1991. In Goya's work, then, Stephen believes we are specifically addressed by the other, to witness the horrors of war, but in ways which draw us beyond despair. Goya, he remembers, healed himself of his mental illness by 'visiting circuses, fiestas, fairs, freak shows, street markets, acrobatic displays, lunatic asylums, bear fights, public executions, any spectacle strong enough to still the shouting of the demons in his ears' (195). Stephen recalls this as he visits a fair with Justine and Adam, where he 'felt dazed by the colours and shapes around him', and notices 'all these mouths shouting, laughing, screaming, eating, drinking; mouths everywhere' (195). Here, Stephen experiences the opposite vision of Ben's photographs of landscapes in which there is no human presence visible. The fairground is a disorienting landscape in which he is compelled to recognise the vibrant, roaring, indefatigable presence of human life. It demands of him an openness to the existence of others as subjects in the here and now, and thus serves as a corrective to his routine nightmares of the dead woman in Sarajevo, and to his instinctual desire to isolate himself from others.

The fairground functions to catapult Stephen's consciousness away from the self-protective individuation into which he retreats to hide from the terrors of the history he has been called upon to witness. But it is not the most decisive moment. That is forced upon him by the act of violence inflicted on Justine, which 'taught him more about his feelings for [her] than months of introspection could have done' (265). It is significant symbolically that Stephen is alone on a hillside, contemplating his book, when he looks down to find that Justine is about to interrupt a burglary, and that 'however hard he ran he wouldn't get there in time' (265). What Stephen learns from this moment is his sense of connectedness to Justine, that instead of thinking of their relationship as one temporarily convenient to both of them individually, he has come to recognise that he loves her. Moreover, the lesson of connectedness doesn't end there, for Justine also ponders the connections implied between her and the burglars. What is meaningless to her as a 'brutal, random eruption of violence' might be entirely predictable in terms of the burglars' lives, but their violent impingement on her life is an irrefutable point of connection: 'Perhaps everything in their lives had led them to that point, but then that was true of her too' (254). It is typical of Barker's fictional strategy that the perspectives of, and possible meanings of this event for, the burglars, are implied, as she practises the sense of interconnectedness which is foisted on Justine and Stephen by this 'random' act.

This takes us back, I believe, to Judith Butler's argument concerning the implications of 9/11 for thinking about the politics of vulnerability, for an important dimension to Butler's position is that violence reminds us of our physical interdependence with others. Butler argues that violence is 'a way a primary human vulnerability to other humans is exposed in its most terrifying way, a way in which we are given over, without control, to the will of another, a way in which life itself can be expunged by the wilful action of another'.[14] Ben and Stephen have testified to that primary human vulnerability in their work representing the terrors of war, of course, but finally Stephen must recognise that vulnerability, and the consequent sense of interdependence, in the place he associates most with safety and isolation. So, too, Justine knows that 'she might feel happy again, but she would never again feel safe' (254). For both Stephen and Justine, then, and for others in the novel too, such as Kate when she crashes her car on icy roads, violence figures that 'vulnerability to a sudden address from elsewhere that we cannot preempt'.[15] It is a reminder of the illusion of individual auton-omy, of the notion of a retreat to the safety of monadism, for what it compels them to understand again is the physical, emotional and moral connectedness of human beings to each other, even when they are most fundamentally unaware of each other's existence. In Stephen's case, the shattered illusion of individualism leads him to reconsider his emotional ties, and to understand his relationship with Justine not as one of mutual self-fulfilment, but as one of love.

Double Vision concludes with the qualified happy ending of Stephen and Justine's finding their love for each other, but it does not represent the full force of the novel's treatment of the theme of vul-nerability and interconnectedness. It is Barker's most far-reaching novel geographically to date, for, although it is set primarily in an apparently more reclusive setting than previous novels, it takes in the disparate and notorious locations of recent world history at one broad sweep: Baghdad, Afghanistan, New York, Sarajevo and The Hague (for the Milosevic trial). The achievement of the novel, as it was the achievement of the *Regeneration* trilogy to imply connections between the 'home front' and the frontline, is to trace a spectrum between the random eruptions of violence in a rural setting in Northeast England and the more predictable campaigns of war and terror in some of the badlands of contemporary world history. Through the photographs and artworks represented in the novel, not least Kate's sculpture of Christ, Barker suggests the connections not just between these very different locations geographically, but also through time. Ben's pho-tographs of an unpeopled border country, for example, are neither apocalyptic nor despairing, as it turns out, but instead signal a sense of interconnected times and places:

> Stephen found himself driving through a landscape that reminded him of Ben's photographs. Border country. That's why Ben had loved it and photographed it so obsessively, Stephen thought, because he came back from whatever war he'd been covering to a place where every blade of grass had been fought over, time and time again, for centuries, and now the shouts and cries, the clash of swords on shields had faded into silence, leaving only sunlight heaving on acres of grass, and a curlew crying. He thought now that he understood Ben's ties to this place; he was beginning to fall in love with it himself. On impulse he reached out and squeezed Justine's hand. (282)

For Ben, Stephen believes, the unpeopled landscapes he photographs were neither retreats from the global wars he covered, nor, as Kate comes to think, the continuation of a bleak obsession with murder and war. Instead, Ben exemplifies a form of rootedness, of belonging, which is at the same time fully conscious of the relationality of time and place, of a sense of connection with other times and other places. The peaceful vision Ben photographs in this landscape, then, is not a solipsistic flight from history, but is deeply alert to the terrors of history and, like Goya, is all the more hopeful because of it.

According to Butler, to think in these terms of our relationality rather than our separateness is to begin to redefine the meanings and forms of community:

> This way of imagining community affirms relationality not only as a descriptive or historical fact of our formation, but also as an ongoing normative dimension of our social and political lives, one in which we are compelled to take stock of our interdependence. According to this latter view, it would become incumbent on us to consider the place of violence in any such relation, for violence is, always, an exploitation of that primary tie, that primary way in which we are, as bodies, outside ourselves and for another.[16]

The challenge of such a view for Butler is particularly acute in the aftermath of 9/11, and necessitates a consideration of the geopolitical distribution of violence. Pat Barker's novel explores the same challenge, of how to cope with the terror of human vulnerability, while retaining the notion of ourselves as interdependent on others, and intimately connected with others, even those who we believe wish to harm us. The happy ending of Stephen and Justine's relationship represents not a resolution to this challenge, but a determination that love too has its place in this newly exposed world of vulnerability, and that love signifies the admission of the other into our lives in such a way as to transform us. The happiness is qualified: Stephen momentarily thinks of the woman in Sarajevo when he lies together with Justine after they have declared their love for each other, and he knows that love has not banished terror absolutely (302). He and Justine will live with the fact of vulnerability, even if they can suspend that knowledge through love. *Double Vision* continues Barker's concern with the micro-narratives of human history and society, with the impact of the global on the local, and with the possibilities of hope and redemption in a world mourning the loss of security and stability. In this respect, *Union Street* and *Double Vision* explore the same social and political dynamics, and the same fragility of human presence in the world, even if *Double Vision* has moved into more explicitly global dimensions. The ideal of human community is shown to be barely imaginable, and only achievable in the most local and provisional ways. But *Double Vision* works hard to maintain the possibility that, through love and art, we can continue to be creative beings, and continue to bear witness to hope in this post-romantic, secular world.

Notes

1 See Barker's comment on *Union Street*, for example, as 'a vat with smooth curving sides. Once you are in the vat, you are in working-class life, and there is no relief', quoted in Sharon Monteith, *Pat Barker* (Tavistock, Northcote House, 2002), 15.

2 Barker, *Union Street*, 260.

3 Alan Sinfield, *Literature, Politics and Culture in Postwar Britain* (London, Athlone, 1997), 272.

4 Barker suggests in an interview with Robert McCrum that the figures of the therapist and the medium in her work stand in for the role of the novelist, in some ways. See Robert McCrum, 'It's a disaster for a novel to be topical', *Observer*, 1 April 2001.

5 Monteith, *Pat Barker*, 96.

6 Hélène Deutsch, 'Some Forms of Emotional Disturbance and their Relation to Schizophrenia', *Psychoanalytic Quarterly*, 11 (1942), 302.

7 Barker continues to explore here the influence of the father figure, in this novel as a dominating figure who overshadows the influence of the mother. In previous novels, particularly *The Man Who Wasn't There*, it is the absence of a father figure that preoccupies Barker.

8 Jean Baudrillard, *The Spirit of Terrorism*, trans. Chris Turner (London, Verso, 2002), 33.

9 President George W. Bush addressed Congress on 21 September 2001. His address can be found at the following source: 'A Nation Challenged: President Bush's Address on Terrorism before a Joint Meeting of Congress', *New York Times*, 21 September 2001, B.4.

10 Judith Butler, *Precarious Life: The Powers of Mourning and Violence* (London, Verso, 2004), 29–30.

11 Sharon Monteith and Nahem Yousaf make an illuminating comparison between *Double Vision* and Virginia Woolf's *To the Lighthouse* in '*Double Vision*: Regenerative or Traumatized Pastoral?', *Critical Perspectives on Pat Barker*, ed. Sharon Monteith, Margaretta Jolly, Nahem Yousaf and Ronald

Paul (Columbia, University of South Carolina Press, 2005), 283–99. My thanks to Sharon Monteith and Nahem Yousaf for allowing me to read a draft version of this chapter.

12 Monteith and Yousaf trace a compelling continuity between the 'soldier-poet' of *Regeneration* and the war correspondent in *Double Vision*. See '*Double Vision*: Regenerative or Traumatized Pastoral?', 285–7.

13 The parallels between *Border Crossing* and *Double Vision* lead Joyce Carol Oates in her review of the latter novel for the *New York Review of Books* to describe the two novels as 'paired', and 'mirror' novels of each other. See Joyce Carol Oates, 'The Mythmaking Realist', *The New York Review of Books*, 1, 20 (18 December 2003).

14 Butler, *Precarious Life*, 28–9.

15 Ibid., 29.

16 Ibid., 27.

9

Critical overview and conclusion

This book has examined the literary career to date of Pat Barker, one of the most important writers in England today. Recent interviews have testified to the fact that she continues to research and plan new work, which means that any conclusions advanced by this study are necessarily tentative and premature. Indeed, one might ask why publish such a study at all while the subject is very much alive, active, and will in all likelihood write a few more novels, which may even alter the way I and other critics see her entire oeuvre? Criticism, however, is inevitably an engagement with the contemporary moment. It derives from the same Greek root for crisis, and must examine what demands our attention in the present. This book has been commissioned and written to reflect the need for a major critical survey of Barker's achievements and standing now. It represents the view that Barker has already become a key figure in contemporary English literature, and if we want to understand what is happening now in literary and cultural representations of England, then we need to include Barker's work as part of that understanding. For over twenty years, Barker has produced novels which have engaged in challenging and critical ways with some of the most momentous changes in modern English history and society. This book has attempted to meet the task of responding to and assessing Barker's achievements from the perspectives of literary and cultural criticism. In this concluding chapter, I want to reflect on the current critical reputation of Pat Barker's novels, and to situate her work in relation to contemporary cultural and theoretical contexts.

Despite Barker's prominence in contemporary British fiction in the 1980s and especially the 1990s, no book-length study of her work appeared until Sharon Monteith published her study in the 'Writers and their Work' series in 2002. Monteith offers a comprehensive evaluation of Barker's career up to *Border Crossing*, and situates Barker within a materialist tradition of interrogative political fiction. She counters the misrepresentations of Barker's oeuvre as divided into realist, women-centred fictions followed by historical, men-centred fictions by arguing that *Regeneration* did not reflect a change in Barker's literary and political interests, but rather a change in cultural tastes: 'Barker published the novel at a point when commemorative and millennial concerns about the First World War were coming to the fore. The novel resonated for readers grappling with a subject disappearing with the last veterans'.[1] Monteith especially champions Barker as an iconoclastic novelist, whose courage in dealing with challenging ideas and events has made her popular with readers. As the first major study of Barker, Monteith's book illuminates the contexts within which Barker's work is best read, and makes clear that Barker's oeuvre is a story of developing, consistent themes, rather than abrupt shifts and departures.

At the time of writing, the only other book-length studies of Barker's work are Karin Westman's *Reader's Guide* to *Regeneration*,[2] which is an introductory study guide to the novel, and a collection of critical essays, *Critical Perspectives on Pat Barker*, edited by Sharon Monteith, Margaretta Jolly, Nahem Yousaf and Ronald Paul, published in spring 2005.[3] The latter includes chapters on all of Barker's novels by many critics, and includes a few previously published journal articles which can be hard to find in libraries, such as Ann Ardis's essay on *Blow Your House Down*. Beyond book-length studies, there have also been a few essays which have offered evaluative surveys of Barker's literary career. Sharon Monteith published one such survey in a short essay for *Moderna Språk* in 1997, which rehearses the argument of her book that Barker continues to develop in the *Regeneration* trilogy the themes of gender, sexuality and community she explored in her early novels.[4] Sharon Carson published a biographical and literary critical introduction to Barker in a volume on British writers, which locates Barker as a historical and political writer, but of an extraordinary kind, one who is interested in 'retrieving the unrecorded and in giving voice to persons silenced in the rush of passing events'.[5] Lastly, Margaretta Jolly compares the work of Barker with that of an ostensibly more postmodern writer, Penelope Lively, in an essay which seeks to address Barker's status as both a feminist and mainstream writer, and ultimately finds Barker's novels more profoundly interrogative of social identity, even if less challenging aesthetically, than Lively's fiction.[6] All of these studies testify to the fact that Barker has achieved a distinctive vision in modern literature, and has gained widespread popularity with readers and critics, although in the course of surveying her career they have all had to counter in some form mis-perceptions of Barker's oeuvre, particularly in accounting for an apparent change of direction in *Regeneration*.

The emergence of critical surveys of Barker's oeuvre, however, can be traced to 1997 and thereafter, which would suggest, as might be suspected, that the success of the *Regeneration* trilogy demanded that her work receive serious critical attention. It was with the Booker Prize award in 1995, in particular, that Barker's achievements gained more widespread recognition. For various reasons, the *Regeneration* trilogy drew more attention from readers and critics than her previous novels. This is evident in any survey of the critical essays and articles on Barker's novels. There are some essays on Barker's early novels, enough to recognise that Barker's impact on contemporary literature was assured prior to the *Regeneration* trilogy: Monica Malm's short article on *Union Street*, which examines how the novel represents women and mothering;[7] Ann Ardis's essay on *Blow Your House Down*, which traces the classroom experience of teaching a novel in relation to political concerns about class and gender;[8] and Jenny Newman's essay on *The Century's Daughter*, which makes the case for reading the novel as an example of postmodern historiographic fiction.[9] Lyn Pykett was the first to examine *The Century's Daughter*, in a wide-ranging essay which positions Barker's novel in relation to other British fiction concerned with the past, but Pykett argues that Barker shares with other women writers a different approach to representing the past than the postmodern deconstruction of the idea of history associated with male writers.[10] In addition, three essays examine the early novels as a coherent batch, which are considered in relation to gender and class issues particularly: Sue Anderson's essay studies these novels as social criticism fictions, which show how 'authoritarian and uncaring society produces damaged personalities';[11] Peter Hitchcock's Bakhtinian analysis of Barker's early fiction situates her work within working-class and feminist traditions, and celebrates it as 'radical writing';[12] and John Kirk's essay on the first three novels again positions Barker in relation to traditions of working-class writing, and finds that, while Barker explores 'productive and illuminating ways of representing working-class community', her third novel, *The*

Century's Daughter, is in danger of sentimentality or idealistic nostalgia.[13] The essays published on Barker's early work placed her within or adjacent to working-class and feminist traditions of political writing, although all of them identify ways in which Barker problematises, extends or exceeds the generic characteristics of those traditions. Equally evident in these essays, especially the latter three, is the sense that Barker's first three novels can be read in sequence in terms of her development of themes of class and gender, and her development of a political analysis within an expanded, reworked form of social realism.

The Man Who Wasn't There does not appear to fit so neatly into that line of development, and perhaps that is why no essay has yet been published on Barker's fourth novel (although two essays, by Sharon Monteith and Pat Wheeler respectively, are about to be published in *Critical Perspectives on Pat Barker*). It is the *Regeneration* trilogy, however, that marks Barker's arrival as a writer of significant critical interest. Not surprisingly, essays on the trilogy have focused principally on three themes: history, gender and psychology. Martin Löschnigg explores Barker's treatment of the past in the trilogy, and argues that she continues to mythologise the First World War in similar ways to war veterans themselves.[14] Anne Whitehead's essay on hypnosis and history in *Regeneration* argues that Barker focuses on the psychoanalytic treatment of trauma as a process which problematises the meaning of history, and our sense of connection with the past.[15] Catherine Lanone, on the other hand, reads Barker's *Regeneration* and *The Ghost Road* in terms of deeper mythologies of sacrifice, but within a feminist perspective on the reworking of sacrificial motifs in contemporary gender relations.[16] Both Greg Harris and Peter Hitchcock analyse Barker's representation of masculinity, in particular her exposure of contemporary ideologies of gender at work during, and prior to, the First World War.[17] As I've suggested in chapter six, on the trilogy, Hitchcock's essay in particular might be read as a counter-argument to Löschnigg's criticism, in the sense that Hitchcock argues that Barker is showing that the war was not the starting point for new understandings of gender identities, but rather played out and manipulated existing social and gender formations. Laurie Vickroy also makes the argument that Barker situates her trilogy at a transitional time, in which social conflicts about the war are intimately connected with conflicts about sexuality and gender.[18] Like Hitchcock, Vickroy also deploys a Bakhtinian analysis of Barker's work, employing in this instance the concept of the carnivalesque to illuminate the transgressive potential of Barker's fictions.

Vickroy's essay appears in a psychoanalytic journal, but an essay more firmly rooted in psychoanalytic concepts is Anne M. Wyatt-Brown's study of transference in the relationship between Rivers and Barker, arguing that whenever Barker diverges from historical and archival facts, 'the issue of father child relationships tends to emerge in that intermediate space'.[19] The psychoanalytic encounter is also the subject of Ankhi Mukherjee's essay on neurosis and narration in *Regeneration*, which finds the rupture of narrative in the psychoanalysis of trauma resonant of Homi Bhabha's arguments concerning the disruptive discourse of the nation.[20] In contrast, Kenneth Pellow's essay, 'Analogy in *Regeneration*', is less interested in theoretical resonances, and focuses instead on the structural patterns of analogy and dialogue in Barker's novel.[21] The range of concerns addressed in these essays is evidence, I believe, that Barker's work has earned widespread critical attention. Critics are now debating the significance of Barker in terms of her representation of history, psychoanalytic ideas, war, violence, gender, identity and myth, and are interested in analysing her novels from formal, theoretical, historiographic, political and biographical perspectives. In addition to the books and essays discussed above, every novel Barker has published from *Regeneration* onwards has been widely reviewed, and she has been the subject of a number of lengthy newpaper and magazine profiles and interviews, some of which are listed in the Bibliography. These are further testimony to Barker's current status as an author who commands a wide readership and popular critical acclaim.

There remain, however, many significant gaps in the critical response to Barker's work. The novels published since the *Regeneration* trilogy have not yet prompted critical essays, although this is perhaps just a matter of time. More seriously, discussion of Barker's influences is tentative, perhaps because of the difficulty in locating her work in relation to existing traditions. Michael Ross's essay on D.H. Lawrence as intertext in Barker's novels is an exception, but it is also only a beginning.[22] Other critics such as Sue Anderson, Margaretta Jolly and Lyn Pykett have cited other writers as possible analogies or points of comparison with Barker's work, and the names of Alice Walker, Virginia Woolf and Toni Morrison are cited with some regularity as possible intertextual sources, but a study of Barker's influences has yet to be undertaken. There has also been little work done on Barker's representation of questions and problems of national identity, beyond Ankhi Mukherjee's suggestive reading of *Regeneration*. Is she a 'national' writer in any meaningful sense? Likewise, critical discussions of her work have not yet studied in detail the relationship between Barker and her contemporaries in the English novel. To what extent might she share common ground with Peter Ackroyd, Graham Swift, Michèle Roberts, Caryl Phillips or Jim Crace? Are there sustainable comparisons to be made with British writers who have achieved international standing, such as Salman Rushdie, Kazuo Ishiguro, Martin Amis or Angela Carter? I have only managed to suggest in the chapters above some of the contemporaries with whom she might fruitfully be compared, but essay-length studies of these comparisons may well help to position her work more precisely.

I have argued consistently, as Sharon Monteith argued already in her book,[23] that Barker has continued to write novels grounded in feminist perspectives throughout her career, despite what Margaretta Jolly observes as her shift 'to male protagonists, a favouring of the masculinised spheres of pub, battlefield, hospital or government, and a leaning towards the epic rather than domestic scale'.[24] Jolly repeats the observations of a number of reviewers that the apparent reorientations of Barker's fiction towards masculine identities and relations 'have distanced her from her feminist profile'. Indeed, one sceptical (and reductive) way of regarding her career from a feminist perspective is that Barker remained a lesser-known contemporary writer until she began to write novels with male central characters. Her earlier women-centred novels are published by a press devoted to celebrating feminist fiction, or women's writing more broadly, while the mark of her canonisation as a major figure in contemporary fiction is that she moved on to mainstream (that is, male) subjects of war, history, and masculinity. It should be clear from the chapters above that this version of her career ignores several key aspects of Barker's work. It ignores the fact that Barker has always focused on questions of gender from feminist perspectives, no matter what the gender of her central characters – one need only think of Bernard's cross-dressing in *The Man Who Wasn't There*, or Rivers's role as a 'male mother' in *Regeneration*, to recognise that Barker's exploration of gender issues in her 'male' novels is continuous with her analysis of femininity in *Union Street* or *Blow Your House Down*. This is an argument which Sharon

Monteith has already made in her book, and upon which I've expanded here. It also ignores the problem of what constitutes a central character in Barker's fiction. How does one typify a novel like *Double Vision* in which Kate begins as the central character but the narrative attention shifts gradually towards Stephen? Or *Union Street*, in which the men for the most part are shadowy, background presences (or absences) and yet remain central to how the novel functions? Or the *Regeneration* trilogy, in which characters like Sarah, her mother and Beattie are arguably as vibrant and rounded as Sassoon or Owen, or perhaps more so?[25] Barker's narrative method of switching from one character's perspective to another's, and of avoiding a controlling central narrative consciousness, is a way of emphasising intersubjective, sometimes collective, viewpoints, and this makes it difficult to individuate central characters as such.

More importantly, however, the sceptical reading of Barker's career as a move away from her earlier feminist profile leaves the nature of Barker's feminism unexamined. What do we mean by feminism, after all? Certainly, one way of defining feminist fiction, emerging from the emphasis on subjectivity in Second Wave feminist theory, is that it should privilege female experience, a woman-centred view. This raises a problem, however, in determining the relationship between women-centred texts and feminism, particularly given the multifarious nature of feminism as a series of political and cultural positions, movements, perspectives and ideologies. Barker's scrupulous attention to the interrelations between class and gender identity places her squarely within a materialist feminism. Her prioritisation of female experience, combined with her radical critique of capitalism, reification and modernity, in her first three novels, clearly finds her also beyond the pragmatic, rights-oriented interests of liberal feminism. Barker's work is much more closely aligned with radical feminist engagements with Marxism and psychoanalysis of the 1970s and 1980s, which sought to challenge the precepts of industrial technocratic society, to reinterrogate the psychological dimensions of gender relations, and to imagine alternative visions of community and social identity.

What is clear from reading Barker's oeuvre is that her radical feminism does not end or dissipate with *The Man Who Wasn't There*. In fact, the extension of her focus to issues of masculine identity and male society is a necessary development of her feminism. Barker's engagement with feminist ideas and principles through her fiction

can be seen in the context of an expanding agenda among radical fem-
inists, the formation of a feminist public sphere, as depicted in Rita
Felski's *Beyond Feminist Aesthetics*:

> This gradual expansion of feminist values from their roots in the
> women's movement throughout society as a whole is a necessary corol-
> lary of feminism's claim to embody a catalyst of social and cultural
> change. While feminist discourse originates from women's experiences
> of oppression and recognizes their ultimate authority in speaking of its
> effects, feminism as a critique of values is also engaged in a more gen-
> eral and public process of revising or refuting male-defined cultural and
> discursive frameworks. The feminist public sphere, in other words,
> serves a dual function: *internally*, it generates a gender-specific identity
> grounded in a consciousness of community and solidarity among
> women; *externally*, it seeks to convince society as a whole of the validity
> of feminist claims, challenging existing structures of authority through
> political activity and theoretical critique.[26]

In the early novels, Barker's exploration of women's experiences of
sexuality, childbirth, community and low-paid work, within class-
bound and regionally inflected contexts, established her as a feminist
author, but the expansion of her oeuvre into the male-dominated
genres of war and historical fiction, into the focus on public trauma
and memory, and into the critique of contemporary discourses of violence and terror in her most recent novels, has represented a continuation and dissemination of the feminist values at the core of her art.
Moreover, her attentiveness to the limitations of any idealistic, uni-
versal, notions of gendered community, specifically in relation to
social inequalities, and her interrogation of gendered assumptions
(about war, society, work, and so on) means that Barker has always
practised a critical feminism in her work.

Barker's move from Virago to Penguin has never fully been
explained, but one way of understanding it might be as a reaction
against the emergence of 'women's writing' in the 1980s as a mar-
ketable commodity. Virago specialised in women's writing at the
same time as bookstores began to shelve books under this category,
and publishers issued catalogues with special sections devoted to the
same.[27] It marked an ambivalent moment in the cultural reception of
feminist ideas. On the one hand, the recognition of a distinctive
sphere of women's writing was an acknowledgement of feminist
claims for cultural validity, and offered women readers an engagement with a gendered community. On the other hand, it risked the

ghettoisation of women's writing, the separate categorisation of which could safely insulate the 'mainstream' against having to deal with feminist claims for equality, or more radical claims for theoretical critique and political transformation of gendered social structures. Barker's change of publisher, whatever the pragmatic motivations, also signals an intention to engage with the mainstream, and her representation of some of the most public and national debates of the 1990s, about war and memory, about social divisions and gender politics, brought her radical feminist critique to mainstream readers.

The same explanation might be a starting point for understanding Barker's commitment, at least in broad terms, to the generic conventions of realist fiction. In the preceding chapters, I have devoted considerable attention to explaining the narrative art of Barker's work, and it will be obvious, I hope, that she does not fit comfortably into any one tradition or genre of writing. Realism comes closest to describing the general tendencies of her fiction, but her brand of realism is one which questions and disturbs the nature of the real, leaves holes and silences where realism promises presence and speech, and integrates modernist symbolism, dialogic structures, and shifts in narrative perspective with the omniscient pretence of the 'classic' realist form. In all of her novels, there are scenes which could easily be described as social realism, representing quotidian experiences in almost documentary detail, but they are always interspersed or perforated with tropes of the extraordinary, supernatural or spectral, which trouble the comfortable readerly experience of verisimilitudinous realism.

Some of the formal and thematic elements of Barker's fictions might, at a stretch, be categorised as postmodern. If postmodern fictions are playful and experimental, and conflate high and low cultural forms, then we might think of how Barker has consistently played with Gothic and detective fictional forms in her work. If postmodernism entails scepticism towards the lofty meta-narratives implied by Victorian realism or European modernism, then Barker's revisionist approach to social and historical myths might be understood as postmodern. If postmodern novels function principally through pastiche, and by conflating the real and the fictive, then we might consider her extensive use of archival and historical material in the *Regeneration* trilogy, for example, as an instance of postmodern historiographic fiction. But Roland Barthes's distinction between the 'readerly' and the 'writerly' text is worth bringing into play here.[28]

Postmodern fiction has conventionally been understood as 'writerly', as problematising meaning, exploding the categories of representation, and disturbing readers' expectations. It questions its own capacity to represent anything beyond the process of signification itself. But clearly Barker's novels do claim to represent the real, or at least to fictionalise aspects of historical and contemporary experience. They do claim to engage the reader in questioning history as well as historicity, real events as well as the nature of reality, and the way gender functions in society as well as the processes by which gender is signified. It is clear that Barker's texts are denotative as well as aesthetic forms, and do invite the reader to understand social processes and historical events through fictional frames.

Barker's fictional strategy, then, is one which embraces the commitment to representing social, political and historical situations, while acknowledging the problematics of representation. It is, I would suggest, a critical realism, a realism which follows in the wake of postmodernism, and has learned from the postmodern critique of nineteenth-century realist forms, as well as from the negative aesthetics of postmodern reflexivity. It is, moreover, a strategy which earns Barker broad appeal, and which enables her to construct and tell complex stories, from radical feminist and Marxist perspectives, largely for a mainstream readership. Barker's novels are 'readerly' texts in the sense that they are accessible, sometimes seductively transparent, and frequently open up a knowable world for readers. They often indicate the limits of narrative knowledge, as well as enabling access, however. They are sometimes also aesthetically self-conscious, although never in ways which render them incapable of connecting with everyday social practices and cultural meanings. Understandably, Peter Hitchcock and later Margaretta Jolly have described Barker's fictional method in Bakhtinian terms as dialogic in an attempt to account for this combination of readerly and writerly aspects or, more significantly, this combination of mainstream and radical aesthetics.[29] From my analysis in the preceding chapters, I would argue that we might consider Barker's work within the terms of critical realism, which embraces the social orientation of realism with the aesthetic and epistemological doubts of postmodernism.

However we situate Barker's work in relation to theoretical debates, aesthetic labels, and the field of contemporary British fiction generally, what can hardly be doubted is the profound engagement in all of her novels with modern British history and society. Barker grew up in a country which is essentially post-imperial, in which the major political issues have seemed to be about the management of economic and cultural decline, and which is riven by social inequalities. It is clear from the alienation Kelly feels in a middle-class environment in *Union Street*, or from the difference social class makes to how the trenches are perceived in the *Regeneration* trilogy, to the debunking of pastoral myths in *Double Vision*, that there is no unifying experience or vision to be had living in Britain. Even the two world wars, often represented officially as emblematic of national unity, around which the nation gathers in union to mourn, are sources of trauma, disunity and pitiful myths in Barker's novels. Yet, as I've emphasised already in this study, although Barker's critique of the ills and divisions of modern Britain is persistent and forceful, it is always tinged with the possibility of change, of redemption. It is the consistency of Barker's vision and the constructiveness of her most devastating fictional explorations of the social problems and divisions engendered in modern Britain which have earned her work the respect and popularity it now enjoys. The implications of her fiction go beyond the specific social and political dynamics of Britain, of course, as the discussion of her critiques of modernity, capitalism and gender relations in the chapters above have shown. It is for her critical fictions of life in modern Britain, however, that Pat Barker's reputation as a novelist of international standing continues to grow.

Notes

1 Sharon Monteith, *Pat Barker* (Tavistock, Northcote House, 2002), 4.
2 Karin Westman, *Pat Barker's* Regeneration: *A Reader's Guide* (New York, Continuum, 2001).
3 Sharon Monteith, Margaretta Jolly, Nahem Yousaf and Ronald Paul (eds), *Critical Perspectives on Pat Barker* (Columbia, University of South Carolina Press, 2005).
4 Sharon Monteith, 'Warring Fictions: Reading Pat Barker', *Moderna Språk*, 91:2 (1997), 124–9.
5 Sharon Carson, 'Pat Barker', *British Writers: Supplement IV*, ed. George Stade and Carol Howard (New York, Simon and Schuster and Prentice Hall, 1997), 45.
6 Margaretta Jolly, 'After Feminism: Pat Barker, Penelope Lively and the Contemporary Novel', *British Culture of the Postwar: An Introduction to Literature and Society, 1945–1999*, ed. Alistair Davies and Alan Sinfield (London, Routledge, 2000), 58–82.

7 Monica Malm, '*Union Street*: Thoughts on Mothering', *Moderna Språk*, 92:2 (1998), 143–6.

8 Ann Ardis, 'Political Attentiveness vs Political Correctness: Teaching Pat Barker's *Blow Your House Down*', *College Literature*, 18:3 (1991), 44–54.

9 Jenny Newman, 'Souls and Arseholes: The Double Vision of *The Century's Daughter*', *Critical Survey*, 13:1 (2001), 18–36.

10 Lyn Pykett, 'The Century's Daughters: Recent Women's Fiction and History', *Critical Quarterly*, 29:3 (1987), 71–7.

11 Sue Anderson, 'Life on the Street: Pat Barker's Realist Fictions', *It's My Party: Reading Twentieth-Century Women's Writing*, ed. Gina Wisker (London, Pluto Press, 1994), 181–92.

12 Peter Hitchcock, 'Radical Writing', *Feminism, Bakhtin, and the Dialogic*, ed. Dale M. Bauer and S. Jaret McKinstry (New York, SUNY, 1991), 95–121. Also in *Dialogics of the Oppressed* (Minneapolis, University of Minnesota Press, 1993).

13 John Kirk, 'Recovered Perspectives: Gender, Class and Memory in Pat Barker's Writing', *Contemporary Literature*, 40:4 (1999), 603–26.

14 Martin Löschnigg, '". . . the novelist's responsibility to the past": History, Myth, and the Narratives of Crisis in Pat Barker's *Regeneration* Trilogy' (1991–1995), *Zeitschrift für Anglistik und Amerikanistik*, 47:3 (1999), 214–28.

15 Anne Whitehead, 'Open to Suggestion: Hypnosis and History in Pat Barker's *Regeneration*', *Modern Fiction Studies*, 44:3 (1998), 674–94.

16 Catherine Lanone, 'Scattering the Seed of Abraham: The Motif of Sacrifice in Pat Barker's *Regeneration* and *The Ghost Road*', *Literature and Theology*, 13:3 (1999), 259–68.

17 See Greg Harris, 'Compulsory Masculinity, Britain, and the Great War: The Literary-Historical Work of Pat Barker', *Critique: Studies in Contemporary Fiction*, 39:4 (1998), 290–304, and Peter Hitchcock, 'What is Prior? Working-Class Masculinity in Pat Barker's Trilogy', *Genders*, 35 (2002): www.genders.org/g35/g35_hitchcock.txt.

18 Laurie Vickroy, 'Can the Tide be Shifted? Transgressive Sexuality and War Trauma in Pat Barker's *Regeneration* Trilogy', *Journal of Evolutionary Psychology*, 23:2–3 (2002), 97–104.

19 Anne M. Wyatt-Brown, 'Headhunters and Victims of War: W.H.R. Rivers and Pat Barker', *Literature and Psychoanalysis: Proceedings of the 13th International Conference on Literature and Psychoanalysis (Boston, July 1996)*, ed. Frederico Pereira (Lisbon, Instituto Superior de Psicologia Aplicada, 1997), 53–9.

20 Ankhi Mukherjee, 'Stammering to Story: Neurosis and Narration in Pat Barker's *Regeneration*', *Critique*, 43:1 (2001), 49–62.

21 C. Kenneth Pellow, 'Analogy in *Regeneration*', *War, Literature and the Arts*, 13:1–2 (2001), 130–46.

22 Michael Ross, 'Acts of Revision: Lawrence as Intertext in the Novels of Pat Barker', *D.H. Lawrence Review*, 26:1–3 (1995), 51–63.

23 Monteith, *Pat Barker*, 1–10.

24 Jolly, 'After Feminism', 59.

25 Karin Westman discusses the women in *Regeneration* in *Pat Barker's* Regeneration, 43–9.

26 Rita Felski, *Beyond Feminist Aesthetics: Feminist Literature and Social Change* (London, Hutchinson Radius, 1989), 167–8.

27 Barker talks about this switch of publishers and the marketing labels applied to her work in interview with Sharon Monteith, in Monteith's 'Pat Barker', *Contemporary British and Irish Fiction: An Introduction through Interviews*, eds Sharon Monteith, Jenny Newman and Pat Wheeler (London, Arnold, 2004), 32.

28 Roland Barthes, *S/Z*, trans. Richard Miller (London, Jonathan Cape, 1975).

29 See Hitchcock, 'Radical Writing', and Jolly, 'After Feminism'.

Select bibliography

Novels by Pat Barker

Union Street (London, Virago, 1982)
Blow Your House Down (London, Virago, 1984)
The Century's Daughter (London, Virago, 1986) Reissued as *Liza's England* (1996)
The Man Who Wasn't There (London, Virago/Penguin, 1989)
Regeneration (London, Viking/Penguin, 1991)
The Eye in the Door (London, Viking/Penguin, 1993)
The Ghost Road (London, Viking/Penguin, 1995)
Another World (London, Viking/Penguin, 1998)
Border Crossing (London, Viking/Penguin, 2001)
Double Vision (London, Hamish Hamilton/Penguin, 2003)

Selected interviews and profiles

Anonymous, 'Pat Barker', *Contemporary Authors*, 122 (New York, Gale, 1987), 40.

Carson, Sharon, 'Pat Barker', *British Writers: Supplement IV*, ed. George Stade and Carol Howard (New York, Simon and Schuster/Prentice Hall, 1997), 45–63.

McCrum, Robert, 'It's a disaster for a novel to be topical', *Observer*, 1 April 2001.

Monteith, Sharon, 'Pat Barker', *Contemporary British and Irish Fiction: An Introduction through Interviews*, eds Sharon Monteith, Jenny Newman and Pat Wheeler (London, Arnold, 2004), 19–35.

——, 'Warring Fictions: Reading Pat Barker', *Moderna Språk*, 91:2 (1997), 124–9.

Morrison, Blake, 'War Stories', *New Yorker*, 22 January 1996, 78–82.

Perry, Donna, 'Pat Barker', *Backtalk: Women Writers Speak Out* (New

Brunswick, Rutgers University Press, 1993), 43–61.

——, 'Going Home Again: An Interview with Pat Barker', *The Literary Review*, 34:2 (1991), 235–44.

Piette, Adam, 'Pat Barker', *Post-War Literature in English: A Lexicon of Contemporary Authors*, Supplement No. 45 (September 1999), 1–24.

Sammon, Geoff, 'Pat Barker: A Modern British Woman Writer', *Neusprachliche-Mitteilungen Aus Wissenschaft und Praxis*, 49:1 (1996), 42–4.

Sinker, Mark, 'Temporary Gentlemen and Pat Barker on the Film Adaptation of her Novel *Regeneration*', *Sight and Sound*, 12 (1997), 22–4.

Barker criticism

Books

Monteith, Sharon, *Pat Barker* (Tavistock, Northcote House, 2002).

——, Margaretta Jolly, Nahem Yousaf and Ronald Paul (eds), *Critical Perspectives on Pat Barker* (Columbia, University of South Carolina Press, 2005).

Westman, Karin, *Pat Barker's* Regeneration: *A Reader's Guide* (New York, Continuum, 2001).

Articles

Anderson, Sue, 'Life on the Street: Pat Barker's Realist Fictions', *It's My Party: Reading Twentieth-Century Women's Writing*, ed. Gina Wisker (London, Pluto Press, 1994), 181–92.

Ardis, Ann, 'Political Attentiveness vs Political Correctness: Teaching Pat Barker's *Blow Your House Down*', *College Literature*, 18:3 (1991), 44–54.

Brannigan, John, 'Pat Barker's *Regeneration* Trilogy: History and the Hauntological Imagination', *Contemporary British Fiction*, ed. Richard J. Lane, Rod Mengham and Philip Tew (Cambridge, Polity Press, 2002), 13–26.

Childs, Peter, *Contemporary Novelists: British Fiction since 1970* (Basingstoke, Palgrave, 2005), 58–79.

Dodd, Kathryn and Philip Dodd, 'From the East End to *Eastenders*: Representations of the Working Class, 1890–1980', *Come on Down? Popular Media Culture in Post-War Britain*, ed. Dominic Strinati and Stephen Wragg (London, Routledge, 1992), 116–32.

Harris, Greg, 'Compulsory Masculinity, Britain, and the Great War: The Literary-Historical Work of Pat Barker', *Critique: Studies in Contemporary Fiction* 39:4 (1998), 290–304.

Hitchcock, Peter, 'What is Prior? Working-Class Masculinity in Pat Barker's Trilogy', *Genders* 35 (2002): http://genders.org/g35/g35_hitchcock.txt

——, 'Radical Writing', *Feminism, Bakhtin, and the Dialogic*, ed. Dale M. Bauer and S. Jaret McKinstry (New York, SUNY, 1991), 95–121.

Joannou, Maroula, 'Pat Barker and the Languages of Region and Class',

Essays and Studies 2004: Contemporary British Women Writers, ed. Emma Parker (Cambridge and Leicester, D.S. Brewer and the English Association, 2004), 41–54.

Jolly, Margaretta, 'After Feminism: Pat Barker, Penelope Lively and the Contemporary Novel', *British Culture of the Postwar: An Introduction to Literature and Society, 1945–1999*, ed. Alistair Davies and Alan Sinfield (London, Routledge, 2000), 58–82.

Kirk, John, 'Recovered Perspectives: Gender, Class and Memory in Pat Barker's Writing', *Contemporary Literature*, 40:4 (1999), 603–26.

Lanone, Catherine, 'Scattering the Seed of Abraham: The Motif of Sacrifice in Pat Barker's *Regeneration* and *The Ghost Road*', *Literature and Theology*, 13:3 (1999), 259–68.

Löschnigg, Martin, '". . . the novelist's responsibility to the past": History, Myth, and the Narratives of Crisis in Pat Barker's *Regeneration* Trilogy (1991–1995)', *Zeitschrift fur Anglistik und Amerikanistik*, 47:3 (1999), 214–28.

Malm, Monica, '*Union Street*: Thoughts on Mothering', *Moderna Språk*, 92:2 (1998), 143–6.

Martin, Sara, 'Regenerating the War Movie? Pat Barker's *Regeneration* according to Gillies Mackinnon', *Literature/Film Quarterly*, 30:2 (2002), 98–103.

Mukherjee, Ankhi, 'Stammering to Story: Neurosis and Narration in Pat Barker's *Regeneration*', *Critique*, 43:1 (2001), 49–62.

Newman, Jenny, 'Souls and Arseholes: The Double Vision of *The Century's Daughter*', *Critical Survey*, 13:1 (2001), 18–36.

Pellow, C. Kenneth, 'Analogy in *Regeneration*', *War, Literature and the Arts*, 13:1–2 (2001), 130–46.

Pykett, Lyn, 'The Century's Daughters: Recent Women's Fiction and History', *Critical Quarterly*, 29:3 (1987), 71–7.

Ross, Michael, 'Acts of Revision: Lawrence as Intertext in the Novels of Pat Barker', *D.H. Lawrence Review*, 26:1–3 (1995), 51–63.

Vickroy, Laurie, 'Can the Tide be Shifted? Transgressive Sexuality and War Trauma in Pat Barker's *Regeneration* Trilogy', *Journal of Evolutionary Psychology*, 23:2–3 (2002), 97–104.

Whitehead, Anne, 'Open to Suggestion: Hypnosis and History in Pat Barker's *Regeneration*', *Modern Fiction Studies*, 44:3 (1998), 674–94.

Wotton, George, 'Writing from the Margins', *Peripheral Visions: Images of Nationhood in Contemporary British Fiction*, ed. Ian A. Bell (Cardiff, University of Wales Press, 1995), 194–215.

Wyatt-Brown, Anne M., 'Headhunters and Victims of War: W.H.R. Rivers and Pat Barker', *Literature and Psychoanalysis: Proceedings of the 13th International Conference on Literature and Psychoanalysis (Boston, July 1996)*, ed. Frederico Pereira (Lisbon, Instituto Superior de Psicologia Aplicada, 1997), 53–9.

General bibliography

Adorno, Theodor, et al., *Aesthetics and Politics* (London, Verso, 1980).

——, *Minima Moralia: Reflections from Damaged Life*, trans. E.F.N. Jephcott (London, Verso, 1978).

Alexander, Flora, *Contemporary Women Novelists* (London, Edward Arnold, 1989).

Anderson, Linda, *Plotting Change: Contemporary Women's Fiction* (London, Edward Arnold, 1990).

Armstrong, Isobel, 'Woolf by the Lake, Woolf at the Circus: Carter and Tradition', *Flesh and the Mirror: Essays on the Art of Angela Carter*, ed. Lorna Sage (London, Virago, 1994), 257–78.

Bainbridge, Beryl, *English Journey, or The Road to Milton Keynes* (London, Flamingo, 1984).

Bakhtin, M.M., *The Dialogic Imagination*, trans. Caryl Emerson and Michael Holquist (Austin, University of Texas Press, 1981).

Barthes, Roland, *S/Z*, trans. Richard Miller (London, Jonathan Cape, 1975).

Baudrillard, Jean, *The Spirit of Terrorism*, trans. Chris Turner (London, Verso, 2002).

Bauman, Zygmunt, *Liquid Modernity* (Cambridge, Polity, 2000).

Bell, Ian (ed.), *Peripheral Visions: Images of Nationhood in Contemporary British Fiction*. (Cardiff, University of Wales Press, 1995).

Belsey, Catherine, *Critical Practice* (London, Methuen, 1980).

Benjamin, Walter, *Illuminations*, trans. Harry Zohn (London, Fontana, 1973).

——, *Charles Baudelaire*, trans. Harry Zohn (London, Verso, 1997).

Bentham, Jeremy, *The Panopticon Writings*, ed. Miran Božovič (London, Verso, 1995).

Berman, Marshall, *All That is Solid Melts into Air: The Experience of Modernity* (London, Verso, 1983).

Bradbury, Malcolm, *The Modern British Novel* (London, Penguin, 1994).

Butler, Judith, *Precarious Life: The Powers of Mourning and Violence* (London, Verso, 2004).

Carr, David, *Time, Narrative, and History* (Indianapolis, Indiana University Press, 1991).

Chambers, Ross, *Story and Situation: Narrative Seduction and the Power of Fiction* (Manchester, Manchester University Press, 1984).

Connor, Steven, *The English Novel in History, 1950–1995* (London, Routledge, 1996).

Cranny-Francis, Anne, *Feminist Fiction: Feminist Uses of Generic Fiction* (Cambridge, Polity Press, 1990).

de Certeau, Michel, *The Practice of Everyday Life*, trans. S. Rendall (Berkeley, University of California Press, 1988).

——, *Heterologies: Discourse on the Other*, trans. Brian Massumi (Manchester, Manchester University Press, 1986).

de Man, Paul, 'Autobiography as De-Facement', *Modern Language Notes*, 94:5 (Dec 1979), 919–30.

Derrida, Jacques, *The Gift of Death*, trans. David Wills (Chicago, University of Chicago Press, 1995).

——, 'Freud and the Scene of Writing', *Writing and Difference*, trans. Alan Bass (London, Routledge, 1978).

Deutsch, Hélène, 'Some Forms of Emotional Disturbance and their Relation to Schizophrenia', *Psychoanalytic Quarterly*, 11 (1942), 301–21.

Duncker, Patricia, *Sisters and Strangers: An Introduction to Contemporary Feminist Fiction* (Oxford, Blackwell, 1992).

Eakin, Paul John, *Fictions in Autobiography: Studies in the Art of Self-Invention* (Princeton, Princeton University Press, 1985).

Felman, Shoshana and Dori Laub, *Testimony: Crises of Witnessing in Literature, Psychoanalysis, and History* (London, Routledge, 1992).

Felski, Rita, *Beyond Feminist Aesthetics* (London, Hutchinson Radius, 1989).

Foucault, Michel, *Discipline and Punish: The Birth of the Prison*, trans. A.M. Sheridan Smith (London, Penguin, 1979).

Freud, Sigmund, 'The Uncanny', *The Penguin Freud Library*, vol. 14, *Art and Literature*, ed. Albert Dickson (London, Penguin, 1985).

——, 'Beyond the Pleasure Principle', *The Penguin Freud Library*, vol. 11, *On Metapsychology: The Theory of Psychoanalysis*, ed. Angela Richards (London, Penguin, 1991).

Fussell, Paul, *The Great War and Modern Memory* (Oxford, Oxford University Press, 2000).

Gasiorek, Andrzej, *Post-War British Fiction: Realism and After* (London, Edward Arnold, 1995).

Gordon, Avery F., *Ghostly Matters: Haunting and the Sociological Imagination* (Minneapolis, University of Minnesota Press, 1997).

Greene, Gayle, *Changing the Story: Feminist Fiction and the Tradition* (Indianapolis, Indiana University Press, 1991).

Haywood, Ian, *Working-Class Fiction: From Chartism to Trainspotting* (Tavistock, Northcote House, 1997).

Hitchcock, Peter, *Working-Class Fiction in Theory and Practice: A Reading of Alan Sillitoe* (Ann Arbor, UMI Research Press, 1989).

——, *Dialogics of the Oppressed* (Minneapolis, University of Minnesota Press, 1993).

Hoggart, Richard, *The Uses of Literacy* (Harmondsworth, Pelican, 1957).

Holmes, Frederick, *The Historical Imagination: Postmodernism and the Treatment of the Past in Contemporary British Fiction* (Victoria, English Literary Monographs, 1997).

Jack, Ian, 'Editorial: Whatever Happened to Us?', *Granta*, 56 (1996), 7–8.

Jameson, Fredric, 'Ideology, Narrative Analysis, and Popular Culture', *Theory and Society*, 4 (1977), 543–59.

——, *The Political Unconscious: Narrative as a Socially Symbolic Act* (London, Routledge, 1986).

Joannou, Maroula, *Contemporary Women's Writing: From* The Golden Notebook *to* The Color Purple (Manchester, Manchester University Press, 2000).

Jung, C.G., *Synchronicity: An Acausal Connecting Principle* (London, Routledge and Kegan Paul, 1972).

Laing, Stuart, *Representations of Working-Class Life, 1957–1964* (Basingstoke, Macmillan, 1986).

Lejeune, Philippe, *On Autobiography*, ed. Paul John Eakin, trans. Katherine Leary (Minneapolis, University of Minnesota Press, 1989).

Luckhurst, Roger and Peter Marks (eds), *Literature and the Contemporary: Fictions and Theories of the Present* (Harlow, Longman/Pearson Education, 1999).

Lukács, Georg, *History and Class Consciousness* (London, Merlin, 1991).

——, *The Historical Novel* (London, Merlin, 1962).

Lyotard, Jean-François, *The Postmodern Condition: A Report on Knowledge*, trans. Geoff Bennington and Brian Massumi (Manchester, Manchester University Press, 1984).

Meaney, Gerardine, *(Un)Like Subjects: Women, Theory, Fiction* (London, Routledge, 1993).

Mengham, Rod (ed.), *An Introduction to Contemporary Fiction* (Cambridge, Polity, 1999).

Middleton, Peter and Tim Woods, *Literatures of Memory: History, Time and Space in Postwar Writing* (Manchester, Manchester University Press, 2000).

Miller, J. Hillis, *Topographies* (Stanford, Stanford University Press, 1995).

Nairn, Tom, *After Britain* (London, Verso, 2000).

Nancy, Jean-Luc, 'Finite History', *The States of 'Theory': History, Art and Critical Discourse*, ed. David Carroll (Stanford, Stanford University Press, 1990).

Nehring, Neil, *Flowers in the Dustbin: Culture, Anarchy and Postwar England* (Ann Arbor, University of Michigan, 1993).

Olney, James, *Memory and Narrative: The Weave of Life-Writing* (Chicago, University of Chicago Press, 1998).

Orwell, George, *The Road to Wigan Pier* (Harmondsworth, Penguin, 1962).

Owen, Wilfred, *The Poems of Wilfred Owen* (London, Chatto and Windus, 1985).

Piette, Adam, *Imagination at War: British Fiction and Poetry 1939–1945* (London, Papermac, 1995).

Ricoeur, Paul, *Time and Narrative*, vol. 3, trans. Kathleen Blamey and David Pellauer (Chicago, University of Chicago Press, 1988).

Segal, Lynne, *Slow Motion: Changing Masculinities, Changing Men* (London, Virago, 1990).

Showalter, Elaine, *The Female Malady: Women, Madness, and English Culture, 1830–1980* (London, Penguin, 1985).

Sillitoe, Alan, *Saturday Night and Sunday Morning* (London, Grafton, 1985).

Sinfield, Alan, *Literature, Politics and Culture in Postwar Britain* (London, Athlone, 1997).

Smith, David James, *The Sleep of Reason* (London, Century, 1994).

Taylor, D.J., *A Vain Conceit: British Fiction in the 1980s* (London, Bloomsbury, 1989).

——, *After the War: The Novel and England since 1945* (London, Flamingo, 1994).

Terdiman, Richard, *Present Past: Modernity and the Memory Crisis* (Ithaca, Cornell University Press, 1993).

Todd, Richard, *Consuming Fictions: The Booker Prize and Fiction in Britain Today* (London, Bloomsbury, 1996).

Watkins, Susan, *Twentieth-Century Women Novelists: Feminist Theory into Practice* (Basingstoke, Palgrave, 2001).

Waugh, Patricia, *Feminine Fictions: Revisiting the Postmodern* (London, Routledge, 1989).

Wheeler, Wendy, *A New Modernity? Change in Science, Literature and Politics* (London, Lawrence and Wishart, 1999).

Williams, Raymond, *The English Novel: From Dickens to Lawrence* (London, Hogarth, 1984).

——, *Writing in Society* (London, Verso, 1983).

Worpole, Ken, *Dockers and Detectives: Popular Reading, Popular Writing* (London, Verso, 1983).

Index